India China Relations

India China Relations
Current Issues and Perspectives

Dr Suresh Chandra

Alpha Editions

Copyright © 2016

ISBN : 9789386019950

Design and Setting By
Alpha Editions
(A Vij Publishing Group Company)
www.vijbooks.com

Contents

Preface

India and China are two of the world's most ancient civilizations. For centuries they shared advanced ideas, inventions, religious and philosophical traditions. But their economies and societies stagnated during the colonial period. In the post-colonial period mutual relations suffered a setback due to political and boundary disputes. In contemporary times they have reemerged as leading techno-economic nations.

Clearly, the simultaneous rise of India and China unfolding on the global stage hold the key to an emerging Asian century. With so much at stake in building a harmonious partnership, India and China are now banking on culture and creativity to act as connectors between people of the two countries. Travel, tourism and people-to-people contacts are poised for an upswing in 2014, which both countries have designated as the Year of India-China Friendship. Buddhism provides civilizational connect and Bollywood bonding is becoming stronger - a festival of Bollywood films was launched in China recently to much acclaim.

The two countries are now looking to sign a pact on the joint production of films, which promises to build a new popular bridge between them and give Indian filmmakers access to the second largest market in the world after the US. All the matter is just compiled and edited in nature.

As the book addresses this crucial issue quite deftly, it is hoped that it would prove to be a source of great information for the reader.

— *Editor*

1
Introduction

INDIA AND CHINA

India and China are two of the world's most ancient civilizations. For centuries they shared advanced ideas, inventions, religious and philosophical traditions. But their economies and societies stagnated during the colonial period. In the post-colonial period mutual relations suffered a setback due to political and boundary disputes. In contemporary times they have reemerged as leading techno-economic nations. It is high time for them to move beyond conflicts and start cooperating politically, economically, and technologically for mutual benefits. Recent developments and exchanges indicate that the ball is already rolling in that direction. Globalization for common good requires coming together rather than falling apart, sharing resources and assets rather than wasting them in endless conflicts. In the context of currently shifting global political and economic power, no two nations are better equipped than India and China to show the world how the common concerns of humanity can be addressed through mutual respect, friendship, healthy competition, and sharing of resources.

India and China are two of the world's most ancient surviving civilizations. The Chinese built the 4000-mile Great Wall some 2000 years ago, about the time of the birth of Jesus Christ. As an awesome marvel of engineering, most of the wall still stands intact, the only man-made object visible from the outer space.

They invented bureaucracy even earlier, thousands of years before Max Weber brought it eloquently to the attention of the western world. There is not a single country anywhere that bureaucracies do not govern, manage or mismanage, corrupt and plunder, redeem or reform. The Terracotta Army built by Emperor Qin in the 3rd century BC is in almost perfect state of preservation to this day. Some of the greatest inventions that we live by even today came from China, including the gun powder – the most infamous of them all, the paper, paper money, printing, viaducts, dams, clocks, the compass, astronomical observatories, and countless other inventions.

As for India, R. K. Narayan, the famous Indian novelist tells the interesting story of his meeting with British philosopher and iconoclast, Sir Bertrand Russell. While extolling the contributions of ancient Chinese thinkers, Russell said to Narayan, "but you Indians created nothing." Narayan vigorously protested this insulting remark. But Sir Russell kept on repeating, "You Indians created nothing, nothing, nothing." Exasperated, Narayan got up and was about to walk out when Russell drew him near, looked him in the eye and said, "You Indians gave us the zero, which stands as the greatest contribution to the development of mathematics, and consequently, that of modern science." Thereupon they embraced each other with delightful twinkle in their eyes. Ancient Medieval Indians contributions to algebra, textile, chemistry, medicine, metallurgy, and astronomy are legion. Sophisticated agricultural practices, architecture, and sewage systems were developed by the engineers in the Indus Valley civilizations of Harrappa and Mohanjadaro. The wisdom of the Buddha flowed from India to China, while Confucius' precepts of right conduct, wise and merciful ruler, compassion and humility influenced the behaviour of Indian rulers, including that of emperor Ashoka who inscribed on his commemorative pillars,*Satya amar jayte* (Truth alone shall triumph).

India and China, along with the rest of the non-western world lost their edge somewhere during the 16th and 17th centuries when the center of scientific and technological activity shifted to Europe, and later to North America. Contacts between these two great civilizations almost ceased during the colonial period because the new rulers of the world did not encourage such contacts. In more recent times, when these contacts revived they turned into conflict and hostility between a democratic India and a totalitarian China over the issues of outstanding territorial claims, the Chinese annexation of Tibet, and the Exile of Dalai Lama in (Dharamsala) India.

RECENT DEVELOPMENT HISTORY

India became a free country through peaceful transition of sovereignty in 1947. China had a proletarian revolution in 1949 led by Mao Zedong. Both democratic India and Communist China embarked upon ambitious science, technology, and economic development programs through centralized planning. Both emphasized self-reliance through local initiatives, restricting the flow of foreign capital and technology for nearly three decades. During this time, the Peoples Republic of China (PRC) controlled its economy and protected it from outside influences far more than India did. For at least 10-15 years since the revolution in 1949, the only source of foreign capital and technology for China was its ideological partner, the Soviet Union. That relationship began to crack in 1962 because of the USSR's reluctance to transfer nuclear technology to the Peoples Republic. China continued its isolation and suffered serious stagnation for 20 or so more years, until after Mao's death in 1976.

During this period, India too strictly regulated its economy, allowing only partial and highly restricted entry of foreign capital and technology. The Indian economy began to open its door a bit more widely by the middle of the 1980s, at about the same time as China. By this time, the global economy had already taken hold of the national economies in North America, Europe, and the Pacific Rim. Post-Independence era regulations proved a mixed blessing for India. It missed 20 years of the information technology revolution that was sweeping the world and driving the global economy – remember how the IBM was kicked out of India in the middle of 1970s. The private sector stagnated under those regulations. The protected government sector thrived despite its magnificent mismanagement. India's industrial development suffered. While these negative trends were the legacy of regulations, government policy of self-reliance helped built a robust infrastructure of techno-economic institutions and personnel that were ready to march forward when the global economy did finally reach India. Through regulations India was also able to protect its local industries and markets from unbridled speculation and exploitation by multinational corporations. Let me return to China for a minute.

Deng Xiaoping took command of China in 1979, three years after Mao's death. With a massive shift of public policy, Deng gave 190 degree turn to the Chinese economy by opening it to foreign capital, technology, and competition. The scene that I witnessed in China when I went there for the first time in 1980 was a totally different scene than what is going on there today. Despite the open door policy, economic modernization remained laggard through the entire decade of the 1980s. Things began to change rapidly in the next decade. Since then, the Chinese economy has been growing at about 9-10% per year, surpassing any other country for a sustained growth at such a high rate. In terms of GDP per capita, it is the world's 4th largest economy, and is likely to overtake Japan within the next five years. It is one of the world's largest exporters of consumer items through retailers like Wal-Mart, Carrefour, Target, and Tesco. Even garlic in the United States is being imported from China. The American Wal-Mart is probably the biggest buyer of consumer goods made in China. "It bought $19 billion worth of Chinese goods in 2004, amounting to some 15% of China's total exports to America in that year. (The Economist, September 23rd, p. 43)

Since 2000, China's contribution to global GDP growth (in purchasing-power-parity terms) has been bigger than America's, and more than half as big again as the combined contribution of India, Brazil and Russia, the three next largest emerging economies. China's massive build-up of American Treasury bonds affects American interest rates and thus Americans' willingness to spend. Its low-priced manufactures give western consumers more buying power. Its thirst for energy has helped push oil prices to record highs. Its entry to the World Trade Organization in 2001 has speeded up the opening of the world's biggest market. (A Survey of China, The Economist, March 25th, 2006, p. 3)

India has finally left behind its "Hindu growth rate" of 3% to hit an annual growth rate of 8+%. Its technological capability is strong. It is the most preferred destination of IT outsourcing, now moving away from being the world's call center to being a vital feeder to the global knowledge industry. India's economic base is vast – 4th largest in the world in terms of purchasing power parity and 12th largest in terms of GDP. It is projected to become one of the five largest economies in the world by 2050 along with China and Brazil. But per capita incomes remain low ($3000.00, approx.) in international comparisons. Income disparities are wide. Nonetheless, the markets are huge, with the current consumer class estimated to be around 350 million, about the size of the entire European Community.

The combined economies of India and China are already bigger than that of the EU countries put together. At the present rate of growth, the combined consumer class in the two countries will reach about a billion people within the next 5-10 years. These developments have far-reaching implications for the two countries themselves and the world at large in the 21st century.

CHINA–INDIA RELATIONS

China–India relations, also called Sino-Indian relations or Indo-China relations, refers to the bilateral relationship between the People's Republic of China (PRC) and the Republic of India. Historically, India and China have had relations for more than 2,000 years, but the modern relationship began in 1950 when India was among the first countries to end formal ties with the Republic of China(Taiwan) and recognize the PRC as the legitimate government of Mainland China. China and India are the two most populous countriesand fastest growing major economies in the world. The resultant growth in China and India's international diplomatic and economic influence has also increased the significance of their bilateral relationship.

China and India are two of the world's oldest civilisations and have co-existed in peace for millennia. Cultural and economic relations between China and India date back to ancient times. The Silk Road not only served as a major trade route between India and China, but is also credited for facilitating the spread of Buddhism from India to East Asia. During the 19th century, China's growing opium trade with the British Raj triggered the First and Second Opium Wars. During World War II, India and China played a crucial role in halting the progress of Imperial Japan.

Relations between contemporary China and India have been characterised by border disputes, resulting in three major military conflicts — the Sino-Indian War of 1962, the Chola incident in 1967, and the 1987 Sino-Indian skirmish. However, since the late 1980s, both countries have successfully attempted to reignite diplomatic and economic ties. In 2008, China emerged as India's largest trading partner and the two countries have also attempted to extend their strategic and military relations.

Despite growing economic and strategic ties, there are several hurdles for India and the PRC to overcome in order to establish favourable relations. Though bilateral trade has continuously grown, India faces massive trade imbalance heavily in favour of China. The two countries have failed to resolve their long-standing border dispute and Indian media outlets have repeatedly reported Chinese military incursions into Indian territory. Both nations have steadily established heavy military infrastructure along border areas. Additionally, India remains wary about China's strong strategic relations with Pakistan while China has expressed concerns about Indian military and economic activities in the disputed South China Sea.

In June 2012, China stated its position that "Sino-Indian ties" could be the most "important bilateral partnership of the century". That month Wen Jiabao, the Premier of China and Manmohan Singh, the Prime Minister of India set a goal to increase bilateral trade between the two countries to US$100 billion by 2015. In November 2012, the bilateral trade was estimated to be $73.9 billion.

According to a 2013 BBC World Service Poll, 36% of Indians view China positively, with 27% expressing a negative view, whereas 23% of Chinese people view India positively, with 45% expressing a negative view.

GEOGRAPHICAL OVERVIEW

China and India are separated by the formidable geographical obstacles of the Himalayas. China and India today share a border along the Himalayas with Nepal and Bhutan acting as buffer states. Parts of the disputed Kashmir region claimed by India are claimed and administered by either Pakistan (Azad Kashmir and Gilgit and Baltistan) or by the PRC (Aksai Chin). The Government of Pakistan on its maps shows the Aksai Chin area as mostly within China and labels the boundary "Frontier Undefined" while India holds that Aksai Chin is illegally occupied by the PRC.

China and India also dispute most of Arunachal Pradesh at the far eastern end of the Himalayas. However, both countries have agreed to respect the Line of Actual Control here; the area just north of Tawang is seen as a potentialflashpoint.

EARLY HISTORY

Antiquity

India and China had relatively little modern political contact before the 1950s. However, both countries have had extensive and close historical cultural contact since the 2nd century BCE, especially with the transmission of Buddhism from India to China. Trade relations via the Silk Road acted as economic contact between the two regions. China and India have also had some contact before the transmission of Buddhism. References to a people called the *Chinas*, now believed to be the Chinese, are found in ancient Indian literature. The Indian epic *Mahabharata* (c. 5th century BCE) contains references to "China", which may have been referring to the Qin state which later became the Qin Dynasty. Chanakya (c. 350-283 BCE), the prime minister of the Maurya Empire and a professor at Takshashila University, refers to Chinese silk as "cinamsuka" (Chinese silk dress) and "cinapatta" (Chinese silk bundle) in his *Arthashastra*.

In the *Records of the Grand Historian*, Zhang Qian (d. 113 BCE) and Sima Qian (145-90 BCE) make references to "Shendu", which may have been referring to the Indus Valley (the Sindh province in modern Pakistan), originally known as "Sindhu" in Sanskrit. When Yunnanwas annexed by the Han Dynasty in the 1st century, Chinese authorities reported an Indian "Shendu" community living there.

Middle Ages

After the transmission of Buddhism from India to China from the 1st century onwards, many Indian scholars and monks travelled to China, such as Batuo (fl. 464-495 CE) — first abbot of the Shaolin Monastery — and Bodhidharma — founder of Chan/Zen Buddhism — while many Chinese scholars and monks also travelled to India, such as Xuanzang (b. 604) and I Ching (635-713), both of whom were students atNalanda University in Bihar. Xuanzang wrote the *Great Tang Records on the Western Regions*, an account of his journey to India, which later inspired Wu Cheng'en's Ming Dynasty novel *Journey to the West*, one of the Four Great Classical Novels of Chinese literature.

Tang and Harsha dynasties

During the 7th century, Tang Dynasty China gained control over large portions of the Silk Road and Central Asia. Wang

Xuance had sent a diplomatic mission to northern India, which was embroiled by civil war just following the death of Emperor Harsha (590–647). After the murder of 30 members of this mission by usurper claiments to the throne, Wang fled, and returned with allied Nepali and Tibetan troops to back the opposing claimant. With his forces, Wang besieged and captured the capital, while his deputy Jiang Shiren (‹„^ÁN) captured the usurper and sent him back to Emperor Tang Taizong (599-649) in Chang'an as a prisoner.

During the 8th century, the astronomical table of sines by the Indian astronomer and mathematician, Aryabhatta (476-550), were translated into the Chinese astronomical andmathematical book of the *Treatise on Astrology of the Kaiyuan Era* (*Kaiyuan Zhanjing*), compiled in 718 CE during the Tang Dynasty. The *Kaiyuan Zhanjing* was compiled byGautama Siddha, an astronomer and astrologer born in Chang'an, and whose family was originally from India. He was also notable for his translation of the Navagraha calendar into Chinese.

Ming Dynasty

Between 1405 and 1433, the Ming Dynasty China sponsored a series of seven naval expeditions. Emperor Yongle designed them to establish a Chinese presence, impose imperial control over trade, and impress foreign people in the Indian Ocean basin. He also might have wanted to extend the tributary system, by which Chinese dynasties traditionally recognised foreign peoples.

Admiral Zheng He was dispatched to lead a series of huge naval expeditions to explore these regions. The largest of his voyages included over 317 ships and 28,000 men, and the largest of his treasure ships were over 126.73 m in length. During his voyages, he visited numerous Indian kingdoms and ports. On the first three voyages, Zheng He visited southeast Asia, India, Bengal, and Ceylon. The fourth expedition went to the Persian Gulf and Arabia, and later expeditions ventured down the east African coast, as far as Malindi in what is now Kenya. Throughout his travels, Zheng He liberally dispensed Chinese gifts of silk, porcelain, and other goods. In return, he received rich and unusual presents from his hosts, including African zebras and giraffes that ended their days in the Ming imperial zoo. Zheng He and his company paid respects to local deities and customs, and in Ceylon they erected a monument (Galle Trilingual Inscription) honouring Buddha, Allah, and Vishnu.

Sino-Sikh War

In the 18th to 19th centuries, the Sikh Confederacy of the Punjab region in India was expanding into neighbouring lands. It had annexedLadakh into the state of Jammu in 1834. In 1841, they invaded Tibet with an army and overran parts of western Tibet. Chinese forces defeated the Sikh army in December 1841, forcing the Sikh army to withdraw from Tibet, and in turn entered Ladakh and besieged Leh, where they were in turn defeated by the Sikh Army. At this point, neither side wished to continue the conflict, as the Sikhs were embroiled in tensions with the British that would lead up to the First Anglo-Sikh War, while the Chinese was in the midst of the First Opium War with the British East India Company. The Chinese and the Sikhs signed a treaty in September 1842, which stipulated no transgressions or interference in the other country's frontiers.

AFTER INDEPENDENCE

Jawaharlal Nehru based his vision of "resurgent Asia" on friendship between the two largest states of Asia; his vision of an internationalist foreign policy governed by the ethics of the Panchsheel, which he initially believed was shared by China, came to grief when it became clear that the two countries had a conflict of interest in Tibet, which had traditionally served as a geographical and political buffer zone, and where India believed it had inherited special privileges from the British Raj.

However, the initial focus of the leaders of both the nations was not the foreign policy, but the internal development of their respective states. When they did concentrate on the foreign policies, their concern wasn't one another, but rather the United States of America and the Union of Soviet Socialist Republics and the alliance systems which were dominated by the two superpowers.

1950s

On October 1, 1949 the People's Liberation Army defeated the Kuomintang (Nationalist Party) of China in a civil war and established the People's Republic of China. On August 15, 1947, India became an independent dominion under British Commonwealth and became a federal, democratic republic after its constitution came into effect on January 26, 1950. Mao Zedong, the Commander of the Liberation Army and the Chairman of the Communist Party of China viewed Tibet as an integral part of the Chinese State. Mao was determined to bring Tibet under direct administrative and military control of People's Republic of China and saw Indian concern over Tibet as a manifestation of the Indian Government's interference in the internal affairs of the People's Republic of China. The PRC sought to reassert control over Tibet and to end Lamaism (Tibetan Buddhism) andfeudalism, which it did by force of arms in 1950. To avoid antagonising the People's Republic of China, Nehru informed Chinese leaders that India had neither political nor territorial ambitions, nor did it seek special privileges in Tibet, but that traditional trading rights must continue. With Indian support, Tibetan delegates signed an agreement in May 1951 recognising PRC sovereignty but guaranteeing that the existing political and social system of Tibet would continue. Direct negotiations between India and the PRC commenced in an atmosphere improved by India's mediation efforts in bringing about a ceasefire to the Korean War (1950–1953).

India established diplomatic relations with the PRC on April 1, 1950, the 16th state to do so. In April 1954, India and the PRC signed an eight-year agreement on Tibet that set forth the basis of their relationship in the form of the Five Principles of Peaceful Coexistence(or *Panch Shila*). Although critics called the Panch Shila naive, Nehru calculated that in the absence of either the wherewithal or a policy for defence of the Himalayan region, India's best guarantee of security was to establish a psychological buffer zone in place of the lost physical buffer of Tibet. It is the popular perception that the catch phrase of India's diplomacy with China in the 1950s was *Hindi-Chini bhai-bhai*, which means, in Hindi, "Indians and Chinese are brothers" but in 1958, Nehru had privately told G. Parthasarathi, the Indian envoy to China not to trust the Chinese at all and send all communications directly to him, bypassing the Defence Minister VK Krishna Menon since his communist background clouded his thinking about China. Therefore, in unison with diplomacy, Nehru sought to initiate a more direct dialogue between the peoples of China and India in various ways, including culture and literature. Around that time, the famous Indian artist (painter) Beohar Rammanohar Sinha from Visva-BharatiSantiniketan, who had earlier decorated the pages of the original Constitution of India, was sent to China in 1957 on a Government of India fellowship to establish a direct cross-cultural and inter-civilisation bridge. Noted Indian scholar Rahul Sankrityayan and diplomat Natwar Singh were also there, and Sarvapalli Radhakrishnan paid a visit to PRC. Between 1957 and 1959, Beohar Rammanohar Sinha not only disseminated Indian art in PRC but also became skilled in Chinese painting and lacquer-work. He also spent time with great masters Qi Baishi, Li Keran, Li Kuchan as well as some moments with Mao Zedong and Zhou Enlai. Consequently, up until 1959, despite border skirmishes and discrepancies between Indian and Chinese maps, Chinese leaders amicably had assured India that there was no territorial controversy on the border though there is some evidence that India avoided bringing up the border issue in high-level meetings.

In 1954, India published new maps that included the Aksai Chin region within the boundaries of India (maps published at the time of India's independence did not clearly indicate whether the region was in India or Tibet). When India discovered that China built a road through the region, border clashes and Indian protests became more frequent and serious.

In January 1959, PRC premier Zhou Enlai wrote to Nehru, rejecting Nehru's contention that the border was based on treaty and custom and pointing out that no government in China had accepted as legal the McMahon Line, which in the 1914 Simla Convention defined the eastern section of the border between India and Tibet. The Dalai Lama, spiritual and temporal head of the Tibetan people, sought sanctuary in Dharmsala, Himachal Pradesh, in March 1959, and thousands of Tibetan refugees settled in northwestern India, particularly in Himachal Pradesh. The People's Republic of China accused India of expansionism and imperialism in Tibet and throughout the Himalayan region. China claimed 104,000 km^2 of territory over which India's maps showed clear sovereignty, and demanded "rectification" of the entire border.

Zhou proposed that China relinquish its claim to most of India's northeast in exchange for India's abandonment of its claim to Aksai Chin. The Indian government, constrained by domestic public opinion, rejected the idea of a settlement based on uncompensated loss of territory as being humiliating and unequal.

1960s

Sino-Indian War

1962 Border disputes resulted in a short border war between the People's Republic of China and India in 20 October 1962. The border clash resulted in a crushing defeat of India as the PRC pushed the Indian forces to within forty-eight kilometres of the Assam plains in the northeast and occupied strategic points in Ladakh, until the PRC declared a unilateral cease-fire on 21 November and withdrew twenty kilometers behind its contended line of control.

At the time of Sino-Indian border conflict, a severe political split was taking place in the Communist Party of India. One section was accused by the Indian government as being pro-PRC, and a large number of political leaders were jailed. Subsequently,

CPI split with the leftist section forming the Communist Party of India (Marxist) in 1964. CPI(M) held some contacts with the Communist Party of China in the initial period after the split, but did not fully embrace the political line of Mao Zedong.

Relations between the PRC and India deteriorated during the rest of the 1960s and the early 1970s as Sino-Pakistani relations improved and Sino-Soviet relations worsened. The PRC backed Pakistan in its 1965 war with India. Between 1967 and 1971, an all-weather road was built across territory claimed by India, linking PRC's Xinjiang Uyghur Autonomous Region with Pakistan; India could do no more than protest, however 1971 war with Pakistan, India won a landslide victory. The PRC continued an active propaganda campaign against India and supplied ideological, financial, and other assistance to dissident groups, especially to tribes in northeastern India. The PRC accused India of assisting the Khampa rebels in Tibet. Diplomatic contact between the two governments was minimal although not formally severed. The flow of cultural and other exchanges that had marked the 1950s ceased entirely. The flourishing wool, fur and spice trade between Lhasa and India through the Nathula Pass, an offshoot of the ancient Silk Road in the then Indian protectorate of Sikkim was also severed. However, the biweekly postal network through this pass was kept alive, which exists till today.

Sri Lanka played the role of chief negotiator to withdraw the Chinese troops from the Indian territory. It is the Colombo proposals which both countries agreed to adopt and settle this dispute.

Later Skirmishes

In late 1967, there were two skirmishes between Indian and Chinese forces in Sikkim. The first one was dubbed the "Nathu La incident", and the other the "Chola incident". Prior to these incidents had been the Naxalbari uprising in India by the Communist Naxalites and Maoists.

In 1967, a peasant uprising broke out in Naxalbari, led by pro-Maoist elements. A pronunciation by Mao titled "Spring Thunder over India" gave full moral support for the uprising. The support for the revolt marked the end for the relations between CPC and CPI(M). Naxalbari-inspired communists organised armed revolts in several parts of India, and in 1969 they formed the Communist Party of India (Marxist-Leninist). However, as the naxalite movement disintegrated in various splits, the PRC withdrew its political support and turned non-committal towards the various Indian groups.

In September 1967, Chinese and Indian forces clashed at Nathu La. According to the Indian account, on 11 September, Indian soldiers were protecting an engineering company that was fencing the North Shoulder of Nathu La, when Chinese troops opened fire on them. This escalated over the next five days to an exchange of heavy artillery and mortar fire between the Indians and the Chinese. 62 Indian soldiers were killed.

Soon afterwards, Indian and Chinese forces clashed again in the Chola incident. On 1 October 1967, some Indian and Chinese soldiers had an argument over the control of a boulder at the Chola outpost in Sikkim (then a protectorate of India), triggering a fight that escalated to a mortar and heavy machine gun duel. On 10 October, both sides again exchanged heavy fire. According to Indian sources, during the whole conflict Indian losses were 88 killed and 163 wounded, while Chinese casualties were 300 killed and 450 wounded in Nathu La, and 40 in Chola.

1970s

In August 1971, India signed its Treaty of Peace, Friendship, and Co-operation with the Soviet Union, and the United States and the PRC sided with Pakistan in its December 1971 war with India. Although China strongly condemned India, it did not carry out its veiled threat to intervene on Pakistan's behalf. By this time, the PRC had just replaced the Republic of China in the UN where its representatives denounced India as being a "tool of Soviet expansionism." India and the PRC renewed efforts to improve relations after Indian Prime Minister Indira Gandhi's Congress party lost the 1977 elections to Morarji Desai's Janata Party. The new Desai government sought to improve long-strained relations with India and the PRC. In 1978, the Indian Minister of External Affairs Atal Bihari Vajpayee made a landmark visit to Beijing, and both nations officially re-established diplomatic relations in 1979. The PRC modified its pro-Pakistan stand on Kashmir and appeared willing to remain silent on India's absorption of Sikkim and its special advisory relationship with Bhutan. The PRC's leaders agreed to discuss the boundary issue, India's priority, as the first step to a broadening of relations. The two countries hosted each other's news agencies, and Mount Kailash and Mansarowar Lake in Tibet, the mythological home of the Hindu pantheon, were opened to annual pilgrimages.

1980s

In 1981 PRC minister of foreign affairs Huang Hua was invited to India, where he made complimentary remarks about India's role in South Asia. PRC premier Zhao Ziyangconcurrently toured Pakistan, Nepal, and Bangladesh.

In 1980, Indian Prime Minister Indira Gandhi approved a plan to upgrade the deployment of forces around the Line of Actual Control to avoid unilateral redefinitions of the line. India also increased funds for infrastructural development in these areas.

In 1984, squads of Indian soldiers began actively patrolling the Sumdorong Chu Valley in Arunachal Pradesh (formerly NEFA), which is north of the McMahon Line as drawn on the Simla Treaty map but south of the ridge which Indian claims is meant to delineate the McMahon Line. The Sumdorong Chu valley "seemed to lie to the north of the McMahon line; but is south of the highest ridge in the area, and the McMahon line is meant to follow the highest points" according to the Indian claims, whilst the Chinese did not recognise the McMahon Line as legitimate and were not prepared to accept an Indian claim line even further north than that. The Indian team left the area before the winter. In the winter of 1986, the Chinese deployed their troops to the Sumdorong Chu before the Indian team could arrive in the summer and built a Helipad at Wandung. Surprised by the Chinese occupation, India's then Chief of Army Staff, General K.Sundarji, airlifted a brigade to the region.

Chinese troops could not move any further into the valley and were forced to move sideways along the Thag La ridge, away from the valley. By 1987, Beijing's reaction was similar to that in 1962 and this prompted many Western diplomats to predict war. However, Indian foreign minister N.D. Tiwari and Prime Minister Rajiv Gandhi travelled to Beijing over the following months to negotiate a mutual de-escalation.

After the Huang visit, India and the PRC held eight rounds of border negotiations between December 1981 and November 1987. These talks initially raised hopes that progress could be made on the border issue. However, in 1985 the PRC stiffened its position on the border and insisted on mutual concessions without defining the exact terms of its "package proposal" or where the actual line of control lay. In 1986 and 1987, the negotiations achieved nothing, given the charges exchanged between the two countries of military encroachment in the Sumdorung Chu Valley of the Tawang tract on the eastern sector of the border. China's construction of a military post and helicopter pad in the area in 1986 and India's grant of statehood to Arunachal Pradesh (formerly the North-East Frontier Agency) in February 1987 caused both sides to deploy new troops to the area, raising tensions and fears of a new border war. The PRC relayed warnings that it would "teach India a lesson" if it did not cease "nibbling" at Chinese territory. By the summer of 1987, however, both sides had backed away from conflict and denied that military clashes had taken place.

A warming trend in relations was facilitated by Rajiv Gandhi's visit to China in December 1988. The two sides issued a joint communiqué that stressed the need to restore friendly relations on the basis of the Panch Shila and noted the importance of the first visit by an Indian prime minister to China since Nehru's 1954 visit. India and the People's Republic of China agreed to broaden bilateral ties in various areas, working to achieve a "fair and reasonable settlement while seeking a mutually acceptable solution" to the border dispute. The communiqué also expressed China's concern about agitation by Tibetan separatists in India and reiterated China's position that Tibet was an integral part of China and that anti-China political activities by expatriate Tibetans was not to be tolerated. Rajiv Gandhi signed bilateral agreements on science and technology co-operation, on civil aviation to establish direct air links, and on cultural exchanges. The two sides also agreed to hold annual diplomatic consultations between foreign ministers, and to set up a joint ministerial committee on economic and scientific co-operation and a joint working group on the boundary issue. The latter group was to be led by the Indian foreign secretary and the Chinese vice minister of foreign affairs.

1990s

As the mid-1990s approached, slow but steady improvement in relations with China was visible. Top-level dialogue continued with the December 1991 visit of PRC premier Li Peng to India and the May 1992 visit to China of Indian president R. Venkataraman. Six rounds of talks of the Indian-Chinese Joint Working Group on the Border Issue were held between December 1988 and June 1993. Progress was also made in reducing tensions on the border via confidence-building measures, including mutual troop reductions, regular meetings of local military commanders, and advance notification of military exercises. Border trade resumed in July 1992 after a hiatus of more than thirty years, consulates reopened in Bombay (Mumbai) and Shanghai in December 1992, and, in June 1993, the two sides agreed to open an additional border trading post. During Sharad Pawar's July 1992 visit to Beijing, the first ever by an Indian minister of defence, the two defence establishments agreed to develop academic, military, scientific, and technological exchanges and to schedule an Indian port call by a Chinese naval vessel.

Substantial movement in relations continued in 1993. The sixth-round joint working group talks were held in June in New Delhi but resulted in only minor developments. However, as the year progressed the long-standing border dispute was eased as a result of bilateral pledges to reduce troop levels and to respect the cease-fire line along the India-China border. Prime Minister Narasimha Rao and Premier Li Peng signed the border agreement and three other agreements, primarily dealing with cross-border trade, and on increased cooperation on environmental issued (e.g. Pollution, Animal extinction, Global Warming, etc.) and in radio and television broadcasting during the former's visit to Beijing in September. A senior-level Chinese military delegation made a six-day goodwill visit to India in December 1993 aimed at "fostering confidence-building measures between the defence forces of the two countries." The visit, however, came at a time when press reports revealed that, as a result of improved relations between the PRC and Burma, China was exporting greater amounts of military matériel to Burma's army, navy, and air force and sending an increasing number of technicians to Burma. Of concern to Indian security officials was the presence of Chinese radar technicians in Burma's Coco Islands, which border India's Union Territory of the Andaman and Nicobar Islands. Nevertheless, movement continued in 1994 on troop reductions along the Himalayan frontier. Moreover, in January 1994 Beijing announced that it not only favored a negotiated solution on Kashmir, but also opposed any form of independence for the region.

Talks were held in New Delhi in February 1994 aimed at confirming established "confidence-building measures" and discussing clarification of the "line of actual control", reduction of armed forces along the line, and prior information about forthcoming military exercises. China's hope for settlement of the boundary issue was reiterated.

The 1993 Chinese military visit to India was reciprocated by Indian army chief of staff General B. C. Joshi. During talks in Beijing in July 1994, the two sides agreed that border problems should be resolved peacefully through "mutual understanding and concessions." The border issue was raised in September 1994 when PRC minister of national defence Chi Haotian visited New Delhi for extensive talks with high-level Indian trade and defence officials. Further talks in New Delhi in March 1995 by the India-China Expert Group led to an agreement to set up two additional points of contact along the 4,000 km border to facilitate meetings between military personnel. The two sides also were reported as "seriously engaged" in defining the McMahon Line and the line of actual control vis-à-vis military exercises and prevention of air intrusion. Talks in Beijing in July 1995 aimed at better border security and combating cross-border crimes and in New Delhi in August 1995 on additional troop withdrawals from the border made further progress in reducing tensions.

Possibly indicative of the further relaxation of India-China relations, at least there was little notice taken in Beijing, was the April 1995 announcement, after a year of consultation, of the opening of the Taipei Economic and Cultural Centre in New Delhi. The centre serves as the representative office of the Republic of China (Taiwan) and is the counterpart of the India-Taipei Association in Taiwan; both institutions have the goal of improving relations between the two sides, which have been strained since New Delhi's recognition of Beijing in 1950.

Sino-Indian relations hit a low point in 1998 following India's nuclear tests in May. Indian Defence Minister George Fernandes declared that "China is India's number one threat", hinting that India developed nuclear weapons in defence against China's nuclear arsenal. In 1998, China was one of the strongest international critics of India's nuclear tests and entry into the nuclear club. During the 1999 Kargil War China voiced support for Pakistan, but also counseled Pakistan to withdraw its forces.

2000s

With Indian President K. R. Narayanan's visit to China, 2000 marked a gradual re-engagement of Indian and Chinese diplomacy.

In a major embarrassment for China, the 17th Karmapa, Urgyen Trinley Dorje, who was proclaimed by China, made a dramatic escape from Tibet to the Rumtek Monastery in Sikkim. Chinese officials were in a quandary on this issue as any protest to India on the issue would mean an explicit endorsement on India's governance of Sikkim, which the Chinese still hadn't recognised. In 2002, Chinese Premier Zhu Rongji reciprocated by visiting India, with a focus on economic issues. 2003 ushered in a marked improvement in Sino-Indian relations following Indian Prime Minister Atal Bihari Vajpayee's landmark June 2003 visit to China. China officially recognised Indian sovereignty over Sikkim as the two nations moved towards resolving their border disputes.

2004 also witnessed a gradual improvement in the international area when the two countries proposed opening up the Nathula andJelepla Passes in Sikkim which would be mutually beneficial to both countries. 2004 was a milestone in Sino-Indian bilateral trade, surpassing the US$10 billion mark for the first time. In April 2005, Chinese Premier Wen Jiabao visited Bangalore to push for increased Sino-Indian cooperation in high-tech industries. In a speech, Wen stated "Cooperation is just like two pagodas (temples), one hardware and one software. Combined, we can take the leadership position in the world." Wen stated that the 21st century will be "the Asian century of the IT industry." The high-level visit was also expected to produce several agreements to deepen political, cultural and economic ties between the two nations. Regarding the issue of India gaining a permanent seat on the UN Security Council, on his visit, Wen Jiabao initially seemed to support the idea, but had returned to a neutral position on the subject by the time he returned to China. In the South Asian Association for Regional Cooperation (SAARC) Summit (2005) China was granted an observer status. While other countries in the region are ready to consider China for permanent membership in the SAARC, India seems reluctant.

A very important dimension of the evolving Sino-Indian relationship is based on the energy requirements of their industrial

22   *India China Relations: Current Issues and Perspectives*

expansion and their readiness to proactively secure them by investing in the oilfields abroad - in Africa, the Middle East and Central Asia. On the one hand, these ventures entail competition (which has been evident in oil biddings for various international projects recently). But on the other hand, a degree of cooperation too is visible, as they are increasingly confronting bigger players in the global oil market. This cooperation was sealed in Beijing on 12 January 2006 during the visit of Petroleum and Natural Gas Minister Mani Shankar Aiyar, who signed an agreement which envisages ONGC Videsh Ltd (OVL) and the China National Petroleum Corporation (CNPC) placing joint bids for promising projects elsewhere. This may have important consequences for their international relations.

On July 6, 2006, China and India re-opened Nathula, an ancient trade route which was part of the Silk Road. Nathula is a pass through the Himalayas and it was closed 44 years prior to 2006 when the Sino-Indian War broke out in 1962. The initial agreement for the re-opening of the trade route was reached in 2003, and a final agreement was formalised on June 18, 2006. Officials say that the re-opening of border trade will help ease the economic isolation of the region.

In November 2006, China and India had a verbal spat over claim of the north-east Indian state of Arunachal Pradesh. India claimed that China was occupying 38,000 square kilometres of its territory in Kashmir, while China claimed the whole of Arunachal Pradesh as its own. In May 2007, China denied the application for visa from an Indian Administrative Service officer in Arunachal Pradesh. According to China, since Arunachal Pradesh is a territory of China, he would not need a visa to visit his own country. Later in December 2007, China appeared to have reversed its policy by granting a visa to Marpe Sora, an Arunachal born professor in computer science. In January 2008, Prime Minister Manmohan Singh visited China and met with PresidentHu Jintao and Premier Wen Jiabao and had bilateral discussions related to trade, commerce, defence, military, and various other issues.

Until 2008 the British Government's position remained the same as had been since the Simla Accord of 1913: that China held suzerainty over Tibet but not sovereignty. Britain revised this view on 29TH October 2008, when it recognised Chinese sovereignty over Tibet by issuing a statement on its website. The Economist stated that although the British Foreign Office's website does not use the word sovereignty, officials at the Foreign Office said "it means that, as far as Britain is concerned, 'Tibet is part of China. Full stop.'" This change in Britain's position affects India's claim to its North Eastern territories which rely on the same Simla Accord that Britain's prior position on Tibet's sovereignty was based upon.

In October 2009, Asian Development Bank formally acknowledging Arunachal Pradesh as part of India, approved a loan to India for a development project there. Earlier China had exercised pressure on the bank to cease the loan, however India succeeded in securing the loan with the help of the United States and Japan. China expressed displeasure at ADB for the same.

2010s

Chinese Premier Wen Jiabao paid an official visit to India from 15–17 December 2010 at the invitation of Prime Minister Manmohan Singh. He was accompanied by 400 Chinese business leaders, who wished to sign business deals with Indian companies.

"India and China are two very populous countries with ancient civilisations, friendship between the two countries has a time-honoured history, which can be dated back 2,000 years, and since the establishment of diplomatic ties between our two countries, in particular the last ten years, friendship and cooperation has made significant progress.

Premier Wen Jiabao at the Tagore International School, 15th December 2010". In April 2011, during the BRICS summit in Sanya, Hainan, China the two countries agreed to restore defence co-operation and China had hinted that it may reverse its policy of administering stapled visas to residents of Jammu and Kashmir.

This practice was later stopped, and as a result, defence ties were resumed between the two nations and joint military drills were expected.

It was reported in February 2012 that India will reach US$100 billion trade with China by 2015. Bilateral trade between the two countries reached US$73 billion in 2011, making China India's largest trade partner, but slipped to US$66 billion in 2012.

In the 2012 BRICS summit in New Delhi, India, Chinese President Hu Jintao told Indian Prime Minister Manmohan Singh that "it is China's unswerving policy to develop Sino-Indian friendship, deepen strategic cooperation and seek common development" and "China hopes to see a peaceful, prosperous and continually developing India and is committed to building more dynamic China-India relationship". Other topics were discussed, including border dispute problems and a unified BRICS central bank.

In response to India's test of a missile capable of carrying a nuclear warhead to Beijing, the PRC called for the two countries to "cherish the hard-earned momentum of co-operation".

A three-week standoff between Indian and Chinese troops in close proximity to each other and the Line of Actual Control between Jammu and Kashmir's Ladakh region and Aksai Chin was defused on 5 May 2013, days before a trip by Indian Foreign Minister Salman Khurshid to China; Khurshid said that both countries had a shared interest in not having the border issue exacerbate or "destroy" long-term progress in relations. The Chinese agreed to withdraw their troops in exchange for an Indian agreement to demolish several "live-in bunkers" 250 km to the south in the disputed Chumar sector.

Chinese Premier Li Keqiang made his first foreign visit to India on 18 May 2013 in a bid to resolve border disputes and to stimulate economic relations. According to Mr. Li, there were three main reasons for his visit. First was to increase diplomatic co-operation. Second was to cement relations in trade and other areas and finally to formulate strategy for common prosperous future.

The relationship between India and China has never been too strong in modern times, though the bilateral trade is expected to touch $1 Trillion by 2050. There have also been speculations on Indian side on how to tackle the rising trade deficit with China which currently stands up at $40 Billion.

SCIENCE, TECHNOLOGY, AND ECONOMY, IN INDIA AND CHINA

The West is becoming alarmist about what is happening in the world's two most populous nations. In the United States, Japan bashing has been replaced by China bashing. It is well-known that China's military machine is one of the most formidable in the world. But it is the Chinese economy that scares both the Indian and the Americans. Many Americans see both India and China stealing American jobs – China stealing manufacturing jobs (textile, shoes, furniture, hand tools, consumer electronics, Christmas trees and ornaments); while India taking away IT jobs. Some in America have gone to the extent of suggesting that China is about to take over the United States' economy by next year; as it was used to be said abut Japan in the 1980s and the 1990s. Of course, there is some truth in these morbid fears as Americans look back to the disappearance of their steel and automobile industries through competition with Japan. And now here comes China, closely followed by India. Not to be left behind in IT outsourcing, China is rapidly developing its English and computer skills to compete with India in the American high-tech industry. Listen to what Tony Blair, the British Prime Minister said in a recent major policy speech in Oxford, England:

But the international competition is intense and getting more so. Chinese R&D has been rising by 20% a year over the past five years. South Korean R&D has increased ten-fold since 1971. Indian R&D is even more astonishing-it has trebled in a decade. Indian engineers are flooding into the world's markets-350,000 a year, forecast to 1.4m a year by 2015.... It is a warning to us that we have to remain world-leaders and that knowledge also needs to be transferred from the academy to the marketplace.

There is intense competition globally for R&D dollars. Technology and industry leaders understand that research and innovation are absolutely necessary for maintaining competitive advantage in their core competencies. Finding and hiring qualified scientists and engineers in the western countries is difficult and prohibitively expensive.

"The truth is, China and India are increasingly attractive places for companies to do research and development." ("Can Anyone Steer this Economy," Cover Story, *Business Week*, Nov. 20, 2006, p. 62) India has an edge over China in attracting R&D investments due to the availability of more well-trained, English speaking scientists and engineers than in China. A high-tech company can hire an engineer in India at one-fourth the cost for a similar hire in North America, for example. Such foreign investments will be growing rapidly in the coming years in both India and China, more so in India than in China.

The American magazine *Business Week* organized its 10th annual CEO Forum in Beijing in early November (1-3) this year. More than 700 global executives and government officials from many countries participated. Much of the discussion focused on competitiveness in China and India and the competition between them for world resources and markets. Is China with its command economy or India as world's largest and most boisterous democracy better poised to utilize foreign domestic investment for sustained social and economic development, was one of the hotly debated points. The experience so far suggests that without much public debate or dissension about its national plans and priorities, China has done much better than India in that respect. From the Indian point of view, the issue is that the values of individual freedoms, self reliance, and social development must not be sacrificed at the altar of economic development. These are indeed fine values to uphold in a democratic society, but the Indian policy planners need to look hard and fast how much they have or have not achieved by way of all-round social development.

The fact is, both of these Asian giants have their own strengths and weaknesses, their own unique cultural traditions and political histories. They both are only half way home and a long way to go, as the saying goes, toward becoming advanced industrial societies. They have serious social and environmental problems to encounter – problems of poverty and disparity, the problem of rapidly deteriorating environments due to rapid industrialization, and a host of other problems like rural-urban disparity, education, housing, health-care, and employment for their large populations. These are the areas where they can cooperate and learn from each other while they compete for world markets and resources.

The CEO Forum in Beijing spent considerable time on the issue of global competition and rivalry between the two Asian superstars.

With the likes of China Mobile (with 300 million subscribers and a $177 billion market capitalization), telecom gear maker Huawei Technologies, and India's Tata Steel on the prowl for acquisitions overseas, China and India are "reshaping the global economy." Can these giants get along? Their rivalry is bound to intensify as India moves more into low-wage manufacturing, a Chinese specialty. Both must create 15 million new jobs every year just to keep their young people employed.

Increasing energy use in India and China due to economic development and rise in automobile ownership is also a source of worldwide concern as well as intense competition between them. The issue is how to satisfy their voracious appetite for oil. With 17% of the world population, only 0.8% oil reserves, and an economy growing at breakneck speed, China is naturally frantic about meeting its energy needs through imports. It is actively courting African leaders and investing in African development and oil exploration. During a recent summit of top African leaders in Beijing, the latter were lavishly treated by the Chinese President,

Hue JinTao. The huge Chinese oil conglomerate, CNOOC, is actively out to buy oil companies overseas, including a failed bid to buy American UNOCAL. It has since invested in oil interests in Russia and the Middle East. India is faced with a similar energy crunch having only meager oil resources of its won. It is competing with China for oil in world markets. But that is also one area where the two countries can effectively cooperate. Such discussions have already taken place between CNOOC and India's Oil and Natural Gas Commission. The Indian energy Minister came up with an interesting idea while discussing cooperative energy exploration and acquisition strategy with China sometime ago. He suggested that there should be a Consortium of Oil Importing Countries to negotiate the supply and price of crude oil for the benefit of heavy developing country oil importers. I don't know what happened to that idea.

The history of border dispute between India and China going back to the war of 1962 is well-known. That dispute is yet to be resolved and continues to be a source of tension and mistrust between them. The friction is exacerbated by China's military and nuclear cooperation with archrival Pakistan. In its economic expansionist mode, China wants to increase its investment in India but is resisted by the Indian government. China claims double standards by India in granting her clearance for FDI (four bureaucratic levels of approval instead of only the Reserve Bank of India clearance for others) and issuing visas to Chinese workers. One of the cases in point is visa problems for 1,800 Chinese engineers from the Chinese Petroleum hired by Reliance India to lay a gas pipeline (I wonder why Reliance could not find Indian engineers to do the job; and whether the visas were finally issued).

Despite these problems, economic cooperation in terms of trade is increasing between the two countries, currently running at $20 billion from only $1.8 billion in 1989-90. A substantial share of India's mobile-phone market is run by Hutchison Telecommunications of China. Huawei Technologies has a software center in Bangalore that employs 1,150 Indian and 50 Chinese engineers. I understand that most of the Diwali lanterns this year came from China. From the Indian side, an estimated 150 companies are currently doing business in China. India claims these business ventures are with other foreign firms operating in China, not with the Chinese companies. China imports iron ore and other minerals from India.

Concluding Remarks

India and China in the context of globalization suggests several things. Nobel Laureate Amartya Sen, reports his teacher Joan Robinson at Cambridge University once telling him, "The frustrating thing about India is that whatever you can rightly say about it, the opposite is also true." Interestingly enough, you can say exactly the same thing about China. It combines capitalism with communism, poverty and disparity with fast economic growth, impressive industrial development with neglect of its environment, and a massive rural-urban divide. These contradictions exist in India as well, with the exception of the first one. But they are due to long-standing historical and social factors, not due exclusively to globalization, as some tend to suggest.

Generally speaking, all modern economies today are global in character. As Robert Reich said in his well-known book, *The Work of Nations*, there are no national economies any more. India and China are no exceptions. Economic globalization is driving and shaping national politics, economies, histories, social structures, environments, and international relations, and connecting them through interdependent networks as never before. There is a worldwide power shift occurring still unseen and unrecognized by many around us. There are two major implications of this power shift. Ideology and politics are becoming the handmaidens of global economic forces, rather than the other way round, as the case used to be. The other development is unraveling of erstwhile hegemonies. The United States of America and Europe are no longer in the drivers' seats. The balance of power is shifting from West to East, from North to South. The recent demographic, economic, and political developments in China, India, Russia, Latin America, and the Middle East (barring some temporary setbacks here and there) all point in that direction.*. This shifting landscape strongly suggests that this century is poised to be an Asian century and India and China, along with Russian will be its biggest winners – unless the trend is spoiled by very bad political and economic leadership in these countries, which is unlikely. The following developments are noteworthy in this context.

- Except in the US, population in the western countries, including Russia, is declining. It is already below replacement level in Russia and the Scandinavian countries. The current demographic balance between the West and the rest is: West = 1 billion; rest = 5.5 billion. It will continue to move in this direction.

- Historically, the small numbers in the west were largely compensated by their huge scientific and technological superiority for nearly one hundred years. But that equation has undergone significant changes because of globalization of technology systems. The West is still enormously creative but has little control over its own inventions and who might benefit most from them. A new discovery or invention knows no national boundaries. It gets rapidly diffused and used globally. The science and technology human resource balance of power has also shifted significantly. While per capita production of qualified scientists and engineers in the West is still well ahead of the world, in sheer numbers China and India surpass the US in approximately 4 to 1 ratio. Look at the numbers for 2004-05: US = 84,898; India = 103,000; China = 292,569 (India-China combined total = 395,569). A recent report from Control Engineering, a free-lance think-tank is instructive:

- "The vast majority of U.S. manufacturers are experiencing a serious shortage of qualified employees, which in turn is causing significant impact on business and the ability of the country as a whole to compete in a global economy.

This is the key finding of the "2005 Skills Gap Survey" reported by the National Association of Manufacturers, Manufacturing Institute/Center for Workforce Success (NAM) and Deloitte Consulting LLP. The problem for U.S. manufacturers is that this challenge is not universal. Countries with rich educational heritages, such as India, China, and Russia, are graduating millions more students each year from colleges than the United States. These highly educated individuals are actively participating in the development of innovative new products without regard for historical barriers, such as geography— thanks to technologies such as broadband, inexpensive Internet-ready laptops, and collaborative tools. With such international talent readily available and significant shortages existing at home, it is clear that the future of U.S. manufacturing may now be at stake, the report suggests. Details behind the talent shortage reveal a stark reality. More than 80% of respondents indicated that they are experiencing a shortage of qualified workers overall—with 13% reporting severe shortages."

- Latin American leaders like Hugo Chavez (Venezuela), Fidel Castro (Cuba), Lula de Sylva (Brazil), and Evo Morales (Bolivia) clearly indicate declining American hegemony in that part of the world. Their more independent (of America) and socialist leaning economic and foreign policies are redefining the nature of global economy in South and Central America.

- The nuclear postures of North Korea and Iran indicate the declining influence of the European Union, NATO, and the United States on world politics. These postures are buffeted by the support of new international power brokers, notably China and Russia, both members of the UN Security Council.

- The enormous economic power of the Middle East and Russia with their oil is going to play a significant role in defining world politics. Saudi Arabia, Iran, and the conglomerate of small Gulf States are bursting with economic activity. So is Russian Federation.

- American and British policy failures in Iraq and Afghanistan clearly indicate the impotence of these two largest military-industrial complexes. Such failures over a span of six years have turned them into paper tigers by their own counter-intuitive actions in world politics.

CHINA AND INDIA AS DRIVERS OF REGIONAL GROWTH

There is little doubt that China's rapidly growing exports to countries outside of Asia-Pacific in Asia has generated equally rapid growth in imports by China from other Asian and Pacific countries, not just from its neighbours in East Asia but also from Australia, India and Indonesia. According to Perlez (2003), Japan's current "recovery is being driven by a surge in exports to China. Australia's healthy economy is being kept that way by Chinese investments in liquid natural gas products.

China is now South Korea's largest trading partner... In Indonesia, Malaysia and the Philippines (and to a lesser extent in Thailand)... China's main interest is to scoop up what it can for its modernization. Indonesians call this new relationship with Beijing as 'feeding the dragon.'" Although India is by far the largest (and rapidly growing) market in South Asia, it is yet to have a major impact on the trade of its neighbours in South Asia in spite of the creation of the South Asian Preferential Trade Area (SAPTA) in 1997. To a significant extent, this reflects the hostile relations between India and the next largest market in South Asia, viz. Pakistan. Pakistan is yet to grant a most favoured nation status to India. Unless the relations between the two normalize, the prospects of SAPTA are not bright. However, India-Sri Lanka bilateral trade and investment have grown rapidly since the conclusion of a free trade agreement between the two became operational in March 2000. Recent signs of a warming of Indo-Pakistani relations, if they lead to their normalization, could make India the engine of growth for South Asia, as China already is in the Asia-Pacific region.

Foreign Direct Investment

China receives a much larger flow of net foreign direct investment (projected at $57 billion in 2003) than India's (under $4 billion in 2001-02). In Srinivasan (2002), I discussed some of the reasons for this difference. In short, as Luce and Kynge (2003) succinctly point out, "whether it is China's cheaper, more reliable power supply or the more rapid turn around at its ports, China remains an incalculably better environment for most manufacturing than India, which is slowly waking up to this." This environment and the bureaucratic obstacles at all levels of government in India in large part explain the huge flow of FDI to China relative to India. The Indian government has recognized FDI as key for achieving the Tenth Plan target of 8% annual growth and appointed a steering committee on FDI in 2001. It reported in 2002 with several recommendations for making India more attractive as a destination for FDI.

Exchange Rates and Foreign Reserves

Although China's trade surplus with the United States has been growing, its overall trade surplus is modest since it is running a growing trade deficit with Asia-Pacific countries that offsets in large part its trade surplus with the US. The economic logic that only a country's overall trade and current account balances have economic significance and not its bilateral balances with any one or a subset of trading partners, has never been understood by politicians anywhere, and in particular, in the US. As Japanese trade surpluses created an anti-Japan backlash in the eighties, it is now China's turn to be at the receiving end of US pressure. China has accumulated a substantial (projected at $383 billion by the end of 2003) foreign exchange reserves, exceeding its annual imports. India has done the same — its reserves, around $92 billion at the end of 2003, exceed by a substantial margin the likely imports of $60 billion. The issues of the appropriate level of reserves, and whether both countries have accumulated far too much relative to what would be needed to smooth volatility in export earnings and import expenditures and to contain any potential financial crisis like the one experienced by East Asia in 19975. Since neither the renminbi nor the rupee is convertible on capital account and capital controls are in place in both countries, prima facie the probability of an exchange rate crisis of the type experienced by countries with open capital account and fully convertible currencies is very low.

This is not to say, of course, that a balance of payments crisis (BOP) that makes the prevailing exchange rate unsustainable cannot arise—after all, despite capital controls and an inconvertible (on capital account) rupee, India experienced a severe BOP crisis in 1991, which resulted in the devaluation of the rupee and other policy changes. Still, given that partial insurance from other sources of external funds (e.g., from the IMF) is in principle available, should self-insurance through reserves be pushed as far as the current level of reserves in China and India seem to have done?

Any attempt to determine the appropriate level of reserves has to be based on an analysis of the appropriate exchange rate regime for either country, and the related issue of whether the benefits from integration with the global financial markets outweigh the costs. Without doing such an analysis myself, let me cite Kenneth Rogoff of Harvard, the former Economic Councillor and Director, Research Department of the IMF, on the issue:

My interpretation of the evidence not just from Asia but from the whole world, from Europe's experience, from floating rates, from the Bretton Woods system, is that policy makers vastly overrate the risks of having volatile exchange rates and vastly underrate the indirect costs that can come from all the policies that they have to try to suppress them. Certainly I wouldn't say that India has gone too far at the moment in accumulating reserves, it has a very strong position but I think all the countries in Asia are reaching a point when they have to start asking the question how much is enough, that basically a lot of the reserves that the Asian economies are accumulating—even outside of Japan—we are talking about close to a trillion dollars, are basically low interest rate loans from the emerging markets to United States and Europe, and this is very costly. There are opportunity costs to the domestic economy. How much is enough and at what point should one risk letting the exchange rate appreciate.

Knowing the multilateral aspects of it, I realize that there are some outside the IMF who call for greater flexibility in Asian currencies in order to strengthen demand from the rest of the world. I think that is an issue worth considering but it is not the one I want to focus on. From the Asian economies' own perspective, and this is true for India, it is true for China, it is true for virtually all the countries in the region, moving to a regime of greater flexibility would be something that is advisable, would not bring the cost many policy makers fear, and in fact would allow the economies to reduce the level of recession and that would have many positive growth effects (Rogoff 2003). Rogoff's conclusion does not imply that US pressure on China to revalue the renminbi was justified or that India should also let its rupee appreciate, but only that greater flexibility in exchange rates would be appropriate in both countries.

The Indian exchange rate regime is one of managed float (although Rogoff prefers to characterize it as a crawling peg), and it does allow some flexibility. It is possible to argue that the Indian central bank (i.e., Reserve Bank of India) has inappropriately intervened to prevent the rupee from appreciating, and this has cost the Indian economy in terms of foregone growth. But this is an argument that the flexibility inherent in the managed float regime has not been utilized appropriately. It is not the same as arguing that India should immediately make the rupee fully convertible and adopt a regime of clean float.

The latter argument is not persuasive for the simple reason that domestic financial sector reforms are incomplete, and it is risky to open the capital account under the circumstances. In any case, there is no country in the world, developed or developing, that allows a clean float of its currency. On the other hand, there are long term benefits from a convertible currency and by credibly committing to a fully convertible rupee for at a not too distant and specified future date, the pressure to complete the financial sector reforms by that date would become significant. What about China? Again, the problems in the financial sector, particularly the overhang of NPLs are serious, and an immediate revaluation might worsen the problem.

Besides, it has not been established by anyone, least of all by the US Treasury, that the current renminbi-dollar exchange rate is too far from a long-run equilibrium rate. If it is not, and China moves to a floating regime, that US Treasury might find, to its surprise, that the exchange rate does not move from its current level! Unfortunately, China is likely to succumb to the pressure to revalue if newspaper reports (*Financial Times*, February 10, 2004) are to be believed.

It is not unlikely that if India's reserves continue to climb, and outsourcing gathers further momentum, there would be charges of "currency manipulation" against Indian authorities, as the Chinese are currently being charged with. China and India should cooperate in resisting such accusations and pressures and decide on their exchange rate policies in their own interests. Finally, as Rogoff rightly points out, by continuing to accumulate reserves in terms of US dollar assets, China, India and other Asian countries are financing US current account deficits.

As Alan Beattie (2003) points out: "In theory, Asians' role in financing the US current account deficit could give them enormous economic or even political leverage, since a sudden shortfall in capital inflows would spark a slide in the dollar and possibly a sharp rise in interest rates." But he rightly concludes that: "A wholesale flight from the dollar, if it drove up interest rates and forced the US into a rapid tightening of consumers' belts, would also hurt one of the principle buyers of Asia's exports." Chinese and Indian policy makers are sophisticated enough to realize this and can be expected to slow the accumulation of reserves, if appropriate, and allow greater exchange rate flexibility in due course.

FUTURE SCENARIOS FOR CHINA AND INDIA AND THEIR IMPLICATIONS

In the country studies for China and India, analysis was undertaken using the Global Trade Analysis Project (GTAP) model and projections of future growth were made to the year 2020. Through this exercise the implications of rapid growth for production and consumption of agricultural products and trading opportunities for other countries in the region and the world have been assessed, based on certain assumptions.

Prospects for Growth and Domestic Implications

The analysis conducted in the China case study projects average annual growth in GDP of 8 percent in 2006 to 2010 gradually slowing to 6-7 percent in the following decade. Several factors favour this strong growth performance, including macroeconomic stability, high domestic savings, increased spending on research and development, continued high levels of FDI, improved market environment and trade liberalization, and the commitment to greater equity — granting higher purchasing power to lower income groups. Also noted are obstacles that will tend to reduce growth particularly in the long run — a decline in the domestic savings rate, an ageing population and pressures on the natural resource base for sustained agricultural production.

While China's growth rate is projected to decline somewhat in the near future, the India study suggests that GDP growth could be rising from the current levels of 6-7 percent to 7-8 percent. It should be noted that these growth projections apply to two economies of considerably different size. Nevertheless, how does one explain the divergence? Part of the explanation is related to the incremental capital output ratio (ICOR). In India it is currently about 4 and expected to decline. In China while the ICOR was 4 in the early 1980s it has steadily risen since then and in 2002 was 5.4. In short, despite reforms in state-owned industries in China, India uses capital more efficiently. Also favouring India is the demographic dividend, with the percentage of the population in the 15 to 59 age group increasing from 59 percent in 2001 to over 63 percent in 2011 which could add 1 percent to GDP growth. In China, by contrast, the ageing population and sharp decline in population growth due to the one child policy will eventually slow overall economic growth.

The picture for agriculture is somewhat mixed. The land area used in crop production is gradually shrinking due to urbanization and in some instances environmental degradation. Thus for staple crops, production growth depends on an increase in yields. China has already achieved high yields in staple crops, and further gains will depend on technological breakthroughs. Indian crop yields are low by comparison with China and other countries. This is attributed in part to the neglect of investments in research and extension beyond the early Green Revolution years.

In both China and India the yields for the principal Green Revolution crops, rice and wheat, have plateaued, due in part to falling groundwater tables and environmental degradation. However, if priority can be given to investment in research and development and infrastructure, there appears to be ample scope, particularly in India, for increasing yields and agricultural productivity.

As a result of continued rapid economic growth and increase in income per capita, demand for high income elasticity products, like milk, livestock and horticultural products will continue to grow. China and India are committed to maintaining cereal grain self-sufficiency. The projections for both economies indicate that food security can be maintained at a national level without resorting to significant imports. The baseline scenario presented in the China study, for example, indicates that in 2020 China will maintain or surpass self-sufficiency in rice, horticulture, pork and poultry, fish and processed foods, and come close to self-sufficiency in wheat, fibre and beef and mutton. In the case of India, despite low current growth rates of output for many crops, the expectation is that self-sufficiency can be maintained in rice, wheat, coarse grains, sugar, cattle and meat, fish and other foods.

The country should also come close to self-sufficiency in other crops (although the model predicts significant decline in both production and consumption of these crops) and milk. However, both countries will need to adopt policies that ensure food security at a regional and household level where hunger and poverty still persist.

China's agricultural production structure is expected to shift more towards labour-intensive products such as vegetables, fruit, fish and processed foods, while self-sufficiency in land-intensive products such as oilseed, fibres and coarse grains is predicted to fall further from current levels. The largest increases in Indian agricultural production are predicted for oilseed, sugar, fibres, milk, fish, other agricultural products and other foods, while negative or low growth rates are expected in cattle and meat, rice, wheat, coarse grains and other crops. Nevertheless, for some of the high growth products India will continue to require significant imports, especially of oilseed, fibres and other agricultural products.

The dollar-a-day-poverty index had fallen to 16 percent in China in 2002 while it was 34 percent in India. Poverty is projected to continue to decline in India. With a GDP growth rate of 8 percent or more the poverty rate should fall from 26 percent in 1999-2000 to 14 percent in 2010 and then to 8 percent in 2015. There appears to be an implicit assumption in these figures that the reduction in poverty will come largely from growth in employment in the non-farm sector. The analysis of the Chinese experience suggests that the impact of rapid economic growth on poverty reduction tends to slacken eventually if the rural sector does not grow hand in hand. As incomes have grown, the impact and effectiveness of general economic growth on poverty reduction have weakened.

Implications for Asia and the Greater   Pacific Region

Trade liberalization, globalization, and pressures to meet WTO and FTA agreements are generating a substantial growth in trade. China will have the largest impact on Asia and the Pacific region because China's economy is two-and-a-half times larger than that of India, it is growing faster and it is more integrated with the rest of the world. For example, China received some US$60 billion of FDI last year while India received only US$5 billion. FDI and multinational investments are a means of importing technology and entrepreneurial and management skills. By 2020 China is projected to be the world's second largest importer and exporter.

At the level of the overall economy, both China and India will be major importers of energy and minerals principally from Australia, the Russian Federation and the Middle East. China is projected to drop from 92 percent self-sufficiency in energy in 2001 to 67 percent in 2020. Recognizing this as a potential constraint to growth, China is taking steps to improve efficiency in the use of energy. The high total factor productivity (TFP) growth projection in the China country report indicates that reliance on energy imports can be reduced by as much as 60 percent and minerals by 50 percent. Aided by FDI and information technologies, China and India along with other developing countries are finding it increasingly easy to transfer technology from developed countries to exercise their comparative advantage in manufacturing. However, both countries have historically made low use of external resources, relative to their economic size, and national initiatives will continue to play an important role in determining their growth paths.

As noted previously, both China and India are projected to be self-sufficient in cereal grains and do not provide a serious threat to global food security. India is projected to continue its current role as a major net exporter of rice. Both China and India will be major importers of oilseed, plant-based fibre and forestry products. Soybean meal, for example, will come from destinations as distant as Brazil. In China there is already a trend in trade away from land-intensive crops such as food and feedgrains and sugar, and towards export of labour-intensive, high value commodities — horticultural crops, livestock, and aquaculture products. The predictions of the two country reports with regard to net exports and imports in 2020. The use of different scenarios in the China report indicates that China presents considerable opportunities for other agricultural exporters under the baseline and high GDP growth scenarios, but these opportunities are significantly reduced under the high TFP growth scenario. The Indian data, on the other hand, under-represent opportunities for catching up in productivity via technological change.

The China report examines changes in the patterns of agriculture and food trade that are likely to emerge by 2020. Interestingly, Chinese exports to India are predicted to increase by 1 179 percent over their 2001 level, while Indian exports to China are predicted to grow by only 79 percent. The Indian study did not undertake a comparable analysis, but the figures presented in the China report tend to reflect the relatively narrow range of India's net agricultural exports at present — mainly rice, followed by wheat and sugar.

The major diversification in China's exports is predicted to take place in Southeast Asia and "other" Asia, while exports to Japan, Republic of Korea, Hong Kong Special Administrative Region, China, and Taiwan Province of China are predicted to remain fairly stable. Less important growth areas for China include the Russian Federation, Australia and New Zealand, and Central and South America.

On the import side, however, major growth in agricultural trade should come from the more developed Asian countries as well as most other parts of the world excepting Southeast and other Asian countries. For the developing countries in Asia, China is emerging as a significant competitor in agricultural products. In particular the current trade surplus in agricultural products that the Southeast Asian region enjoys with China is predicted to turn negative. Meanwhile many Asian countries will find it difficult to compete with non-agricultural exports from India and China such as textiles, given the comparatively low wages in these two economies.

2

China-India Relations: Contemporary Dynamics

The major source of cultural and religious inspiration for China historically, China's attention in modern times has been preoccupied with the West and Japan, often because the latter forced themselves onto Chinese territory and consciousness. This has not changed much in China's reform era and catching up with the developed economies of the West and Japan has been a major factor motivating China's continuing quest for modernity and identity. Until recently, this Chinese outlook toward Japan and the West contrasted with the preoccupation with China shown by some Indian thinkers.

SINO-INDIAN RELATIONS: A CHRONOLOGY

On the eve of the 11th meeting of the Sino-Indian Joint Working Group (JWG) to discuss bilateral relations, with special reference to the pending border dispute, it would be useful to analyse the set-back to the bilateral relations since May, 1998, and the Chinese perception of its relations with India in the bilateral and global context after the Pokhran II nuclear tests. An attempt has been made to cover all important Chinese statements since May 1998 in this chronology. From the chronology, one could notice three phases in the Chinese reactions. In the first phase (May to July, 1998), there was a strong barrage of criticism of the statements of George Fernandes, the Indian Defence Minister, and Prime Minister

Atal Behari Vajpayee's letter to President Clinton portraying the threat from China as a motivating factor for the Pokhran II nuclear tests.

The characterisation of the Chinese threat was condemned by China as hurting the Chinese people and projected as a mere pretext to cover India's hegemonistic ambitions. The tests were viewed as also indicative of India's desire to acquire a new political status through the possession of nuclear weapons. During this phase, the Chinese criticism of India related to the bilateral (damage to Sino-Indian relations) as well as global (damage to the global non-proliferation regime) aspects. There was rigidity in the Chinese attitude to both these aspects. In the second phase (July-middle to December, 1998), there were signs of a mellowing down of the Chinese rigidity on the bilateral aspect. There was once again stress on the importance of Sino-Indian relations and repeated calls to India to make amends in a suitable manner so that the bilateral relations could be put back on track. After the initial hard-line comments on Kashmir suggesting a multilateral conference on the issue, Beijing reverted back to its 1996 and pre-1996 stance of neutrality as between India and Pakistan on this issue.

In the third phase (since January, 1999), while welcoming the Indian initiatives for mending the damage to bilateral relations, Beijing continued to be rigid in its insistence that the international community should not accept India's concept of a minimum nuclear deterrence and that India and Pakistan should sign the NPT and the CTBT unconditionally and immediately. There was also a note of concern in Chinese pronouncements that other permanent members of the UN Security Council might ultimately accept India's need for a minimum nuclear deterrence.

During all these phases, Chinese inconsistencies in possessing a nuclear and missile capability for itself and opposing a similar capability for India were sought to be explained as follows:

- The Chinese capability was acquired in self-defence in the context of the cold war. China did not view the capability as conferring a political status on it. Moreover, China was already a permanent member of the Security Council.

• On the other hand, the Indian capability was acquired after the cold war was over when the contemporary trend was towards peace, harmony and non-proliferation. The Indian nuclear aspirations marked a revival of its hegemonistic designs and had the ulterior motive of seeking a new political status in the international community.

It is evident from the chronology that China's two-pronged policy is to continue to oppose India's nuclear aspirations and deny it any new political status at par with that of China through its emergence as a de facto nuclear weapon power, while at the same time not allowing this to affect the bilateral relations.

The Chronology

The setback process started with a statement by George Fernandes, the Indian Defence Minister, in the beginning of May 1998, in which he reportedly described China as a major military threat to India. However, he subsequently claimed that his observation made to a private TV channel was distorted.

On May 5,1998, Zhu Bangzao, a spokesman of the Chinese Foreign Office, described Mr.Fernandes' remarks as "absolutely ridiculous and unworthy of refutation" and added that China had noted with the "utmost regret and resentment" his statements on China since coming to office.

He said:" The remarks by the Indian Defence Minister George Fernandes have seriously sabotaged the friendly atmosphere for improving bilateral relations between China and India…China does not pose any threat to neighbouring countries. His accusation concerning China's relations with relevant countries is utterly fictitious and has no basis in facts…His statement that China has built a sophisticated electronic surveillance base in Myanmar's Coco Islands and has installed missiles in Tibet targeting India is absolutely fictitious and entirely baseless…. It is extremely irresponsible."

On May 8,1998, an unidentified spokesman of the Chinese Foreign Office told pressmen that China had twice protested to India through the Indian Embassy in Beijing over the "ridiculous and fragile" statements of Fernandes.

On May 12,1998, Lin Shanglin, the Chinese CDA in New Delhi, issued a written statement at New Delhi stating as follows:" The so-called issue that China has been building a naval base in Myanmar is utterly fictitious, whose aim is to find grounds to the so-called China threat...Allegations of Chinese involvement in the development of Pakistan's Ghauri missile are a fabrication. It is irresponsible to assume that China is engaged in nuclear proliferation. The co-operation between China and Pakistan in the peaceful utilisation of nuclear energy is under the safeguards and supervision of the International Atomic Energy Agency (IAEA) and conforms to the international general practices."

After the suspected leakage to the "New York Times" by the US State Department of the letter written by Indian Prime Minister Atal Behari Vajpayee to President Clinton citing India's perception of a possible threat from China as one of the reasons for Pokhran II, Chinese Government spokesmen, govt-controlled media and strategic analysts started a barrage of vigorous criticism of India.

The Xinhua news agency said on May 18,1998: "Political analysts are of the view that with the nuclear explosion, India seeks to develop nuclear weapons, barge into the world's club of nuclear powers and then seek regional hegemony."

Ye Zhengjia, a former Chinese diplomat posted at New Delhi and subsequently posted to the Chinese Foreign Ministry's Institute of International Studies, told Japan's Kyodo news service on May 18,1998: " By presenting a China threat scenario, India is trying to extract mileage out of ideological differences between China and the West while New Delhi is actually masking its own contradictions with the West to lessen the blow of sanctions." He denied that China's nuclear tests were carried out to raise the country's political status in the new world order. He added: " In any case, a country's international standing does not depend upon its capability to do a nuclear test. That time has passed." The official "China Daily" wrote on May 20,1998: " India's improper move of attributing its nuclear tests at Pokhran to potential threat from China has made the international community realise that the new Indian Government is not only irresponsible, but also immoral. This is the first time in history that a nuclear country has denied its own responsibility for its nuclear tests and shifted the blame to others..To justify its series of nuclear tests, India uses the political tactic of making India-China ties tense....China had been taking a reserved attitude towards provocative statements from India in order to push forward Sino-Indian ties. However, India took China's forbearance as weakness."

Xinhua reported on June 2,1998, that at a meeting between the Chinese Vice-Premier Qian Qichen and the US National Security Adviser Sandy Berger both sides "believed that the international community must take effective and feasible measures to halt the nuclear arms race in the South Asian region and prevent nuclear proliferation in order to restore and safeguard peace and stability in the region." Sandy Berger had gone to Beijing to prepare the ground for Clinton's visit.

In an interview to the AFP news agency on June 3,1998, President Jiang Zemin denied that China had helped Pakistan make nuclear bombs and said: "The nuclear co-operation between the two countries is strictly peaceful in the area of technology of nuclear reactors and all the installations concerned are under the control of the IAEA."

He recalled his historic visit to India in 1996 "after a number of signals of friendship from New Delhi" and said he had received a warm welcome, " but the Prime Minister then was not the same person as the one today."

Jiang further said that Pokhran II which clearly showed that "India is targeting China and Pakistan" surprised him He added: "China hopes that Pakistan will not respond and will make a wise decision. But the Pakistani Government is faced with strong public pressure on the subject."

In an article on June 5,1998, the "Liberation Army Daily", the journal of the PLA, accused George Fernandes of recklessly using China's name as an excuse for India's nuclear ambitions and warned: " If this arrogant boast and military expansionism are not effectively checked, the consequences will be serious."

A signed editorial in the "China Daily" of June 6,1998, urged India to show wisdom by renouncing its nuclear weapons programme and said that a 14 per cent rise in India's defence budget was an unwise decision which would further escalate the arms race in South Asia.

It added: "Such a rise in defence spending reveals the South Asian country's ambition to be a military power and is adding fuel to the already heated arms race...It is unwise for the Indian Government to develop nuclear weapons and raise defence spending with no regard for its relations with the international community." It described Fernandes' statement in the Indian Parliament about the occupation of Indian territory by China as a "concocted excuse."

In an interview to the "Newsweek" on June 21,1998, Jiang Zemin said: "In November 1996, I paid a successful visit to India. I was accorded a very friendly reception by the Government and people of India. That visit has left me with very good memories. I was very surprised that they conducted the nuclear tests. I was even more surprised that they cited China as a reason for their nuclear testing. I really don't know what kind of threat China poses."

Jiang also said that if Clinton raised the question of alleged Chinese supply of missiles to Pakistan, "the answer very simply is that we don't plan to sell missiles."

A joint statement issued by Jiang Zemin and President Clinton on June 27,1998, after the latter's visit to Beijing in the last week of June, 1998, said: "Recent nuclear tests by India and Pakistan and the resulting increase in tension between them are a source of deep and lasting concern to both of us.

"Our shared interests in a peaceful and stable South Asia in a strong global non-proliferation regime have been put at risk by these tests, which we have joined in condemning.

"We have agreed to continue to work closely together, within the P-5, the Security Council and with others, to prevent an accelerating nuclear and missile arms race in South Asia, strengthen international non-proliferation efforts and promote reconciliation and the peaceful resolution of differences between India and Pakistan.

"The P-5 joint communiqué of June 4, which was endorsed by UN Security Council Resolution 1172, set out clear and comprehensive objectives and a plan for action to address the threat of a South Asian nuclear and missile arms race.

"We pledge our full support for the steps outlined in the joint communiqué and again call on India and Pakistan to stop all further nuclear tests and adhere immediately and unconditionally to the CTBT, to refrain from weaponisation or deployment of nuclear weapons and from testing or deployment of missiles capable of delivering nuclear weapons and to enter into firm commitment not to weaponise or deploy nuclear weapons or missiles capable of delivering them.

"The United States and China remain firmly committed to strong and effective international co-operation on nuclear non-proliferation, with the NPT as its cornerstone.

"We will continue to bolster nuclear non-proliferation efforts and reiterate that our goal is adherence of all countries, including India and Pakistan, to the NPT as it stands, without any modification.

"States that do not adhere to the treaty cannot expect to be accorded the same benefits and international standing as are accorded to NPT parties. Notwithstanding their recent nuclear tests, India and Pakistan do not have the status of nuclear weapon states in accordance with the NPT." Speaking at the Beijing University on June 29,1998, Clinton said: "We (the US and China) are now pursuing a common strategy to move India and Pakistan away from further testing and engage in a dialogue to resolve all outstanding issues."

Commenting the same day on the reference in the Clinton-Jiang statement to the nuclear issue in South Asia, the "China Daily" said that the US-China understanding on this subject "signified a healthy, stable China-US relationship." It added: " Such a relationship is not only in the interest of China and the US, but of the world peace and stability at large. "

Tang Guoqiang, a spokesman of the Chinese Foreign Office, rejected on June 30,1998, India's criticism of the Clinton-Jiang statement. He said that as major powers, the US and China had to act in the common interest of the international community to prevent a nuclear arms race in the region and promote reconciliation between New Delhi and Islamabad.

Accusing India of starting a nuclear arms race in South Asia, he said: "The joint statement expresses the strong determination of China and the US in further preventing nuclear proliferation and also promoting reconciliation and peaceful settlement of the differences between India and Pakistan.

"There is nothing reproachful about the joint statement on South Asia. While India opposed the joint statement, Pakistan has welcomed it. However, we have taken note of India's comments."

Writing in "The Hindu" of July 2,1998, F.J.Khergamvala, its Tokyo correspondent, quoted Robert Manning and James Przystup, former senior US State Department officials, who had visited China, as having stated in an article in the "Wall Street Journal" (date not mentioned) that during their visit a prominent Chinese analyst told them that "transferring material or technology to Iran is negotiable, but Pakistan is our Israel", implying thereby that Pakistan's security was as important to China as Israel's was to the US.

However, in an interview to the State-run China Central Television before leaving China, Clinton said that the US and

China had agreed to work together to prevent the spread of nuclear and missile technologies to countries like Pakistan that might misuse it.

He added: "China has agreed to work with the US to stop the transfer of technologies to countries that might misuse it, to not assist unsafeguarded nuclear facilities like Pakistan's and to consider joining the worldwide system that prevents the exportation of dangerous technologies."

At a meeting of the leaders of China, Russia, Kazakhstan, Kyrgyzstan and Tajikistan held at Almaty in Kazakhstan on July 3, 1998, Jiang Zemin failed to have a critical reference to the nuclear and missile arms race in South Asia included in the final communiqué. However, during a joint press conference by the leaders after the summit he condemned India for starting a nuclear race in South Asia.

While briefing pressmen on July 9,1998, Tang Guoqiang, the Chinese Foreign Ministry spokesman, avoided commenting on India's offer of a pledge of no-first-use of nuclear weapons. He merely said: "The most urgent task for India is to immediately abandon its nuclear programme and sign the NPT and the CTBT unconditionally as soon as possible."

However, in an interview to K.K.Katyal and C.Raja Mohan, the New Delhi correspondents of "The Hindu" the same day, Zhou Gang, the Chinese Ambassador to India, gave the first indication of the beginning of a mellowing down of the Chinese criticism of India. He made the following points:

- "It is up to the doer to undo the knot". Beijing would like India to provide responsible explanations for totally "unreasonable and groundless" accusations against China and, thus, create a favourable atmosphere for a new beginning in bilateral relations. The initiative for this must be taken not by China, but by India. It was China's set policy to develop a "constructive and co-operative partnership" with India towards the new millennium.

- It was impossible to call for a dialogue and establish best relations while keeping up attacks on China, which had been the victim of baseless accusations. China would like these charges to stop and "actual actions" initiated. China would not like the present situation to go on. "As two big powers, the high-level political contacts between India and China should be normal."

- He hoped that India and Pakistan would peacefully resolve their differences "including the Kashmir issue" through talks. "The position of the Chinese side is consistent". After the nuclear tests by India and Pakistan, the growing tension on Kashmir and the issue of peace and security in South Asia had caused widespread concern in the international community. "We will do whatever is beneficial for the improvement of India-Pakistan relations and peace and stability in South Asia, but never do otherwise."

- China's ties with Pakistan were State-to-State relations between two sovereign countries. China had not transferred to any country equipment or technology that could be used for making nuclear weapons. Some of India's concerns over Sino-Pakistan military co-operation were caused by misunderstandings and others arose out of unnecessary misgivings. China would like to exchange views on this subject with India through diplomatic channels, as used to be done in the past. He disapproved of the resort to media and exaggerations based on "rumours from the West."

- There was peace and tranquillity on the India-China border. "We hope the two sides would make joint efforts to maintain this situation." China had taken "a series of flexible measures" on Sikkim and he hoped that the Indian side " would also adopt a positive and flexible attitude so as to create a proper atmosphere and conditions for the disposal of this issue."

In a lead article on July 14,1998, the "China Daily" called for " a multilateral meeting attended by India, Pakistan, the US, China and Russia to help resolve the Kashmir dispute, over which India and Pakistan have fought two wars since 1947."

The article, quoting Ma Jiali of the China Institute of Contemporary International Relations, said: "Indian Government officials should stop spreading the China menace theory which will create suspicion and hostility between the two peoples. The Indian Government's unreasonable attacks on China deeply hurt the feelings of the Chinese people and undermined the mutual trust the two countries have been trying to build over generations." Quoting Ouyang Liping, another expert of the same Institute, the article said that China had consistently adhered to the policy of non-proliferation of nuclear weapons and denied that China was aiding Pakistan's clandestine nuclear programme.

Commenting on the annual report of the Defence Ministry of the Government of India for 1997-98, the article said: "In the report, the Indian Government did not examine its mistake in provoking a dangerous nuclear arms race. It vilified China as the main reason for the deterioration of South Asia's security environment instead."

The article described the BJP-led Government as head strong and alleged that the real purpose of Pokhran II was to gain regional hegemony.

It further quoted Ouyang Liping as saying: "India's recent nuclear explosions reflect a dangerous ultra-nationalism and its ambition to build a regional hegemony and become a major political power."

The article added: "Continuously denying its faults and spreading lies will not win sympathy or trust from others, but will make the international community more vigilant against its ambitions. India should first abandon its nuclear development plan unconditionally so as to convince Pakistan to follow in its foot steps."

The article again quoted Ouyang Liping as saying that the international community must press India and Pakistan to completely abandon their nuclear programmes and convert South Asia into a non-nuclear area. In this connection, he cited the examples of South Africa and Ukraine and said: "They (South Africa and Ukraine) abandoned their nuclear capability in the 1990s under international pressure and for the good of their own peoples."

Despite this article, there was another indication of a possible mellowing down of the Chinese official criticism in an address by Zhou Gang, the Chinese Ambassador, in the India International Centre at New Delhi on July 25,1998. He made the following points:

- India's nuclear tests had led to "temporary difficulties" in Sino-Indian ties, but had not diluted Beijing's commitment to building a long-term friendly relationship with New Delhi." It is a firm policy of the Chinese Government to develop with India a long-term neighbourly and constructive partnership of co-operation for the 21st century.

- India and China could play an influential role in promoting Asian stability. "As the two most populous developing countries in the world, China and India can exert important influence in the affairs of South Asia and Asia as a whole."

- China did not seek hegemony in the region though it was naturally interested in the developments between India and Pakistan. China had normal relations with Pakistan, which were based on the five principles of peaceful co-existence. Pakistani nuclear weapons programme could not be linked to China's. Pakistan had, however, received conventional weapons from China, but the quantum of these exchanges was much smaller to the defence trade between India and a "powerful country" (an apparent reference to Russia).

- "Friendly relations between China and any country are not directed at any third country." China did not pose any security threat to India. "Fictitious charges against China have gravely hurt the feelings of the Chinese people and harmed Sino-Indian relations."

- China wished India "stability, progress and development" and sought "neighbourliness, friendship and progress" from New Delhi. The Chinese pronouncements were a refutation of some wanton attack and accusations by certain personages in India. They were meant to "safeguard the friendly relations between our two countries and bring them back on track."

Co-operation between India and China must diversify and should not be held hostage to the pending resolution of the border dispute. The boundary question could be resolved on the principle of mutual understanding and mutual accommodation. The Peace and Tranquillity accord of 1993 and the subsequent agreement of 1996 on confidence-building measures continued to be the cornerstone of the Sino-Indian security relationship.

In an interview to the "Al Ahram" of Cairo on July 26,1998, Prime Minister Zhu Rongji said: "I assure there is no Chinese threat to India. I confirm our keenness on good neighbourly relations and peaceful co-existence. Beijing had no time to threaten or scare other countries, as it is busy with its own economic development. Any view on China's fearful size came only from India. No other State took this view. India has utilised this theory as a pretext to conduct its nuclear tests. However, the real target behind the nuclear tests is practice of hegemony as well as settling the internal crisis facing the ruling party. Due to limited economic capabilities, China sets aside a limited percentage of its resources for defence purposes. It is less than that allocated by India and Japan. In fact, China needs some defence capabilities."

Jaswant Singh, who attended the ASEAN meeting at Manila as the Indian Prime Minister's special representative, met Tang Jiaxuan, the Chinese Foreign Minister, on July 27,1998. A Chinese spokesman later said that "both sides conducted frank discussions on the Indian nuclear explosions and Sino-Indian relations." He added that during the discussions, the Chinese Foreign Minister stressed that India, running counter to the world trend, conducted nuclear tests and that India, "in an attempt to find an excuse for the tests, groundlessly alleged that China poses a threat to India."

A joint statement issued by Tang Jiaxuan and his Filipino counterpart, Domingo Siazon after bilateral talks on August 2,1998, expressed the support of the two countries for the Security Council Resolution 1172 of June 6,1998. The two countries expressed "their grave concern over and strongly deplored the recent nuclear tests in South Asia. These had exacerbated tensions in the region and raised the spectre of a nuclear arms race." In a statement in the Lok Sabha, the lower House of the Indian Parliament, on August 4,1998, Prime Minister Vajpayee said India was keen on improving its relations with China and asserted that his Government had never dubbed China as an enemy or a threat. He also said that India wanted to accelerate the efforts for a solution to the border problem.

Commenting on this statement on August 7,1998, Tang Guoqiang, spokesman of the Chinese Foreign Office, said: "We have taken note of the Prime Minister's statement in Parliament. We hope that the Indian side will take concrete actions so that the bilateral relations will return to normal." Replying to a question on the Kashmir issue on August 11,1998, the same spokesman distanced himself from the views mentioned in the "China Daily" article and re-stated the traditional Chinese position. He said: " Kashmir is an outstanding issue between India and Pakistan. The Chinese position on that is consistent. The Chinese side hopes that India and Pakistan will solve their dispute through peaceful negotiations and maintain calm and restraint before the solution of the problem."

Addressing a meeting of industrialists organised at New Delhi on August 12,1998, by the Federation of Indian Chambers of Commerce and Industry, Zhou Gang, the Chinese Ambassador, made yet another reassuring statement. He said that despite the setback to the Sino-Indian bilateral relations, there was scope for increased bilateral trade and economic relations "because the reforms and the opening up of the economy in both the countries have provided great opportunities for expanding trade and economic relations." He expressed his optimism that "on the eve of the next century trade and economic relations and cooperation between China and India would be pushed on to a new high." However, while talking to journalists after the meeting, he added that India's nuclear tests had severely damaged bilateral relations and "this will spill over to the economic relations also."

In reply to questions during the daily press briefing on August 13,1998, Tang Guoqiang, the Chinese Foreign Office spokesman, again evaded comments on China's reaction to India's no-first-use of nuclear weapons offer and repeated the Chinese demand that India should first give up its nuclear programme and sign unconditionally the NPT and the CTBT.

Addressing a meeting at the Bharat Chamber of Commerce at Calcutta on September 14,1998, Zhou Gang, the Chinese Ambassador, said differences between the two countries should not be seen as an obstacle to fostering trade. He added: "Expansion of economic relations, trade and technological co-operation between our two countries is beneficial for the overall development of bilateral relations and in conformity with the fundamental interests of the people of our two countries." He also claimed that China's nuclear tests were undertaken in the interest of self-defence.

China reacted sharply to a courtesy call by the Dalai Lama on Prime Minister Vajpayee in the third week of October 1998. On October 22,1998, a Chinese Foreign Office spokesman described it as a violation of India's commitment to keep itself away from the Dalai Lama's anti-Chinese activities. Rejecting the Chinese criticism, a spokesman of the Indian Foreign Office pointed out the next day that the Dalai Lama had been received in his capacity as a religious leader by successive Indian Prime Ministers and that leaders of other countries had similarly received him too. The 11th meeting of the JWG, which should have been held in the second half of 1998, could not be held due to the misunderstanding in the bilateral relations. While talking to a group of visiting American journalists at New Delhi in the middle of November, 1998, a diplomat of the Chinese Embassy said that China had adopted an "active approach" to the subject and that the matter was under discussion through diplomatic channels.

In his briefing for the US journalists, the unnamed Chinese diplomat reportedly made the following points:

- China acquired a nuclear weapon capability in the context of the cold war. After the end of the cold war the trend was towards non-proliferation.
- The Indian tests were against the contemporary historical trend and seriously affected peace and stability in South Asia. The Indian tests had also dealt a heavy blow to international nuclear disarmament and the global non-proliferation regime.
- China did not agree that there was a nuclear apartheid. "The nuclear status of the five permanent members of the UN Security Council is a product of history. In our opinion, favouring the NPT doesn't mean that the nuclear weapon states will enjoy the permanent privilege of possessing nuclear weapons. China had all along urged countries with the largest nuclear arsenals to speed up the process of nuclear weapon reduction. As a nuclear state, China will never shirk its own responsibility for the complete prohibition and thorough destruction of nuclear weapons in the end."
- "China has always been committed, on the basis of the Five Principles of Peaceful Co-Existence, to the development of good neighbourly and friendly relations with its neighbouring countries, including India. China has made unremitting efforts to improve and develop Sino-Indian relations. This stand of China has not changed. Before and after India's nuclear tests, the Indian Defence Minister and other senior officials preached the China threat theory and made wanton accusations against China. All this cannot but affect the normal development of the bilateral relations. The responsibility for upsetting Sino-Indian relations at present is totally on the Indian side. As the ball is now in the Indian court, we hope that apart from

expressing its willingness to improve the relations in words, what is more important for the Indian side is to take concrete actions to improve the relations."

A joint declaration signed by Russian President Boris Yeltsin and Jiang Zemin, at the end of the latter's visit to Russia on November 25,1998, cited South Asia along with Kosovo, Afghanistan and Korea as regions of "the most acute conflict situations, which, if they escalate, may pose real threats to the international community." It added: "On South Asia, Russia and China confirm their position expressed in the UN and at other international fora and stress the paramount importance of the NPT and the CTBT for the global efforts to promote the non-spread of nuclear arms and nuclear disarmament. Russia and China call upon all countries which have not yet joined these treaties so far to do so without delay and without conditions."

Russian Foreign Office officials tried to play down the significance of the reference by saying that they had succeeded in toning down a harsh statement which Jiang wanted and in ruling out any reference to India by name. According to them, since Jiang insisted on some reference to it in the joint declaration they had to agree to a mild formulation which need not cause embarrassment to India.

In a letter to Jaswant Singh on December 15,1998, congratulating him on his taking over as the Minister for External Affairs, Tang Jiaxuan, the Chinese Foreign Minister, hoped that Sino-Indian relations could be consolidated and further developed during Singh's tenure. In his reply to the message, Jaswant Singh said:" India remains committed to the process of dialogue to address and resolve outstanding issues." He referred to his meeting with Tang at Manila and said that he looked forward to "continuing our interaction to further mutual understanding, co-operation and friendship, so essential for our two countries and peoples."

In his first press conference after taking office, Jaswant Singh stated that India was committed to improving its ties with China so that all outstanding issues were resolved in accordance with the five principles of peaceful co-existence.

In his daily press briefing on December 28,1998, Zhu Bangzao, the spokesman of the Chinese Foreign Office, said: " We welcome Minister for External affairs Jaswant Singh's remarks. China has always attached importance to the growth of its good neighbourly, friendly and co-operative ties with India on the basis of the five principles of peaceful co-existence. Normalisation of Sino-Indian relations complies with the fundamental interests of the people of both the countries."

The "Jane's Defence Weekly" reported in the last week of December, 1998, that the Chinese authorities had assessed that India would take at least 10 years to establish an operational nuclear strike capability and, hence, India did not pose an immediate threat to China's security.

China strongly expressed its annoyance over the remarks of Ram Jethmalani, the Indian Urban Affairs Minister, that there was a strong case for India to recognise Taiwan as an independent country. He made these remarks in an interview to "The Week" of Kerala in the last week of December 1998.

The "People's Daily" wrote on December 31,1998: "We strongly urge certain Indian politicians to stop interfering in China's internal affairs and work towards improving rather than damaging the bilateral ties. Jethmalani's remarks have further hurt the feelings of the Chinese people. "

In a despatch on January 1,1999, Xinhua described Jethmalani's remarks as "evil-minded and dangerous." In an article on January 6,1999, the "China Daily" asked Indian leaders "not to test China's patience with irresponsible comments" and to adopt a coherent policy towards China. It added: "China's goodwill and repeated patience should not be returned with vile language." The criticism came down after the Government of India, through the Indian Embassy in Beijing as well as through its press spokesman in New Delhi, assured China that there was no change in India's policy on Taiwan. There were clear indications in January 1999, that while showing readiness to restore the pre-Pokhran II normalcy to the bilateral relations, China remained determined in its opposition to India's acquiring any nuclear deterrence capability. Addressing a meeting of non-proliferation experts in Washington in the middle of January 1999, Sha Zukang, head of the Department of Arms Control and Disarmament in China's Foreign Office, reportedly stated as follows:

- "It is a direct violation of UN Security Council Resolution 1172 to negotiate, or to even discuss, with India on India's so-called minimum nuclear deterrence capability."

- "It is also unhelpful to publicly support India's permanent membership in the UN Security Council soon after its nuclear tests."

- The South Asian tests had become a litmus test for the effectiveness of the global non-proliferation regime. The international community should do its best to stop and reverse the nuclear weapons programmes of India and Pakistan.

- There were two essential requirements for the success of the international nuclear diplomacy in the sub-continent. First, " the international community should have sufficient patience and perseverance and should not lose hope because of the lack of progress in the short run." Second, "the major powers must have a consensus view and take concerted actions in this matter."

- "If any country seeks to exploit the South Asian situation to obtain unilateral, short-term political, economic or strategic benefits at the expense of the other countries and the international solidarity, it can only further undermine the already badly-damaged international non-proliferation regime, and, in the end, the long-term interests of that country will also be jeopardised."

- "We have noted with concern that after the Indian nuclear tests, some Nuclear Suppliers' Group members have taken a more pro-active stand on issues of nuclear co-operation with India. We hope that these countries could be more cautious in this area."

In an interview to the "Handelsblatt" of Germany on February 2,1999, Tang Jiaxuan, the Chinese Foreign Minister, rejected indirectly the idea of a Russia-India-China strategic triangle to which Prime Minister Yevgeny Primakov had referred during his visit to India in December, 1998. Tang spoke of China's "very good strategic partnership with Russia, which is full of vitality and regularly produces new elements" but clarified that Beijing's partnership with Moscow "includes neither alliances nor confrontation with third countries such as the US."

He described relations with India as far from ideal and blamed India for the deterioration in the relations. He urged India "to take practical steps towards the restoration of normal and healthy relations."

In an interview to the Press Trust of India on February 4,1999, Zhou Gang, the Chinese Ambassador to India, said: "India, instead of maintaining the so-called minimum nuclear deterrent, must accede to the CTBT and the NPT without delay and conditions."

Referring to speculation about the possible easing of sanctions against India by the US in the wake of the latest round of Jaswant Singh-Strobe Talbott discussions, he said:"Basically, China does not advocate sanctions."

On Primakov's strategic triangle idea, the Ambassador said:" China handles international affairs by proceeding from the fundamental interests of the people of China and the whole world and does not enter into alliances with any big power or group of countries. China's developing relations with any other country are not directed against another country." In his daily press briefing on February 23, 1999, a spokesman of the Chinese Foreign Ministry welcomed the Vajpayee-Nawaz Sharif summit and the resulting Lahore Declaration. He added: "We hope the two sides will keep the momentum of dialogue and solve their differences through peaceful negotiations and consultations."

In his inaugural address to the budget session of the Indian Parliament on February 22,1999, President K.R.Narayanan said that India "seeks to strengthen and deepen its historic and friendly relations with China" and "is looking forward to continuing the dialogue with that country."

Addressing a seminar on Sino-Indian relations at New Delhi on February 25,1999, Zhou Gang, the Chinese Ambassador, said as follows:

- "We have consistently believed that the problems that cropped up in the Sino-Indian relations are temporary and can be surmounted. There exist extensive common interests between China and India and our commonalties far outweigh our differences."

- 'The outstanding issue between China and India is no more than the boundary dispute left behind by history." These differences could be resolved on the basis of the five principles of peaceful co-existence and in accordance with the principle of mutual understanding and mutual accommodation.

- "We have noted that the Indian side has recently expressed its willingness to attach importance to its relations with China, not to view China as an enemy,and resume the dialogue, so as to find solutions to mutual concerns."

- China was not involved in the Pakistani nuclear and missile programmes."All co-operation between China and Pakistan in the field of peaceful uses of nuclear energy is under the safeguards of the IAEA. Non-existent is the issue of nuclear and missile proliferation to Pakistan. In fact, the Chinese side has already taken note of some concerns of the Indian side and, proceeding from the overall interests of friendly relations between China and India, it has taken a positive, flexible and pragmatic approach and made proper re-adjustment of certain policies concerned."

- The entire historical baggage of Sino-Indian differences could not be shed overnight, but only on the basis of reciprocity in a step by step manner. "All this needs a favourable atmosphere in our bilateral relations. Therefore, we hope that the Indian side will also adopt a flexible and pragmatic approach and solve the Chinese side's concerns earnestly."

• The attribution of a Chinese threat to justify India's nuclear tests by some personalities was mainly responsible for the recent deterioration in the Sino-Indian relations. "All this has deeply hurt the feelings of the Chinese people and seriously harmed the Sino-Indian relations. This is the main cause upsetting Sino-Indian relations."

The Ambassador's presentation coincided with the visit of a team of officials of India's Ministry of External Affairs to Beijing for three days from February 25,1999, to prepare the ground for holding the delayed JWG meeting.

In the daily press briefing on March 1,1999, Ms. Zhang Qiyue, a spokesperson of the Chinese Foreign Office, commented as follows on the talks with the Indian team: "Both sides discussed India's tests and their impact on Sino-Indian ties and expounded their respective positions on the issue. The two sides also focused on bilateral issues and re-affirmed their faith in the five principles of peaceful co-existence. The two sides agreed to work for the restoration and improvement of bilateral relations."

A spokesman of the Indian Embassy in Beijing said that India stoutly defended its position on the Pokhran tests and added: "We pointed out to them India's rejection of the UN Security Council resolution and our stand on the NPT and the CTBT." Addressing a press conference during the session of the National People's Congress, Tang Jiaxuan, the Chinese Foreign Minister, said on March 7.1999: "I expect, may be soon, the JWG on the boundary question between China and India will resume its activity." He again appealed to India and Pakistan to roll back their nuclear programme.

Addressing a seminar on "India, China and Russia in the 21st century" organised by the Indian Council of World Affairs at New Delhi on March 9,1998, Zhou Gang, the Chinese Ambassador, said:

- The recent consultations in Beijing between officials of the two Foreign Offices marked a "new starting point" to improve bilateral relations.
- "We have noted that the Indian side has recently expressed its willingness to attach importance to and improve relations with China and not view China as its enemy. All this is welcome."
- China was pursuing an independent foreign policy vis-à-vis Russia, the US and India. "As powers of major influence and permanent members of the UN Security Council, China and the US share common interests on major issues related to peace and development in the Asia-Pacific region and the world as a whole. The two sides have decided to work together for the establishment of a constructive strategic partnership."
- The concept of a Sino-Russian strategic partnership did not have any military connotations. "Building a Sino-Russian strategic partnership is not aimed at forming an alliance and is not directed at any third party, but is aimed at abandoning confrontations between the two countries so as to create conditions for the broadest equal exchanges and co-operation."
- "It is the firm policy of the Chinese Government to develop with India, a long-term neighbourly, constructive and co-operative partnership into the 21st century. The two countries had the foundation and potential for evolving mutually beneficial co-operation. India and China shared similar or common views on such issues as peace and development, human rights, environmental protection and population control."
- "Strict adherence to the five principles of peaceful, co-existence, mutual trust and shedding a threat image of each other were the key for laying a credible foundation for a healthy Sino-Indian relationship."
- China hoped that "South Asian countries will treat one another on an equal footing, live in harmony, develop

friendly co-operation and settle their differences and disputes through peaceful means."

• When the bilateral relations were developing without a hitch, some personalities in India accused China of posing a threat to India's security so as to justify the nuclear tests. This was the main cause for upsetting the bilateral relations. Beijing's policy was defensive in nature and any fear of a China threat was entirely "unfounded and fabricated with ulterior motives."

In an interview to the PTI on March 21,1999, Sha Zukang, Director-General of the Department of Arms Control and Disarmament in the Chinese Foreign Office, said:

• "We have never posed a threat to India and history clearly shows that...We didn't have New Delhi in mind when we decided to go nuclear."

• Since China became a nuclear power, it had never threatened any country. "On the contrary, because of our own bitter experience of being blackmailed, we have declared to the world that we would never be the first to use nuclear weapons. To say China's nuclear weapons are threatening the security of India is hurting."

• China was willing to resume dialogue with India in the post-Pokhran phase, provided New Delhi took concrete actions to normalise strained bilateral relations. "We are prepared to enhance dialogue with India so as to clear misgivings, further mutual understanding and promote the goal of establishing a constructive and co-operative partnership between China and India. We hope that the Indian side will also take concrete actions in the same direction."

• "We continue to maintain that India and Pakistan should fully implement the UN Security Council Resolution 1172. To maintain peace and stability in South Asia and establish a nuclear-weapon-free world, both South Asian neighbours should abandon their nuclear weapons programmes and unconditionally accede to the NPT and the CTBT."

In an address to the United Services Institution (USI) of New Delhi on March 24,1999, Zhou Gang, the Chinese Ambassador, said as follows:

- "There exists profound traditional friendship between the people of the two countries. China and India sympathised and supported each other during their struggles of national independence and liberation against foreign aggression. The two countries share similar or identical views on many major issues such as economic development, human rights, environmental protection, combating drug trafficking and crime and population control."

- "There is nothing abnormal about some differences between the two countries. As long as both sides proceed from the overall interests of bilateral friendly relations and handle these concerns on the basis of mutual trust, with a positive, flexible and pragmatic approach and in a truth-seeking and forward-looking spirit, the differences will be narrowed gradually and problems resolved instead of coming in the way of the normal development of the bilateral relations."

- "Good neighbourly relations between India and China will not only conform to the fundamental interests of the two countries, but will encourage peace, stability and development in Asia and the world at large."

- "The outstanding issue between China and India is no more than the boundary dispute left behind by history. The Chinese Government has maintained that while positively seeking a solution to the boundary issue, the two sides should work hard to develop bilateral relations in various fields so as to create a favourable atmosphere for the final solution of the boundary issue. China stood for a peaceful, fair and equitable solution to the boundary issue on the basis of the five principles of peaceful co-existence, in accordance with the principle of mutual understanding and mutual accommodation through friendly talks, while taking into account the historical background and the present reality and the national feelings of the people of the two countries."

- "China welcomed the resumption of talks between the two Foreign Office officials in February. This useful meeting provides a new starting point for the improvement of Sino-Indian ties." He hoped that the two sides trust each other and treat each other with sincerity and strictly adhere to the five principles of peaceful co-existence.

Talking to pressmen on April 2,1999, Brajesh Mishra, Principal Secretary to the Indian Prime Minister, said that an official dialogue with Beijing had already commenced and that the forthcoming JWC meeting might result in a visit to China by the Indian Minister for External Affairs.

During a meeting with a visiting delegation of the Congress (I) led by K.Natwar Singh, at Beijing on April 8,1999,Hu Jintao, the Chinese Vice-President, asked India to pursue a long-term policy on Sino-Indian relations in view of the "complex and dynamic international situations unfolding at the turn of the century." He said that under the changing international situation today, India and China should "look closely at and handle the relations between the two countries from the historical perspective and a long-term viewpoint." He noted that the bilateral relations had progressed on the normal track over the past decade "thanks to the joint efforts of the leaders of the two countries ", and regretted the chill in the bilateral relations after Pokhran II. The process of progress had consequently suffered "undesirable disturbances", he said.

Reports of Chinese reaction to the Agni II missile test available so far indicate that the spokesman of the Chinese Foreign Office expressed regret and concern at the test which, he pointed out, was a violation of the Security Resolution 1172 and added:" We have taken note of the remark by the Indian Prime Minister that this test is not directed against any country."

The annual report of the Indian Defence Ministry for 1998-99 released on April 16,1999, said as follows on Sino-Indian relations:

- Sino-Indian relations have improved in recent years and New Delhi regards China as "a great neighbour."

- India does not regard China "as an adversary and would like to develop mutually friendly relations with it."
- India has expressed its interest time and again in resolving its boundary dispute with China peacefully and through bilateral negotiations as quickly as possible.
- The September 1993 agreement on peace and tranquillity and the subsequent accord on confidence-building measures provided a reliable framework for the maintenance of peace and tranquillity in the border areas.
- Contacts between the two sides such as the meeting between Jaswant Singh and Tang Jiaxuan at Manila and the earlier visit to India by the Chinese Chief of General Staff serve the objective of furthering mutual understanding between the two countries and reassuring each other about their peaceful intentions.

SINO-INDIAN RELATIONS 1950-1959

The Sino-Indian relationship from 1950 to 1959 was particularly warm, and several reasons for these cordial relations existed. Arguably the most important was the hasty diplomatic recognition of the PRC in December 1949 by India, making them the second nation in the world after Burma to do so. This conferment of legitimacy was helpful in establishing a cooperative environment with China, as many nations chose instead to recognize the Republic of China (ROC) in Taiwan. Furthermore, India's existence as a socialist and not a capitalist state, allowed for greater cooperation with the PRC since they did not come into direct conflict with Maoist ideology like the U.S. This basis of diplomatic and ideological congruency led Prime Minister Nehru to attempt to revolutionize international affairs by producing the Panchsheel Agreement between China and India in 1954. The Panchsheel Agreement stressed five points; (1) mutual respect for each other's territorial integrity and sovereignty; (2) mutual non-aggression; (3) non-interference in each other's domestic affairs; (4) equality and mutual benefit, and finally; (5) peaceful coexistence. This agreement originates from Nehru's optimism that post-colonial nations could invalidate the precepts of a bipolar world, and that the regional powers of Asia can contradict the validity of traditional balance of power politics.

The diplomatic and ideological reasons for Sino-Indian cooperation are bolstered by shared historical experiences. Both China and India share a long and uninterrupted cultural and historical tradition. Both nations at one time were great powers. Most importantly though, both nations were invaded by Western imperialists and consummately humiliated and exploited. This occupation and exploitation by the West caused the growth of significant nationalist forces within India and China, and the desire to gain independence. The ROC received its independence in 1912, and the later consolidation of the PRC in 1949 ushered in a new era of Chinese sovereignty and independence from imperialism. Likewise, India achieved its independence from Britain in 1947.

Due to their history of Western occupation, China and India had additionally failed to develop independent industries. Their occupations meant that the Chinese and Indian economies were still largely agrarian, and dependent on the import of finished goods. This led the Indian government to implement a form of democratic socialism, while the PRC engaged in agrarian based communism, or Maoism. Regardless of their system's differences, both nations abhorred capitalism creating an ideological common ground. Their common historical experience produced a familiar perspective upon which Indian and Chinese policymakers could relate to one another.

This environment of common history and diplomatic cooperation producing positive relations would be challenged by the Chinese policy of taking back historical possessions. The 1950 invasion and takeover of Tibet by the PRC would begin to show strains in the relationship. Trepidation over Tibet's seizure by the PRC was based in the idea of a historical Indian-Tibetan relationship, but the Seventeen Points Agreement of May 1951 ironed out their differences with India recognizing China's historical sovereignty over Tibet while still preserving Indian economic and social interests in Tibet. The agreement appeared to settle a possible dispute over Tibet between the two powers, but right-wing elements in the Indian parliament expressed this viewpoint of the PRC invasion, "the final action of the Chinese, in my judgment, is a little short of perfidy". This underlying opinion of the Tibet invasion by the PRC would bring forward another issue heightening tension in the relationship.

This issue was the definition of China's border with India in the Northeast and Northwest. Maxwell argues that one of China's diplomatic priorities was defining diplomatically agreed boundaries, as "boundaries are one of the first expressions of a modern state" and the PRC sought this validation of modernity. However, to not endanger Sino-Indian relations over the border question, Nehru and Zhou Enlai agreed to leave the border issue between mid-level bureaucrats to be mediated at a later date paving the way for the 1954 Panchsheel Agreement.

Thus, this issue remained on the back-burner of Indian foreign policy until the PRC began to make moves towards its historical conception of Sino-Indian boundaries south of the McMahon Line in 1957. Two years later Tibet rose up in a massive revolt against Chinese authority.

China's People's Liberation Army (PLA) moved in to put down the rebellion by breaking popular will in the capital of Lhasa. March 31, 1959 the Dalai Lama fled from Tibet into India where he was granted political asylum. This course of events angered the Indian public as they saw it as a renunciation of Indian trade and cultural access to Tibet guaranteed in the Seventeen Points Agreement. PRC officials chaffed at India's meddling in their domestic affairs by granting asylum to the Dalai Lama and thereby violating the 1954 Panchsheel agreement. The Tibetan revolt combined with gradual Chinese assertion of borders in 1957 due to diplomatic impasse, are the primary factors contributing to a hostile Sino-Indian diplomatic relationship from 1959 to the outbreak of hostilities.

Important the Systems Theory

Now that a historical context for Sino-Indian relations during the 20th Century has been established, it is necessary to define the systemic level theory from which the case will be analyzed. A systemic level of analysis eschews the individualities of states and the impact of individual leaders on foreign policy outcomes. Instead it focuses on the structure of the international system, and how this structure forces states to conform to a set of probable responses regardless of their individual differences.

In Kenneth Waltz's seminal work, *Man the State and War*, he lays down the foundation for a levels-of-analysis framework for studying international relations. Waltz does not contend to have created this framework, but instead argues that different theories of international relations promote one or another level of analysis over the other. The basis of this assertion is in Waltz's take on how is politics best to be studied, "Can man in society best be understood by studying man or by studying society"? If one believes that man in society can best be understood by studying man then you will focus on individuals and reject the influence of society on them, and vice versa. This idea is then refocused from the question of man and politics to the question of why states go to war.

Classical realists like Hans Morgenthau believe that war is driven essentially by the natural evilness of man. Essentially the "ubiquity of evil in human action arising from man's ineradicable lust for power and transforming churches into political organizations ...revolutions into dictatorships... love for country into imperialism". From this perspective, society and government are not influential forces in history, but instead magnifiers of mans collective malevolence when grouped into nations. From a classical model states cannot cooperate because "passion often obscures the true interests of states as of men," and not because "states are never honorable and peaceful". Waltzian neo-realism departs from these ideas by exploring the other half of the question. Believing that "Man is born and in his natural condition remains neither good nor bad," but is influenced by society to one extreme or the other, as states are influenced by a society of states (the international arena) to engage in war or not.

Neorealist systems theory is driven by one primary characteristic: in no matter what form the system is structured, the system is driven by the essential existence of anarchy. The source of this anarchy is the absence of an overarching international body with the power to force the conformity of the units of the structure (the states). As such the United Nations and other international organizations are not important and have no bearing on the system since they lack the capability of shaping the unit actors decisions. Acknowledging this, states are the only relevant actors, and the anarchic system leaves them with two realities. The first is that states are responsible for their own security, and secondly that threats to this security are unending.

Additionally, neo-realism departs from classical realism in that classical realists view power itself as the ultimate goal of the state, whereas neorealists view power as a means with the end being security. Peace in an anarchic system is fragile, and therefore each state must provide for its own security. However, providing for one's own security through military power or alliances often times undermines the security of neighboring states. This paradox where increasing a states security undermines the perception of security in another state is known as the "security dilemma," and is a major structural explanation for the outbreak of war. This is due to the fact that one can never be certain if additional security measures are defensive or offensive in the anarchic system. Another cause on the systemic level for the outbreak of war is the failure of deterrence. Deterrence strategy implies a buildup of military force adequate enough in perception or reality to prevent a state from threatening another states security. If any state misperceives the deterrent capability of another, or believes it has a greater offensive capability war is likely to break out.

In addition to these universal characteristics of the systemic structure is the variable concept of how power in the international system is actually divided. In the period of the Sino-Indian war the world was locked in a bipolar balance of power led by the U.S. and the Soviet Union. In a bipolar system states are rigidly aligned to either pole, but states in each camp have great flexibility of strategy. This was caused by the zero-sum nature of a bipolar system, in that the gain of one side is the loss of the other. As such, the leader of either faction is unwilling to allow client members to fail in policy endeavors. Finally, in a bipolar system states that refuse to join either faction drastically increase their security dilemma unless they have the power to challenge the international structure towards a multi-polar balance. Now that the neorealist systemic level theory is defined it shall be applied to explain the variables causing the outbreak of the Sino-Indian war.

Derivation and Events Leading to Border Dispute

The 1914 Simla Convention between Britain and Tibet established the McMahon Line as the official border between British India and China, denying the right of Chinese suzerainty over Tibet. However, the line's namesake McMahon, was ordered back to London in disgrace over the "chicanery" he exercised in border negotiations in which he presented a different map to the Chinese envoy, thus distancing Britain from the legitimacy of the negotiated border. Thirty years later British cartographers began drawing the McMahon Line as the border between British India and China, thus reviving the lines legal legitimacy.

When India gained its independence from Britain in 1947 it inherited all of the British territorial agreements, and as such inherited the McMahon Line as the border between it and China. Indian belief in the legitimacy of the McMahon line dated back to the Simla Convention of 1914, as well as to the numerous maps of British India with the line delineating its northern border. As such Nehru shrugged off Chinese insistence in border negotiation during the 1954 agreement stating that "the McMahon line marked their border with China, where was the need" ? Despite India's view of the McMahon Line's legitimacy, China had not signed the Simla Convention and under no circumstances consented to any bilateral agreement between Tibet and Britain because it violated their sovereignty. Indian intransigence on negotiating a border acceptable to both parties led the PRC to act independently in areas south of the McMahon line. The justification for this was that in the absence of mutually negotiated borders, the true national boundary was a line of actual control represented by the extent of either nation's ability to administrate the territory.

Practical assertion of this idea was first revealed to India in 1957 when an Indian patrol discovered an all-weather road which had been constructed in the Aksai-Chin Plain connecting Xinjiang and Tibet. The Indian government launched diplomatic protests asserting a violation of their territorial integrity; however the PRC "considered [Aksai-Chin] to have long been Chinese territory". This issue was not resolved as the Indian government refused to engage in territorial negotiations until Chinese forces completely withdrew from the Aksai-Chin Plain. The PRC refused to do so, and instead of a diplomatic solution India began to pursue a more confrontational approach to assert their territorial claims.

The rebellion in Tibet helped to drastically sour relations between the PRC and India, but the border dispute widened due to a change in Indian military strategy. This change in military strategy was to create forward-posts behind the Chinese claim line, and in strategic locations to flank Chinese military positions.

These posts were constructed to assert Indian territorial claims in the Ladakh region and to threaten the Xinjian-Tibet road in Aksai-Chin. By September, 1962 a similar series of forward posts had been built beyond the Chinese claim line in Tibet, and four such posts were built even beyond the McMahon Line. This resulted in an inability to claim that these posts were simply to defend Indian territorial integrity. The territorial dispute from India's perspective, coupled with the building of forward military posts by the Indian military caused the 1954 Panchsheel Agreement to not be renewed in 1961. Crossing both the claim and McMahon lines, both nations were in violation of each other's territorial conception, and India was now physically challenging Chinese sovereignty in Tibet.

STRONG ECONOMIC GROWTH IN RECENT YEARS

India's strong economic growth in recent years has begun to gain the world's attention. Henry Kissinger predicted that in the twenty-first century the international system will be dominated by six major powers: the US, Europe, China, Japan, Russia and India. Similarly, Samuel Huntington foresees that during the coming decades, "India could move into rapid economic development and emerge as contender for influence in world affairs." According to a variety of indicators, India is clearly a rising power, even though this power may not have been fully realized or recognized by key actors in the international society. These indicators include, among others, the world's second-largest population and soon the largest and the fourth-largest army. Since the economic reforms began in 1991, the Indian economy has left the Hindu rate of growth behind and accelerated, becoming the third largest economy in the world in purchasing power parity terms.

The potential of Indian entrepreneurship has been noted from Mumbai to London. India's development and its expanding influence have begun to attract attention and concern from China, not the least because marketers of India have tended to accentuate China's political differences with India. In the marketplace, Sino-Indian trade has expanded rapidly but Chinese and Indian firms can also be found competing against each other and quite a bit of the Indian press coverage of Chinese moves has tended to give way to zero-sum discussions of who might eat the other's lunch (e.g., in outsourcing). Meanwhile, India's involvement and growing role in Asia, especially in East Asia have brought forth different perceptions of its rise and impact.

We offer a preliminary review of Chinese scholars' perspectives on India's rise and its role in Asia: how does Beijing look at India's economic development model and competition with China, and respond to its expanding influence in Asia and beyond? We also draw on data from the Chicago Council survey on the rise of China and India to provide the opinions of the general public.

Different Perspectives Views of India

In some contrast with the views of Indians with regard to China, Chinese public perceptions of India are generally benign, even bordering on benign neglect. When the Chicago Council survey on global public attitudes asked the Chinese to evaluate the level of influence now (2006) and ten years from now on a scale of 0 to 10 (with 0 meaning not influential at all and 10 meaning extremely influential), the Chinese ranked China second behind the United States now but pulling level with the U.S. in ten years. Yet they ranked India at the bottom of the top nine despite allowing for some growth in Indian influence in a decade's time.

In contrast, the Indians ranked India as the second most influential after United States. However, appear to have a more elevated assessment of India's influence. Many Chinese analysts hold the view that India's rise as a global power is inevitable in the long run, and that this development would be compatible with China's preference for a multi-polar world. Based on this premise, they adopt a forward-looking approach to India's rise and advocate greater Sino-Indian cooperation. There is growing recognition that China and India share many common views on regional and international affairs, and that "while their politicians both dislike American hegemony, particularly in Asia, they have no intention to challenge the existing international order led by the United States, because both of them are developing countries and need a stable international environment for their domestic economic construction". The benign elite view of Sino-India interests are reflected in the Chicago Council survey of public attitudes. 56 percent of the Chinese public surveyed believe that China and India are mostly partners while only 30 percent think they are rivals. Chinese perceptions are thus more positive than those of Indians and especially of Americans.

Indeed, a majority of the Chinese public surveyed support India's growth both economically and even militarily. When asked whether it was mainly positive or mainly negative for India to become significantly more powerful economically, 56 percent of the Chinese surveyed believed it was, only second behind the Indians surveyed. Most remarkably, when asked whether it was mainly positive or mainly negative for India to become significantly more powerful militarily, 56 percent of the Chinese surveyed also believed it was, only second behind the Indians surveyed and in sharp contrast to the views of the South Koreans and Americans. Chinese analysts, however, are cautious about India's ambitions.

They suggest that although ad hoc management of the bilateral relationship is possible, the long-term prospect of rapprochement is overshadowed by India's continued nuclear and missile programs, the Tibet issue, territorial disputes and the absence of mutual trust. Ma Jiali also pointed out that as India rises, "the enhancement of India's strategic position will reduce China's strategic influence to some extend, especially in the Third World, thus will weaken China's strategic role, making it more complicated for China to deal with major powers". However, most of their analyses focus not so much on any immediate threat that India poses to China, but on the patterns and trends of developments in India that could transform it into a formidable adversary in the long run, thus potentially diverting Chinese resources from its top policy priorities (economic development and the eventual resolution of the Taiwan issue) and making any settlement of the border issue more elusive than ever. Not surprisingly, there are also some Chinese analysts with more ambivalent views on Sino-India relations. They believe that "conditional engagement with India certainly is preferable to open conflict, with the prospect of pushing New Delhi further into the U.S. camp." They hold that "India has various strategic suspicions toward China, and because of these suspicions, India has no will and determination to establish strategic partnership relations with China, even has not recognized China's market economic status.

As a result, Sino-India's bilateral trade value is only about 10 percent that of Sino-Japan's bilateral trade." This group of analysts has little expectation of near-term normalization, because many issues seem to defy any easy resolution. In general it appears that most Chinese analysts from government research institutes, universities, civilian think tanks and business circles hold the view that China should develop normal relations with India and seek ways to resolve bilateral differences through negotiations and cooperation. This includes government officials affiliated with the Ministry of Foreign Affairs, such as retired diplomats and analysts who have worked and written on Sino-Indian relations and South Asian affairs. This set represents the majority Chinese perspective on India.

THE CURRENT RELATIONSHIP BETWEEN INDIA AND CHINA

There is an overall positive trend in Sino-Indian relations, as seen in supporting statistics. In 2004-2005, total trade figures jumped from 13 billion dollars to 20 billion. In 2008, China became India's largest trade partner, and last year trade between the two countries reached $62 billion annually. In the field of defence, China and India have also established an annual defence dialogue and hold regular joint counterterrorism exercises. Setbacks in the relationship do occur but it is difficult to say how much of this is due to real concerns and how much is a tit-for-tat game. The border clearly remains an unresolved dispute. China, for its part, still lays claim to most of the Indian state of Arunachal Pradesh, which China asserts is part of Tibet and since 2007 has referred to the area as "South Tibet." Similarly, while India has acknowledged China's sovereignty over Tibet, it has not changed its stance on the McMahon Line as the boundary. Since 2003, fourteen rounds of talks have been held on the border issue and, while no breakthrough has been reached, the mechanism provides a forum through which the two countries can address complaints about incursions and the build-up of defenses.

Despite the occasional flaring up of bilateral tensions and acrimony in the press, policy in India toward China has so far been highly pragmatic and driven primarily by economic concerns, leading to an issue-based attitude toward coalition building within multilateral fora like the World Trade Organization. A key concern for India, however, is the large Indian trade deficit. In 2010 alone, India's exports to China were $20 billion lower than those of China to India. The concerns over the trade deficit are compounded by the fact that a huge proportion of Indian exports to China are raw commodities — ores, slag, ash, and cotton — with little value adding capacity. India's imports from China are much higher value-added manufacturing items which is in part due to China's greater manufacturing efficiency but also due to Chinese non-tariff barriers.

China Perceived by The Indian People

The living memory of the Indian forces' traumatic defeat in the 1962 border war with China continues to affect Indians' opinion of China. When George Fernandes, former Indian defence minister, described the Chinese as "India's enemy number one" in the 1970s, the statement drew a sympathetic chord among many Indians. However, more recent surveys reveal a picture that is more nuanced and complex.

A Pew Global Survey in 2010 showed that 42 percent of Indians see Lashkar-e-Taiba as the greatest threat to India, followed by Pakistan at 33 percent, then the Naxalites at 16. Only 3 percent of Indians see China as the greatest threat. The report also notes that the United States enjoys a largely positive image, with nearly two-thirds expressing a favorable opinion, although this was down from 76 percent in 2009. By contrast, only 34 percent see China favorably.

While opinion surveys have their shortcomings, when several surveys concur, even partially, they help build a trend. The Pew findings have a distinct echo in polling from BBC World Service. There has been a steady decline of mutual positive perception between China and India over the years. The most significant fall is in Chinese opinions of India, where between 2009 and 2010, approval fell by 14 percent. Indian opinion of China has risen from a low of 22 percent in 2008 to 30 percent in 2010. Both are now roughly at the same level of around 30 percent approval, which is lower than the high point of 2005. In regards to India's opinion of China, the trends can perhaps be explained by growing anxiety about China's rise, especially in terms of the competition for energy resources and manufacturing capabilities.

While a strong lobby in India argues that China's growing economy is good for the region and for India, the Indian government has been cautious regarding Chinese foreign direct investment. China's expanding military might is also viewed with a growing sense of wariness that has manifested publicly, including in a 2009 statement by Admiral Suresh Mehta, India's naval chief, warning that India was no match for China militarily.

INDIA'S RELATIONS WITH CHINA: THE GOOD, THE BAD AND THE (POTENTIALLY) UGLY

Indian Prime Minister Manmohan Singh will travel to Beijing. The visit will cap a year that has been full of ups and downs in India's relations with China.

The tale of three trips is representative. One in May by Chinese Premier Li Keqiang, his first abroad, was intended to signal the importance Beijing placed in the Sino-Indian relationship. But it took place in the aftermath of—and some would say was overshadowed by—a border standoff between the two countries' militaries. In July, the Indian defence minister visited Beijing to rebuild trust and defence ties. Media coverage, however, focused on warnings to India issued by a PLA general, which Chinese officials had to rush to dismiss.

And Singh will be travelling from a country that is largely preoccupied domestically. When discussions do turn to China, they have focused on concerns about Indian capacity vis-à-vis that country, Indian politicians accusing the government of being soft on China and Chinese scholars labeling India's border infrastructure upgrades as provocative. These and other developments have highlighted what Indian policymakers acknowledge—that there are elements of cooperation, competition and concern in the China-India relationship. There have been good signs for those interested in stable, cooperative Sino-Indian relations.In the spring, just after he'd formally taken office, Chinese President Xi Jinping proposed a five-point formula to improve ties between the two countries. "Positive vibes" were detected at Xi's subsequent meeting with Singh on the sidelines of the BRICS summit in Durban in March.

There have been numerous public Chinese declarations of the importance of the relationship—perhaps not seen since the first half of the 1950s. The Chinese ambassador to India unusually took to the editorial pages of an Indian newspaper to emphasize, "To strengthen good-neighbourly and friendly cooperation with India is China's strategic choice and established policy which will not change."

Chinese officials have indicated that greater efforts should be made toward a boundary settlement. The two countries have strategic and economic dialogues in place. They restarted their defence dialogue earlier this year and are expected to resume joint military exercises shortly. China and India also have specialized dialogues on issues like Afghanistan, Central Asia and counterterrorism.

The agreement to discuss Afghanistan was considered a departure from previous Chinese policy; Beijing had earlier been reluctant to add it to the agenda because it would have likely meant talking about Chinese ally Pakistan. Along with regional discussions, China and India have also cooperated in the multilateral realm, including on issues like trade and climate change.

Premier Li chose India as his first overseas stop, with the Chinese government indicating that the choice was very deliberate. Hosting an Indian youth delegation, Li put a personal spin on the choice, noting the "the seeds of friendship sown" when he visited India 27 years ago—a trip that he said left a "lasting impact." During the May visit, he stressed the need to build trust and especially emphasized the economic benefits of greater ties.

Those economic ties have already grown. China is one of India's largest trading partners. Bilateral trade in goods has gone from less than $3 billion in 2000 to $66.57 billion in 2012. While investments haven't kept the same pace, they have also grown. In India, the interest in doing business with China is evident beyond the private sector and the central government— along with visits by a number of Indian CEOs, China has also seen visits from chief ministers of a number of Indians states, including Andhra Pradesh, Bihar, Karnataka and Madhya Pradesh.

Narendra Modi, current chief minister of the state of Gujarat and prime ministerial candidate for the forthcoming national election for the BJP (India's largest opposition party), has also traveled to China. While Modi has expressed hawkish views on China on the geopolitical front, he has expressed admiration for that country's economic achievements.

The governments of both countries have reasons for wanting stable ties: the desire for a peaceful periphery in order to focus on domestic socio-economic objectives; the need for stability in South Asia, especially with the impending American drawdown of forces from Afghanistan; existing and potential economic ties; and the prospect for cooperation in the multilateral realm. For Delhi, in addition, a stable relationship with China opens up the possibility that Beijing might use its leverage with Islamabad to shape Pakistan's behaviour in a way that might benefit India.

For Beijing, there's desire to limit India's burgeoning relationships with the United States and Japan, as well as with other countries in what Beijing considers its backyard. Moreover, as China is preoccupied with eastern maritime disputes and the North Korean situation, stable relations on its southern and southwestern flank would also help the Chinese leadership.

This year has, however, also shown how quickly the bad in the relationship can steal the spotlight from the good—with the potential to turn ugly. In April, less than two weeks after an Indian observer commented on the "upswing in relations" between China and India, their long-standing boundary dispute flared once again. While the two countries communicated through the crisis and resolved it diplomatically, and Li's visit proceeded as planned, the border incident reinforced the mistrust that many in India feel toward China and its intentions. Furthermore, it was a reminder that despite increased engagement, bilateral differences have the potential to stall, if not reverse, progress toward more stable relations.

Differences are not restricted to the boundary dispute. Tibet remains a key source of tension between the two countries though the two countries have found a way to manage their differences on the issue for now. In addition, China's relationship with Pakistan has been a major source of concern in India. Its role in strengthening Pakistan's conventional, missile and nuclear capabilities is especially highlighted. India also disapproves of China's assistance to Pakistan in developing projects and infrastructure in area disputed between India and Pakistan.

China's growing political and economic ties with India's neighbours are also a subject of concern. Delhi watches warily increasing Chinese interactions—political and commercial—with and involvement in countries like Afghanistan, Bangladesh, Myanmar, Nepal and Sri Lanka. Concern about a military dimension being added persists. Beijing's increasing interest in operating in the Indian Ocean, which India has traditionally considered its backyard, has also not gone unnoticed. While China emphasizes that these activities have benign goals—economic development, security for its ships, etc.—some in India who tend to take a hawkish position are not convinced; others are taking a wait-and-see attitude. Even beyond the neighborhood, there are concerns about competition with China for markets, influence and resources across the globe.

Closer to home, water is the resource that has become the subject of tension—specifically Chinese dam construction on its side of the Brahmaputra River. Indian officials have publiclycalled for Beijing to reassure India on this matter. Domestic critics, however, perceive the Indian government as being too tolerant of the construction. They argue that China has not respected information sharing agreements on this front and warn of more ambitiousChinese river diversion plans.

Economic ties, which many envisioned as the driver of good Sino-Indian ties, have also not escaped trouble. Bilateral trade in goods actually fell almost 10 percent from 2011 to 2012. In India there's much concern about the trade imbalance. The overall trade deficit has gonefrom $28 billion in 2010-2011 to $40.8 billion in 2012-2013.

While investments have grown, they remain limited compared to the investment relationships that both China and India have with other countries. In India, there have also been complaints about market access in China and the treatment of Indian labor there, concern about Chinese investment in "strategic" sectors in India, accusations about visa abuses by Chinese companies and restrictions on Chinese labor. Indian companies also privately express concerns about cyber-espionage. Overall, reports of cyber-attacks on Indian government and military networks — allegedly emanating from China — have done nothing to decrease distrust that persists, especially among the public.

There is also an overall sense that China does not respect India and/or that it will seek to prevent India's rise. As evidence, critics point not only to China's relationship with Pakistan, which is seen as driven by a desire to keep India tied up in South Asia, but also note China'sreluctance to endorse India's demand for a permanent seat on the U.N. Security Council or its objections to India being given membership in the Nuclear Suppliers Group.

Another overarching problem: the lack of trust in China and its intentions. This is especially evident among the public. According to a Pew poll last year, more Indians have an unfavorable view of China than a favorable view. In a more recent Lowy Institute poll, China ranked only second to Pakistan in terms of countries that people considered threatening to India, with 60 percent indicating China would be a major threat over the next decade (an additional 22 percent identified it as a minor threat). 73 percent of those surveyed identified "war with China" as a big threat over the next ten years. Almost three-quarters believed that China wants to dominate Asia. 58 percent felt that China's growth had not been good for India. This reinforces what the Pew poll found last year. In that poll, two-thirds of urbanites who expressed an opinion on the subject believed that China's growing economy was a bad thing.

Overcoming this mistrust continues to be a major obstacle. The legacy of history remains a problem. Every time there is a border incident it reinforces the narrative that has prevailed in many quarters in India since the 1962 China-India war: that China only understands strength; that while Beijing's leaders say China and India "must shake hands," they cannot be trusted — that one hand held out might just be a precursor to the other stabbing one in the back. This problem is made worse by limited connectivity and communications, and little knowledge about the other country — even though these have improved. Media coverage about China and the relationship can also get quite heated, with a tendency to focus on the negative. All these problems are exacerbated by the lack of transparency when it comes to Chinese decision-making. This has led to uncertainty about Chinese behaviour and motivations, which was evident in the debate about why the border incident in April occurred — and this uncertainty exists even among policymakers.

Thus, Indian governments have tried to follow a multi-pronged strategy. The emphasis might have differed somewhat, but for the last two governments in India — one a coalition led by the BJP and the current one led by the Congress — the general approach towards China has been to co-operate, if possible, and to compete, if necessary. Indian officials have joined with Chinese counterparts to increase ties, build trust and improve communications. Simultaneously, policymakers note that competition in and of itself is not all bad. As former Indian Prime Minister Vajpayee noted in Beijing, "a sense of competition between two close and equal neighbours" might indeed be natural. There is also, however, a realization that beyond cooperation and competition, there is a potential for conflict. Thus, while hoping and working for the best, there has been some attention on planning and preparing for the worst—i.e. the possibility that China will emerge as an explicit threat. There is a desire to do this cautiously, however, with policymakers quite conscious of the potential for provocation, miscalculation and exacerbation of the security dilemma.

In practice, this overall approach has meant increasing engagement with China—political, economic and even military-to-military—at the bilateral, regional and multilateral levels. Simultaneously, this approach has translated to a series of actions including strengthening India's military, as well as its border infrastructure and border regions, maintaining a nuclear deterrent, and consolidating or expanding ties and influence in India's near abroad.

India has also tried to step up its game in China's neighborhood. Indian policymakers underplay the strategic aspects and goals of India's "Look East" policy—which the Indian foreign ministry describes as "oriented towards deepening India's engagement with the countries of East and Southeast Asia"—and emphasize its cultural and economic aspects. However, these elements and the link to China have not been entirely missing in action. The Indian government and companies are increasingly interested and engaged in the region, especially focusing on countries like Indonesia, Japan, Singapore, Thailand and Vietnam. In recent months, India-Japan ties have probably been in the spotlight the most, with another round of the U.S.-India-Japan trilateral dialogue and Singh's visit to Japan in May. India has also sought to be more engaged with multilateral fora in the region. Officials from some Southeast Asian countries, however, want India to do much more. Channeling some of their frustrations, Hillary Clinton, when she led the State Department, called for "India not just to look east, but to engage East and act East as well."

Another key aspect of India's approach has been the pursuit of closer relations with the United States. Of course, these ties with the United States are not solely driven by China. India indeed has no desire to make a choice between its relations with China and the United States. However, the United States plays a useful role as an offshore balancer. Furthermore, Indian policymakers believe that a strong U.S.-India relationship gives them leverage with China and sends a signal to that country. Some also note that China takes India more seriously because the United States does. India, however, still has doubts about U.S. reliability as a potential partner, especially given the level of Sino-U.S. engagement, and prefers to maintain a diversified portfolio of partnerships.

So, where do India's relations with China go from here? In the near term, during the Prime Minister's visit, the two sides might sign a border defence cooperation agreement. The accord would essentially be a way to manage rather than resolve the boundary question, which the Indian foreign secretary has noted continues to be "a particularly difficult issue." The trans-border rivers question is also likely to be discussed. In addition, given the two countries' priorities, bilateral and global economic and financial issues will be high on the agenda. Potentially, there also might be agreements that could facilitate greater people-to-people ties, including a cultural and visa pacts. Regionally, developments vis-à-vis Afghanistan and the Middle East that concern both governments are likely to be discussed. Finally, on the multilateral front, trade and climate change issues might be on the agenda, given upcoming international summits in those two areas.

As for the longer term, the scenarios usually outlined are deepening cooperation, increasing competition that might lead to conflict, or continuity with both competition and cooperation in evidence. There is a debate in India—inside and outside government—about China, which scenario might prevail, the future of the relationship and what approach to take with China. The differences are evident in the Lowy poll—almost equal numbers of those surveyed believe that India "should join with other countries to limit China's influence" and "should cooperate with China to play a leading role in the world together."

How the relationship plays out will depend on a number of internal, bilateral, regional and global factors. In the meantime, Shyam Saran, a former foreign secretary and currently chairman of the National Security Advisory Board, has called for India to manage relations with China "with prudence but firmness." An air force chief described the way forward as "play cool and continue to develop capabilities."

3

India-China Relations and the Re-construction of Strategic Partnerships

India's perceptions and policies with respect to the People's Republic of China (PRC), as well as India-China relations, as they stand today, have been (and in many ways, continue to be) primarily determined and defined by two critical events, the border conflict of October 1962 and the Indian nuclear explosions of May 1998.

The former wrenched the relationship out of the idealistic and unsustainable *'bhai-bhai'* framework and brought it firmly in the realm of 'realpolitik' and at the same time made the PRC, India's single most important security threat and challenge. The latter shaped and molded the strategic dimensions of the relationship – it had in fact been primarily motivated by the threat perception from the north and the obvious power asymmetry between the two. There have certainly been some modifications as well as some major shifts in this perception since the late 1980s. Officially, India and China do not consider each other a security threat; however, military/security issues still continue to influence India-China relations.

The forces of economic globalization, which acquired a new impetus after the disintegration of the Socialist Bloc and the end of the political-economic ideological divide, were paralleled by a transformation in international relations. They also imparted a greater momentum to the far-reaching domestic economic reforms underway in the PRC since the late 1970s and substantially boosted its 'policy of opening up to the outside world', the objective of which was, among others, expanding its economic engagement with the advanced industrialized countries and the capitalist world economy. The cumulative effect of the domestic economic reforms and an export-led strategy over the last two and a half decades, has led to the phenomenon of the "rise of China," which is now the one of the defining characteristics of the global order. India, and also the world, now has to deal with this new scenario. Nonetheless, it is useful to recall, that the discourse of a "rising" China was preceded by the phenomenal expansion of the East Asian and Pacific region and the emergence of an Asia-centric world order. It was thus a new resurgence of Asia that was underway. Moreover, China is rising in an era of economic globalization– a period, which has witnessed economic integration and interdependence among nation-states to a hitherto unprecedented degree – there are factors therefore, which will be simultaneoussly constraining China's rise, even as they are assisting and promoting it.

THE PRC'S STRA TEGIC OBJECTIVES

Not unexpectedly, the PRC's chief strategic objective is to regain what it feels is its rightful status as one of the dominant global powers – but, as the PRC leaders aver on every possible occasion, it would be a responsible and responsive power that will never seek to exercise hegemony either globally or regionally or indulge in power politics. This would require the continuation of the rule by the Communist Party of China, which in turn would seek to preserve and enhance its legitimacy through continued high growth rates and raising the living standards of ever increasing segments of its population. This has necessitated the adoption of policies that contribute to the maintenance of internal social stability and the creation of a "harmonious society" to enable the leadership to sustain its reform and open door policies.

Externally, the PRC has focused on "the creation of a favourable international environment" conducive to its strategy of inviting foreign direct investment and access to export markets, building of linkages which ensure a steady flow of the economic inputs necessary for its continued high growth (and internally to create conditions under which foreign capital would not be tempted to exit the country), strengthening its regional power and presence, and maintaining and modernizing its defence capabilities to protect and "preserve China's independence, sovereignty and territorial integrity." All together, as a country in the process of modernization, the orientation of the PRC may be said to be fundamentally defensive, except when its core national interests are concerned.

The Economic Rise of China

The phenomenon of the 'rise of China' must be understood first in economic terms. It is universally acknowledged as the fastest growing economy in the world, which has demonstrated its ability to sustain historically unprecedented high rates of growth – almost ten percent per annum-for over a quarter of a century. This has catapulted it to the rank of the world's fourth largest economy, with real per capita output having increased nearly nine times since 1978.

During the same period, China's foreign trade volume multiplied 24 times with a turnover of over US$1 trillion and foreign exchange reserves now exceeding US$ 300 billion. This high growth has translated into an appreciable improvement in virtually all indices of human development: a marked reduction in overall poverty, a life expectancy of 71 (much higher than most developing countries) and a literacy rate of more than 90 percent (compared to 66 percent at the end of the 1970s, which was far ahead of India at 36 percent at the same time.) Furthermore, its per capita GDP in 2005 was $1,700 (though compared to the United States, which has a per capita GDP of $42,000, it still has a lot of catching up to do). It is estimated that if current rates of growth are maintained, the Chinese economy would, by 2045 or even earlier, surpass the U.S. economy, though estimates vary somewhat and, even then, its per capita income would still not be as great at the United States.

Analysts have also pointed out that if that were to happen, by dint of sheer size, and not in high per capita income terms, China would emerge as an economic superpower, alongside the United States and the European Union.

Internal Challenges

Among the Chinese leadership's greatest worries is unequal growth and, hence, macro-economic imbalance. This is reflected in the frequent exhortations at the highest levels to build a "harmonious society" and address regional and income imbalances. There are increasing qualms about the stability of the agricultural sector, which is witnessing a swelling of the ranks of the unemployed. Unemployment estimates indicate that a floating population of nearly 150-200 million unemployed or underemployed Chinese labourers, can, and have, created extremely unstable and precarious economic and political conditions. The income gap is now a chasm. Of China's 1.3 billion people, the most affluent fifth earns half of total income, according to one official study, while the bottom fifth takes home a piddling 4.7 percent. Incidents of protest are on the rise – 87,000 reported in 2005– that's an average of more than 200 protests a day on such issues as official corruption, health problems, environmental degradation, mistreatment by employees, home evictions, an unravelling social security net, the privatization of higher education, the impact of market reforms in the healthcare sector, which has virtually collapsed in rural areas and the rise of communicable diseases.

Clearly, there is a highly mixed and uneven record as far as China's socio-economic scenario is concerned. This is potentially one of the most serious challenges for China's leadership and has been reflected and voiced in almost all the major official documents and government work reports over the last few years. Upheaval in China will have terrible repercussions both domestically and internationally, as the spill over costs would be tremendously destabilizing for the region.

Regardless, it must also be stated that China does not appear to be on the verge of a collapse. So far, the leadership has demonstrated a remarkable ability to take timely measures to address emerging concerns. The internal challenges however suggest that there are critical forces, which could possibly come together to place some checks or brakes on the pace of growth. There is thus an interrelated problem: the legitimacy of the ruling Communist Party rests on its ability to sustain high growth and spearhead the modernization and development process.

But these high growth rates are at present dependent on a set of policies, which are proving increasingly unsustainable. The ruling elite now faces the problem of opposition from segments of the populations that had traditionally constituted its social base – peasants and workers – who have not benefited from the reform. Finally, there are a host of issues stemming from the authoritarian nature of the Chinese state and its hard-line stance on political reforms. Opposition is also emerging from an as yet small, but increasingly vocal, globalized, liberal intelligentsia and civil society. Given all these aspects, the leadership maintains that their rise is not a foregone conclusion and that they must be counted in the ranks of the developing countries. They hope to achieve the status of a medium power by the middle of the 21st century.

The Energy Factor

After several decades of self-sufficiency and several years of oil exports, China became a net oil importer in 1993. In 2004, the PRC became the world's second largest petroleum consumer after the United States. Roughly 40 percent of world oil demand is attributable to China's rising energy needs. It has been estimated that by 2020, oil imports will reach 8 million barrels per day, requiring one-half to three-quarters of domestic consumption to be met by imports. With India's growth also moving into double-digit figures, and keeping in mind that India's energy imports exceed China's, this is one sector where Chinese and Indian interests are likely to compete, if not clash. Over the last few years, India and China have been positioned against each other in bidding for the acquisition of oil fields abroad, though of late some cooperation and coordination of policies has taken place.

China's efforts to achieve energy security have led to concern in India, particularly with regard to China's activities in the Indian Ocean. The so-called "string of pearls" strategy, wherein China has secured naval bases in the littoral states, particularly with India's neighbours – Myanmar, Bangladesh, Sri Lanka, Seychelles, and Pakistan – must be carefully assessed. While it is obvious that acquiring these bases is largely driven by China's need to ensure the safety of the sea lanes of cooperation (SLOCs) through which the bulk of its imports pass and is therefore linked to China's overall economic security, the strategic and security ramifications for India are evident.

Moreover, in the context of the rather troubled relations that India has with each of these countries, their use of China as a countervailing force or a hedging strategy cannot be discounted. Under these circumstances, India's best strategy would be to simultaneously endeavour to resolve the tension spots in its neighbourhood and improve its relationship with its neighbours and to continue on the trajectory of normalization of relations with China. The objective should be to gradually reduce and eliminate the scope for China's countervailing role and, over time, acquire some presence in these strategic bases.

GROWING ON INDIA-CHINA RELATIONS

There is a growing perception now that the global economic gravity has shifted to Asia and that India and China, the emerging economic powerhouses in the region, will shape the Twenty-first century. In making such feelings a reality however, the nature of the future dynamics of domestic conditions as well as external relations of the two nations appears a crucial factor; this article attempts to focus in particular on the future prospects for India-China ties on the premise that this, along with the roles of other Asian powers like Japan, is going to be important in the matter of guaranteeing the stability and prosperity of the region as well as rest of the world.

The article tries to present the Chinese side with Indian perspectives of key developments. Chinese perspectives are already being made available in India in a similar manner. The writer feels that put together, such exchanges will facilitate creation of a better mutual understanding between the two sides, impacting favourably on the overall India-China relationship.

Growing Optimism

Broadly speaking, India-China ties at government levels remain stable at this juncture; New Delhi and Beijing have established a 'strategic and cooperative partnership for peace and prosperity' and signed a document on 'shared vision for the 21st century', signifying that the Sino-Indian ties have gone beyond the bilateral context and acquired a global character. Accordingly, India and China are cooperating on international issues related to the diversification of global energy mix, climate change, arms control and disarmament, non-traditional security threats, counter-terrorism, WTO, WMD, human rights and South-South Co-operation.

Bilaterally, the two sides now aim at building 'a relationship of friendship and trust, based on equality, in which each is sensitive to the concerns and aspirations of the other'. They are not viewing each other as a security threat and are by and large satisfactorily implementing confidence building measures in the disputed border, besides carrying out joint military exercises. Special Representatives of India and China have so far held thirteen rounds of border talks, though with no tangible results. Most important is that with an attitude of promoting ties looking beyond the unsolved and 'complex' border dispute, India and China are speeding up their trade and economic contacts. Bilateral trade is fast gathering momentum, with the volume to the tune of US$ 40 billion now and projections for US$ 60 billion by 2010.

China has emerged as India's largest trading partner, replacing the US, in April 2008- February 2009 period. Also significant is the ongoing momentum in their exchanges of high level visits reflecting the desire of each party to forge stronger ties, of which the recently concluded state visit of Indian President Ms Patil to China is a prominent example. Notwithstanding the encouraging picture brought out above, there are issues deeply dividing India and China; resolving them once for all is of utmost necessity, to further strengthen their relations. There are some talks in India about the past civilisational contacts helping resolution of the issues; they however lack substance. As modern nation states, the India and China have developed geo-political interests, which often tend to clash. What follows is a discussion on the conditions contributing to India-China frictions and the likely scenario in bilateral ties in future.

Problem Areas—Boundary Issue

As this writer sees, the boundary issue comes foremost in the list of problem areas. It is most sensitive one for both India and China as it relates closely to territorial integrity and sovereignty in respect of each side. It therefore needs to be handled carefully by the two nations. China's understanding of Indian perspectives on the boundary issue will remain incomplete if it does not take into account the traditional doubts prevailing in India on China having been territorially ambitious. Examples being quoted in India in this regard include Mao's description of China's 'palm' (Tibet) and 'five fingers' (Nepal, Sikkim, Bhutan, NEFA and Ladakh); references are also being made in India to the PRC's sense of 'historical loss' of territories expressed through their maps and atlas series, published in eighties. Such maps had even been seen claiming that India's Assam, even Andamans, were 'historically' parts of China. Proceeding from 'doubts' to substantive points, it is being seen in India that the border positions of India and China are in conflict with each other and hence are difficult to solve. China's claims are based on its historical stand – all its borders, including with India, are as defined during the Qing dynasty period which ended in 1912. The root of the border problem with India lies in Beijing's position that a large chunk of its territory, especially the 90,000 Sq km area in the Eastern sector, were illegally taken away by the British India, after the 1914 Simla Convention and that India inherited the British legacy. This has provided the rationale for Beijing in rejecting the McMahon line, a product of the Convention and in claiming the entire Arunachal Pradesh state of India as part of Chinese territory, called by it as 'Southern Tibet' Authoritative scholars in China have categorically stated that Beijing cannot recognize the McMahon line; if it did so, it would amount to Chinese admission of the 1962 conflict as a 'war of aggression' as well as an implicit acknowledgement that Tibet was once independent of China. On the other hand, for India, McMahon line remains the 'de facto' border with China.

The Sino-Indian border problem remains complicated with the Chinese claiming recently the 2.1 Sq km 'finger area' of Sikkim, the status of which as an Indian state has already been recognized by Beijing 'de facto'. On the current scenario, meriting attention are India's concerns arising from various factors – the reported Chinese intrusions, said to number 270 in 2008, into the Indian border, the adverse reaction of Beijing to the visit of the Indian Prime Minister Dr. Manmohan Singh to Arunachal Pradesh, China's bid to stop the loans for Arunachal Pradesh from the Asian Development Bank and strong Chinese state-controlled media criticisms of India's dispatch of additional troops to and positioning of advanced fighter aircraft in its Eastern border. Adding to India's discomfort has also been the rise in the level of Chinese media rhetoric against India, noticed in 2009; this has however subsided now.

Sino-Indian border talks, despite thirteen rounds of talks so far between two Special representatives, have not led to any tangible result in finalising a 'frame work' for a boundary settlement in accordance with the Agreement on Political Parameters, reached in 2005. While Beijing's stand is to approach the border issue in the spirit of 'mutual understanding and mutual accommodation', India wants 'ground realities' to be taken into account. About the reported Chinese claim over Tawang, an interesting argument is that besides strategic factors, the same has been due to the China's fears that Buddhist monasteries in the border including the one in Tawang have been centres of Tibetan resistance to the Chinese authority and as such, they should be taken over by it. Interestingly, the Chinese have introduced some new elements to the border question by questioning the already agreed position of keeping areas with settled populations out of the dispute. Is China ready for accommodation on the border issue? The statement made by the PRC Ambassador to India in November 2006 that both sides should make compromises on the 'disputed' Arunachal may be meaningful in this regard.

China's general stand is to 'shelve' the difficult border issues like the one with India and instead work for 'common development'. For e.g the PRC wants to 'shelve' the South China Sea territorial dispute, leave the Senkaku issue with Japan for 'future generations' to solve and 'put aside the Sino-Indian border dispute waiting for a suitable climate for solution' (Deng Xiaoping to the then Indian leader Vajpayee, Beijing, 1979). What is being noticed in India is that China never gives up its claims on sovereignty over disputed areas. An example is Japan-China settlement on exploring the disputed Chunxiao gas field in the East China Sea.

Though Beijing has agreed for joint development of the field, it has declared that China's sovereignty over the field is indisputable. The Chinese 'shelving' formula needs close scrutiny of India in particular. As this writer views, this formula has inherent flaws – for some at least, the projected completion of China's military modernization in 2050 may create new pressures on the leaders in Beijing at that time to become aggressive on all border issues. What are therefore needed are serious efforts from India and China at their border talks, leading to a 'compromise' based solution to the issue, much sooner than later.

Other Bilateral Issues —Tibet Issue

Tibet issue is prominent among other problems. It can be said that with India accepting the Tibet Autonomous Region as an integral part of China and standing firmly against any anti-China activity of the Dalai Lama from India's soil, this issue does not figure in Sino-Indian state to state relations. However, Beijing appears to be having reservations on India's motives with respect to the Dalai Lama. The State-controlled media allegation, made on the eve of Manmohan Singh – Wen Jiabao meeting in Thailand, that the Dalai Lama is colluding with India whenever Sino-Indian border talks are held, along with the Chinese official view that the proposed visit to Arunachal Pradesh by the Dalai Lama in November 2009, 'further exposes the anti-China and separatist nature of the Dalai clique' and a subsequent authoritative comment that such visits cast a new shadow on Sino-Indian relations, firmly point to Beijing's approach linking the Dalai Lama factor with the Sino-Indian border question.

China's fears need to be understood in the context of March 2008 unrest in Tibet, posing a challenge to China's sovereignty over that territory, even weakening Beijing's position in its border negotiations with India. Also, the question as to why India is tolerating the Tibetan Government in Exile in its soil, seems to be bothering China. Premier Wen Jiabao's description of the Tibet issue as a 'sensitive' one in relations with India, assumes significance in the context of what has been said above. The writer feels that Chinese suspicions on India-Dalai Lama relations are not going to disappear soon; the picture may change if talks between Beijing and the exiled spiritual leader succeed, but chances in this regard appear to be bleak at least for the moment.

China-Pakistan Nexus

China-Pakistan nexus is the next major bilateral issue. A better understanding is required in China about India's sensitivities on this account. The Chinese military, missiles and nuclear help to Pakistan continues, but Beijing is not in a position to give a guarantee to India that Pakistan will not leverage such support from China, to fight against India. Not surprisingly, New Delhi perceives that China's military assistance to Pakistan has direct implications for India.

China's Defence Modernisation

On the third issue of China's military modernization programme, India's concerns are being expressed through its important government documents, for e.g. the Defence Ministry's Annual Report (2008-2009) has said that the programme has implications for India's defence and security. Asking Beijing to show greater transparency in its defence policy and postures, particularly on the double-digit growth in defence spending in last two decades, it has observed that China's stated aim in its Defence White Paper for 2008 to develop missiles, space based assets and blue water naval capabilities will have an effect on the overall military environment in the neighbourhood of India. The Chinese side should properly address such concerns of India.

China's Policy towards India's Neighbourhood

India's concerns also relate to China's attempts to establish a strategic presence in India's neighbourhood, for e.g port projects like Gwadar (Pakistan), Hambantota(Sri Lanka), Chittagong (Bangladesh). They are giving rise to fears in India of a Chinese encirclement of the country, under what has come to be known as a 'string of pearls strategy'. The PRC has taken care to officially repudiate such concerns, by asserting that it has no plans to try for domination of the shipping lanes in the Indian Ocean and has no intentions to establish a chain to encircle India. An India-China understanding on the issue is a must for further improving bilateral relations.

India-US Relations

Chinese critical positions on the India-US relations are also a matter of India's concern. The Chinese have welcomed the India-US Strategic Dialogue and are themselves promoting ties with the US. Still, China seems to nurture fears about US-India collusion against it. Its official media description of India's policy as one 'befriending the far and attacking the near' is unmistakably an indirect, but strong criticism of the developing strategic relations between India and the US.

East Asia Integration

It would be necessary for China to pay attention to the Indian perception that it hesitates to accept India's leading role in the East Asian regional integration process on the plea that the process should only be based on ASEAN+3 (China, Japan and South Korea) cooperation, and that ' outsiders' like India, Australia and New Zealand have no place in it.

India's Defence Strategy

Reports in India about the country's defence strategy visualizing war on two fronts- Pakistan and China, have been commented upon in China. A Chinese comment (China Youth Daily) has said that India's real target is China, not Pakistan. Indian strategic planners have only done a scenario building; war is not an option for India, which wants to settle its historic problems with its two neighbours peacefully. Under the strategy, both land and sea power are getting emphasis in India, which reflects a logical consideration of the country's geopolitical position.

How to Read Chinese Media?

The Indian public does not understand the reasons for appearance of hawkish views on India in some of China's strategic journals/websites. Global Times and writers like Colonel Dai Xu, have often given controversial views on India. How far such views reflect official thinking remains a question in India. Is the People's Liberation army (PLA) influencing China's foreign policy making? Even the US Defence Secretary Robert Gates has hinted to such possibilities (Shangrila Dialogue, Singapore, 2010).The answer to such misgivings may lie in the need for reporting transparency in China.

Economy

Questions are being asked in China on how India will use its economic power. They are similar to doubts in India and abroad about China's intentions once its modernization programme gets completed, say in 2050. China has announced peaceful development as its goal. India's objectives are on the same lines – enriching the entrepreneurial and economic potential of the country through a suitable reform strategy as well as integrating the country with the world's economic system under a new order. India's increasing role in G-20 mechanism speaks for the latter in particular. Another basic point relates to attempts to compare the development models of India and China. Which one is the better? A debate may be unending in this regard- generally, the Indian model based on democracy is being viewed favourably from a long term point of view than that of China which rests on a one-party system. The main difference is that while China has been following a model based on investment flow from abroad and exports. India has been giving a boost to entrepreneurship and free enterprise. In the opinion of the writer, the Indian superiority in the service sector notwithstanding, it will not be easy for India to catch up fast with China, which has already emerged as a manufacturing giant.

What will be India's global interests as an emerging power is another topic getting focus in China. As Dr Manmohan Singh, the Indian Prime Minister puts it, India's goal is to gain its rightful place in the comity of nations, making full use of the opportunities offered by a globalised world, operating on the frontiers of modern science and technology and using modern science and technology as important instruments of national economic and social development. The emerging India's partnerships with the US, China and other powers, India's role in the G-20 mechanism etc stand to explain its interests in the 21st century. Realising its responsibilities as a growing power, India is cooperating with other nations on addressing issues of global concern like terrorism, climate change, disarmament, world trade etc. In conclusion, it can be said that there are mixed views on China in India; Indians are noticing the prevailing good atmosphere in bilateral relations at state levels, but their concerns are continuing on China's strategic intentions vis-à-vis India. More and more people to people contacts between the two sides can bring a beneficial change to such conditions.

CHINA AND INDIA : DIFFERENT APPROACHES, DIFFERENT OUTCOMES

What the above discussion of the divergence and convergence between Sino-Indian interests reveals is the success of China in attaining its foreign policy objectives and the failure of India to preserve its vital interests vis-à-vis China. This cannot simply be attributed to China's economic and military strength. While China is definitely the bigger player in the region and the world at large but its success vis-à-vis India owes as much to its power as to the way that power has been cultivated and used. While realizing fully well that it would take China decades to seriously compete with the US, it has focused strategic energy on Asia. Its foreign policy is aimed at enhancing its economic and military prowess to achieve hegemony in Asia. China's recent emphasis on projecting itself as peaceful power is merely aimed at allaying the concerns of neighbours lest they try to counterbalance it. China's readiness to negotiate with other regional states and to be an economically "responsible" nation is also a signal to other states that there are greater benefits in bandwagoning to China's growing regional weight rather than opposing its rise in any manner.

However, while declaring that it will be focusing on internal socio-economic development for the next decade or so, China has actively pursued policies of preventing the rise of other regional powers. In case of India, this manifests itself in its cultivation of Pakistan as a close ally. From supplying it nuclear and missile technologies to building its military infrastructure, China has done all it can to build Pakistan as a counterweight to India. This policy has largely succeeded as India no longer enjoys its earlier conventional superiority vis-à-vis Pakistan possession of nuclear weapons by both nations ensures that any step that India takes to strengthen its nuclear weapons profile is viewed by the international community as highly destabilizing in the context of the "nuclear flashpoint" that South Asia has become for the world at large. China has thereby been successful in emerging as a "responsible" global player, despite its abysmal nuclear and missile proliferation record while the international community rails at India for making the world much more dangerous.

China's attempts to increase its influence in Nepal, Bangladesh, and Myanmar, its persistent refusal to recognize parts of India such as Arunachal Pradesh, its lack of support for India's membership to the United Nations Security Council and other regional and global organizations, all point towards China's attempts at preventing the rise of India as a regional and global player of major import.

It is this strategy that China has consistently and successfully pursued without any apologies. In fact, this strategy has been so successful that today China no longer believes that India can be a serious rival for Asian hegemony and some have pointed out, India is off of China's diplomatic radar.

In contrast to China's well-laid out policy vis-à-vis India, India has from time to time oscillated from one extreme to another. George Tanham has famously pointed out that India has shown little ability to think strategically on national security. In the case of India's China policy, it needs to be realized that there is nothing really sinister about China's attempts to expand its own influence and curtail India's. China is a rising power in Asia and the world and as such will do its utmost to prevent the rise of other power centres around its periphery like India that might in the future prevent it from taking its rightful place as a global player. This is not much different than the stated US policy of preventing the rise of other powers that might threaten its position as a global hegemon. Just as the US is working towards achieving its strategic objective, China is pursuing its own strategic agenda.

There is also nothing extraordinarily benign in China's attempts to improve its bilateral relations with India in recent times. After working to curtail India's influence in various ways, China would not like to see India coming close to the US in order to contain China. In this geopolitical chessboard, both the US and China are using India towards their own strategic ends. India must resist the tendency of reacting to the actions of other. India's attempt to come up a coherent strategy towards China based on identified strategic objectives is of paramount importance. Prime Minister Manmohan Singh declared that it wants to have friendly relations with China, a reasonable foreign policy objective. However, without a clear articulation of India's national security objectives, pursuit of friendly relations with China should not become an end in itself. It should be a means towards achieving India's larger strategic objective of emerging as a major regional and global player.

India's China policy is also symptomatic of a larger misunderstanding in the Indian and political establishment with regard to a nation's foreign policy. For the left-liberal strand in the Indian polity, foreign policy is merely an extension of domestic policy. As such since India is a secular, democratic, and peace-loving nation, India's pursuit of its relations with other states should merely be a reflection of these virtues. This has given rise to much of the moral rhetoric in foreign affairs. On the other hand, the Indian right, because of its preoccupation with establishing a "Hindu" nation and minority bashing, have extended its narrow sectarian view to foreign policy. The consequence has been its obsession with Pakistan as evil incarnate in its foreign policy agenda and its inclination to view the world in black and white, friends and enemies, evil and noble. Shaped by these forces, Indian foreign policy has merely been one of responding to events around it rather than anticipating them and evolving long-term strategies to deal with them. India's China policy is a casualty of this reactionary approach.

India needs to develop its economic and military might without being apologetic. It needs to clearly articulate its national interests and engage China on a host of issues, from the border problem to the alleged dumping of cheap Chinese goods in the Indian market. India needs to recognize that appeasing China is neither desirable nor necessary even as a direct confrontation with China is not something India can afford, at least in the near future. It must also be recognized that while for India, managing its relations with China is at the top of its foreign policy agenda, China does not view India as a significant global player and is largely indifferent to India's growing profile.

India is a rising power in Asia and there is nothing wrong in demanding its rightful place in the inter-state hierarchy. Simply put India and China are two major powers in Asia with global aspirations and some significant conflicting interests. As a result, some amount of friction in their bilateral relationship is inevitable. The geopolitical reality of Asia makes sure that it will be extremely difficult, if not impossible, for *Hindi-Chini* to be *bhai-bhai* (brothers) in the foreseeable future. This reality should be accepted by the Indian policy makers, rather than wished away. India should make a serious attempt to manage this friction by expanding the zone of cooperation with China even as it tries to steadfastly pursue its national interests. India should display the confidence to craft a foreign policy that best serves its national security interests without always looking over the shoulders to make sure that China is not displeased. Again, India can learn a lot by examining how China has managed its relationship with the US in the last few years. While India certainly needs to engage China in an effort at reconciling security and political perspectives, it is naïve to assert, as many do, that India should first be sensitive to China's concerns, real or imaginary, before defining its foreign policy goals and strategic agenda. Does China consult India in its pursuit of its own strategic objectives? It does not and neither should India expect it to. In a similar vein, India should define its foreign policy agenda in view of its own national security imperatives.

But for this to happen, the government of India will have to formulate a clear China policy and, more importantly, a broader national security strategy. Ad-hocism just won't do. This should be the top foreign policy priority of the Indian government if it wants India to emerge as a global power of any reckoning. India should heed to Sun Tzu's advice and recognize that a merely tactical foreign policy approach without the backing of a sound strategy will only lead to nowhere.

CHINA'S STRATEGY OF CONTAINING INDIA

On the surface, relations between India and China are positive. India's economic ties with China are booming. China is set to emerge as India's leading trade partner in the near future, leaving its current number one partner, the United States, behind. Between 2000 and 2005, trade with China registered a hike of 521 percent, whereas India's trade with the U.S. increased by only 63 percent during the same period. There are regular high-level meetings between Asia's two rising powers. India and China have just concluded their second round of bilateral "strategic dialogue" and declared 2006 as a Sino-Indian friendship year. More importantly, they have agreed to cooperate, rather than compete, for global energy resources. The incipient Sino-Indian entente has prompted some to argue that it has the potential to alter Asian geopolitics radically.

Long-time observers of India-China relations, however, maintain that some improvement in the rhetoric and atmospherics notwithstanding, India-China ties remain fragile and as vulnerable as ever to a sudden deterioration. The combination of internal issues of stability and external overlapping spheres of influence forestall the chances for a genuine Sino-Indian rapprochement. Though both sides are working to expand and deepen economic cooperation, there is as yet no strategic congruence between the two giants. Indeed, the issues that bind the two countries together are also the issues that divide them and fuel their rivalry because they have different positions in the international system, contrasting strategic cultures, world views, political systems, and competing geostrategic interests.

In the power competition game, China has clearly surged far ahead of India by acquiring potent economic and military capabilities, and the existing asymmetry in power and status serves Beijing's interests; therefore, China has resisted any Indian attempts to narrow the power gap. Unlike China, India's fractious polity continues to limit its economic and military potential. Nor has New Delhi been able to lend a strategic purpose to its foreign and economic policies. Beneath the surface, frictions and tensions are simmering between the two countries over some fundamental issues: the territorial dispute, the nuclear issue, the U.N. Security Council reform issue, to name a few. Both remain locked in a classic security dilemma: one country sees its own actions as justifiably self-defensive, but these same actions appear aggressive to the other. In the past year, India has found itself ranged against China at the United Nations, the International Atomic Energy Agency over Iran's nuclear program, the East Asia Summit and the Nuclear Suppliers Group (N.S.G.) over the issue of India's membership.

Three major developments which shook the ground beneath South Block (India's External Affairs Ministry building) in New Delhi recently were the emergence of a pro-China axis comprising Pakistan, Nepal, and Bangladesh at the 13th South Asian Association for Regional Cooperation (S.A.A.R.C.) Summit in Dacca, China's opposition to the July 2005 India-U.S. nuclear energy agreement, and Beijing's moves to confine India to the periphery of a future East Asia Community at the first East Asia Summit in Kuala Lumpur in mid-December 2005. Add to this Beijing's worldwide campaign against India's (and Japan's) bids for permanent membership in the U.N. Security Council, the continuing stalemate in the India-China border negotiations, coupled with their ever-expanding economies and widening geopolitical horizons, it is clear that the bilateral relationship between the two rising Asian giants continues to be characterized more by competition and rivalry than by cooperation. Despite the hype over India's burgeoning trade with China, it consists mostly of raw materials, iron ore, steel, and like commodities that are used to fuel China's economic growth while China exports manufactured goods, electronics and machinery to India. Even in the information technology sector, the focus of Chinese diplomacy remains on leveraging India's strengths to China's advantage without any quid pro quo in the technology hardware or manufacturing sectors.

Neither power is comfortable with the rise of the other. Each perceives the other as pursuing regional hegemony and entertaining geographical expansion. Each puts forward its own proposals for multilateral cooperation that exclude the other. Both vie for influence in Central, South and Southeast Asia, and for leadership positions in global and regional organizations. More than ever before, the state of the India-China relationship is increasingly being influenced by "the U.S. factor" as the Southern and Central Asian region becomes an arena of strategic competition in Asia.

SYMPATHETIC CHINA'S STRATEGY

China's leaders do not explicitly provide an overarching "grand strategy" that outlines strategic goals and the means to achieve them. Such vagueness may reflect a deliberate effort to conceal strategic planning, as well as uncertainties, disagreements, and debates that China's leaders themselves have about their own long-term goals and strategies. Still, it is possible to make some generalizations about Chinese "grand strategy" based on strategic tradition, historical patterns, statements and official papers, an emphasis on certain military capabilities, and recent diplomatic efforts.

Strategy with Chinese Characteristics

At the core of China's overall strategy rests the desire to maintain the continuous rule of the Chinese Communist Party (CCP). A deep-rooted fear of losing political power shapes the leadership's strategic outlook and drives many of its choices. As a substitute for the failure of communist ideology, the CCP has based its legitimacy on the twin pillars of economic performance and nationalism. As a consequence, domestic economic and social difficulties may lead China to attempt to bolster support by stimulating nationalist sentiment which could result in more aggressive behaviour in foreign and security affairs than we might otherwise expect. – *Deng Xiaoping's "24 Character Strategy*

Chinese leaders and strategists rarely use a Western "ends-ways-means" construct to discuss strategy. Rather, they discuss strategy in terms of two central concepts: "comprehensive national power" (CNP) and the "strategic configuration of power." These concepts shape how Chinese strategic planners assess the security environment, gauge China's relative position in the world, and make adjustments to account for prevailing geopolitical trends.

CNP. China's strategic planners use CNP scores to evaluate China's standing in relation to other nations. These scores are based on qualitative and quantitative measures of territory, natural resources, economic prosperity, diplomatic influence, international prestige, domestic cohesiveness, military capability, and cultural influence. China's leading civilian and military think tanks apply slightly different criteria for CNP. A 2006 report by the Chinese Academy of Social Sciences, for example, used economic, military, and diplomatic metrics to rank China sixth among the world powers.

Since the early 1980s, China's leaders have described their national development strategy as a quest to increase China's CNP. They stress economic growth and innovation in science and technology as central to strengthening CNP.

The "24 Character" Strategy

In the early 1990s, former paramount leader Deng Xiaoping (d. 1997) gave guidance to China's foreign and security policy apparatus that, collectively, has come to be known as the "24 character" strategy: *"observe calmly; secure our position; cope with affairs calmly; hide our capacities and bide our time; be good at maintaining a low profile; and never claim leadership."* Later, the phrase, "make some contributions (*you suo zuo wei*)" was added.

Elements of this strategy have often been quoted by senior Chinese national security officials and academics, especially in the context of China's diplomacy and military strategy. Certain aspects of this strategy have been debated in recent years – namely the relative emphasis placed upon "never claim leadership" or "make some contributions." China's increased international profile, especially since the 2002 16th Party Congress, suggests Beijing is leaning toward a more assertive, confident diplomacy. Taken as a whole, Deng's strategy remains instructive in that it suggests both a short-term desire to downplay China's capabilities and avoid confrontation, and a long-term strategy to build up China's power to maximize options for the future.

Key assumption of this strategy is that economic prosperity and stability will afford China greater international influence and diplomatic leverage as well as a robust, modern military. A commentary in the official *Liberation Army Daily* in April 2006 shed some light on the relationship between CNP, military modernization, and China's international status: "As China's comprehensive strength is incrementally mounting and her status keeps on going up in international affairs, it is a matter of great importance to strive to construct a military force that is commensurate with China's status and up to the job of defending the interests of China's development, so as to entrench China's international status."

"Strategic Configuration of Power." The "strategic configuration of power," or "*shi*," is roughly understood as an "alignment of forces," although there is no direct Western equivalent to the term. Chinese strategic planners continuously assess the "strategic configuration of power" for potential threats (e.g., potential conflict over Taiwan that involves the United States) as well as opportunities (e.g., the collapse of the Soviet Union) that might prompt an adjustment in national strategy.

China's leaders describe the initial decades of the 21st Century as a "20-year period of opportunity," meaning that regional and international conditions will generally be peaceful and conducive to economic, diplomatic, and military development and thus to China's rise as a great power. Closely linked to this concept is the "peaceful development" campaign to assuage foreign concerns over China's military modernization and its global agenda by proclaiming that China's rise will be peaceful and that conflict is not a necessary corollary to the emergence of a new power.

Stability, Sovereignty, and Strategy

The perpetuation of CCP rule shapes Beijing's perceptions of China's domestic political situation and the international environment. Regime survival likewise shapes how Party leaders view instability along China's periphery – e.g., North Korea, Central Asia – which could escalate or spill over into China. Concern over maintaining legitimacy also influences how Beijing treats the status of China's land and maritime territorial claims, since any challenge to Chinese sovereignty could undermine the strength and authority of the Party.

China has settled territorial disputes with many of its neighbours in recent years. However, disputes with Japan in the East China Sea, with India along their shared border, and with Southeast Asian nations in the South China Sea remain. Although China has attempted to prevent these disputes from disrupting regional relations, occasional statements by PRC officials underscore China's resolve in these areas. For example, on the eve of President Hu's historic October 2006 visit to India, PRC Ambassador Sun Yuxi told Indian press, "the whole of what you call the state of Arunachal Pradesh is Chinese territory... we are claiming all of that – that's our position."

Balance, Position, and Strategy

Beyond China's efforts to maintain stability on its borders and assert its territorial claims, Beijing seeks to advance its strategic interests into the "greater periphery" encompassing Central Asia and the Middle East. The security goals behind this emphasis include maintaining access to resources and markets, and establishing a regional presence and influence to balance and compete with other powers, including the United States, Japan, and India in areas distant from China's borders.

Similarly, China's strategy for the developing world seeks to secure access to resources and markets, build influence in multilateral bodies such as the United Nations, and restrict Taiwan's diplomatic space. To build these relationships, China emphasizes its self-proclaimed status as the leader of the developing world and one that can sympathize with local dissatisfaction over the effects of globalization and perceptions of a widening "north-south" gap.

Resource Demands and Strategy

As China's economy grows, dependence on secure access to markets and natural resources, particularly metals and fossil fuels, is becoming a more urgent influence on China's strategic behaviour. At present, China can neither protect its foreign energy supplies nor the routes on which they travel, including the Straits of Malacca through which some 80 percent of China's cruse oil imports transit – a vulnerability President Hu refers to as the "Malacca Dilemma."

China relies on coal for some two-thirds of its energy, but its demand for oil and gas is increasing. In 2003, China became the world's second largest consumer and third largest importer of oil. China currently imports over 40 percent of its oil (about 2.5 million barrels per day in 2005). By 2025, this figure could rise to 80 percent (9.5 – 15 million barrels per day). China began filling a strategic petroleum reserve in 2006. By 2015, Beijing plans to build reserves to the International Energy Agency standard of 90-days supply, but with poor logistics and transportation networks, this may still prove inadequate.

Nuclear power and natural gas account for smaller, but growing, portions of energy consumption. China plans to increase natural gas utilization from 3 percent to 8 percent of total consumption by 2010. Similarly, China plans to build some 30 1,000-megawatt nuclear power reactors by 2020.

China's reliance on foreign energy imports has affected its strategy and policy in significant ways. It has pursued long-term energy supply agreements in Angola, Central Asia, Chad, Egypt, Indonesia, Iran, Nigeria, Oman, Russia, Saudi Arabia, Sudan, and Venezuela. China has used economic aid, diplomatic favours, and, in some cases, the sale of military technology to secure energy deals. China's desire to meet its energy needs, moreover, has led it to strengthen ties with countries that defy international norms on issues ranging from human rights, support for international terrorism, and proliferation.

In the past few years, China has also offered economic assistance and military cooperation with countries located astride key maritime transit routes. Concern over these routes has also prompted China to pursue maritime capabilities that would help it ensure the safe passage of resources through international waterways.

Other Factors Influencing Chinese Strategy

Economic Reform. Economic success is central to China's emergence as a regional and global power, and is the basis for an increasingly capable military. However, underlying structural weaknesses threaten economic growth. Demographic shifts and social dislocations are stressing an already weak social welfare system. Economic setbacks or downturns could lead to internal unrest, potentially giving rise to greater reliance on nationalism to maintain popular support.

Political Reform. In an October 2005 White Paper on Political Democracy, China's leaders reaffirmed the "people's democratic dictatorship," and declared that China is "against the anarchic call for 'democracy for all.'"

However, internal pressures for political liberalization persist. Party leaders criminalize political dissent, censor the media and internet, suppress independent trade and labour unions, repress ethnic Tibetan and Uighur minorities, and harass religious groups and churches not recognized by the regime. The Party is wary of any unsanctioned organization in China, even if non-political, fearing these organizations could facilitate organized opposition. *Non-Traditional Security Challenges.* Non-traditional security challenges such as epidemic disease (e.g., HIV, avian influenza), systemic corruption (according to official Chinese press, more than 17,500 government officials were prosecuted for corruption in the first eight months of 2006 alone), international crime and narcotics trafficking, and environmental problems (e.g., pollution, water shortages, and renewable resource depletion) could exacerbate Chinese domestic unrest and serve as sources of regional tension and instability.

FORCE TRANSFORMATION AND SECURITY IN THE TAIWAN STRAIT

The security situation in the Taiwan Strait is largely a function of dynamic interactions among policies and actions taken by the mainland, Taiwan, and the United States. China's emergence as a global economic force, increased diplomatic clout, and improved air, naval, and missile forces strengthen Beijing's position relative to Taipei by increasing the mainland's economic leverage over Taiwan, fostering Taiwan's diplomatic isolation, and shifting the cross-Strait military balance in the mainland's favour. Taiwan, meanwhile, has allowed its defense spending to decline in real terms over the past decade, creating an increased urgency for the Taiwan authorities to make the necessary investments to maintain the island's self-defense capabilities. The U.S. Government has made clear that it opposes unilateral changes to the status quo by either side of the Taiwan Strait, does not support Taiwan independence, and supports peaceful resolution of cross-Strait differences in a manner acceptable to the people on both sides of the Taiwan Strait.

In accordance with the Taiwan Relations Act [Public Law 96-8, (1979)], the United States has taken steps to help maintain peace, security, and stability in the region. In addition to making available to Taiwan defense articles and services to enable Taiwan to maintain a sufficient self-defense capability, the U.S.

Department of Defense, through the transformation of U.S. Armed Forces and global force posture realignments, is maintaining the capacity to resist any effort by Beijing to resort to force or coercion to dictate the terms of Taiwan's future status. For its part, Taiwan has taken important steps to improve its joint operations capability, strengthen its officer and non-commissioned officer corps, build its reserve stocks, and improve crisis response capabilities.

Taiwan has bolstered its defensive capabilities by taking delivery of the final two of four KIDD-class DDGs in September 2006. These improvements have, on the whole, reinforced Taiwan's natural defensive advantages in the face of Beijing's continuing build-up. However, Taiwan has yet to acquire other major end items offered for sale by the United States in 2001, namely, Patriot PAC-3 air defense systems, P-3C Orion anti-submarine aircraft, and diesel electric submarines. These systems would enable Taiwan to make necessary improvements to its air and missile defense and anti-submarine warfare capability. In the six years since the offer was made, China has continued to make significant advances, some unexpected, in the capability areas these systems are designed to protect against.

China's Strategy in the Taiwan Strait

Beijing appears prepared to defer unification as long as it believes trends are advancing toward that goal and that the costs of conflict outweigh the benefits. In the near term, Beijing's focus is likely one of preventing Taiwan from moving toward *de jure* independence while continuing to hold out terms for peaceful resolution under a "one country, two systems" framework that would provide Taiwan a degree of autonomy in exchange for its unification with the mainland. Beijing is pursuing these goals through a coercive strategy – with elements of persuasion – that integrates political, economic, cultural, legal, diplomatic, and military instruments of power.

Although Beijing professes peaceful resolution as its preferred outcome, the PLA's ongoing deployment of short range ballistic missiles, enhanced amphibious warfare capabilities, and modern, long-range anti-air systems opposite Taiwan are reminders of Beijing's refusal to renounce the use of force. The sustained military threat to Taiwan serves as an important backdrop to the overall campaign of persuasion and coercion. Exercises, deployments, and media operations all contribute to an environment of intimidation. For example, in a March 2006 speech before military deputies to the National People's Congress plenary, China's Minister of National Defense, General Cao Gangchuan, noted that the Taiwan Strait situation was "still very grim and complicated," and proclaimed that, "all PLA officers and men must enhance their sense of imminent danger as well as their sense of mission and sense of responsibility, lose no time in making military preparations for military struggle, and resolutely safeguard national sovereignty and territorial integrity!"

The circumstances in which the mainland has historically warned it would use force against the island are not fixed and have evolved over time in response to Taiwan's declarations and actions relating to its political status, changes in PLA capabilities, and Beijing's view of other countries' relations with Taiwan.

These circumstances, or "red lines," have included: a formal declaration of Taiwan independence; undefined moves "toward independence"; foreign intervention in Taiwan's internal affairs; indefinite delays in the resumption of cross-Strait dialogue on unification; Taiwan's acquisition of nuclear weapons; and, internal unrest on Taiwan. Article 8 of the March 2005 "Anti-Secession Law" states Beijing would resort to "non-peaceful means" if "secessionist forces... cause the fact of Taiwan's secession from China," if "major incidents entailing Taiwan's secession" occur, or if "possibilities for peaceful reunification" are exhausted.

The ambiguity of these "red-lines" appears deliberate, allowing Beijing the flexibility to determine the nature, timing, and form of its response. Added to this ambiguity are political factors internal to the regime in Beijing that are opaque to outsiders.

Beijing's Courses of Action Against Taiwan

The PLA's capabilities to pursue a variety of courses of action are improving. In the absence of direct insights into PLA contingency planning, some analysts hold that Beijing would signal its readiness to use force imminently in an attempt to menace Taiwan in accordance with Beijing's dictates. Others assess that the likely Chinese course of action would be designed to create military and political pressure toward a rapid resolution on Beijing's terms before the United States or other countries would have a chance to respond. If a quick resolution is not possible, Beijing would seek to deter U.S. intervention or, failing that, delay such intervention, defeat it in an asymmetric, limited, quick war; or, fight it to a standstill and pursue a protracted conflict. Rough outlines for these courses of action are presented below.

Limited Force Options. A limited military campaign could include computer network attacks against Taiwan's political, military, and economic infrastructure to undermine the Taiwan population's confidence in its leadership. PLA special operations forces infiltrated into Taiwan could conduct acts of economic, political, and military sabotage. Beijing might also employ SRBM, special operations forces, and air strikes against air fields, radars, and communications facilities on Taiwan as "nonwar" uses of force to push the Taiwan leadership toward accommodation. The apparent belief that significant kinetic attacks on Taiwan would pass below the threshold of war underscores the risk of Beijing making a catastrophic miscalculation leading to a major unintended military conflict. *Air and Missile Campaign.* Surprise SRBM attacks and precision air strikes against Taiwan's air defense system, including air bases, radar sites, missiles, space assets, and communications facilities could support a campaign to degrade Taiwan defences,

Factors of Avoidance

China is deterred on multiple levels from taking military action against Taiwan. First, China does not yet possess the military capability to accomplish with confidence its political objectives on the island, particularly when confronted with the prospect of U.S. intervention. Moreover, an insurgency directed against the PRC presence could tie up PLA forces for years. A military conflict in the Taiwan Strait would also affect the interests of Japan and other nations in the region in ensuring a peaceful resolution of the cross-Strait dispute.

Beijing's calculus would also have to factor in the potential political and economic repercussions of military conflict with Taiwan. China's leaders recognize that a war could severely retard economic development. Taiwan is China's single largest source of foreign direct investment, and an extended campaign would wreck Taiwan's economic infrastructure, leading to high reconstruction costs. International sanctions could further damage Beijing's economic development. A conflict would also severely damage the image that Beijing has sought to project in the post-Tiananmen years and would taint Beijing's hosting of the 2008 Olympics, for which China's leaders would almost certainly face boycotts and possibly a loss of the games. A conflict could also trigger domestic unrest on the mainland, a contingency that Beijing appears to have factored into its planning. Finally, China's leaders recognize that a conflict over Taiwan involving the United States would give rise to a long-term hostile relationship between the two nations – a result that would not be in China's interests.

Blockade. Beijing could threaten or deploy a naval blockade as a "non-war" pressure tactic in the pre-hostility phase or as a transition to active conflict. Beijing could declare that ships en route to Taiwan ports must stop in mainland ports for inspections prior to transiting on to Taiwan. It could also attempt the equivalent of a blockade by declaring exercise or missile closure areas in approaches and roadsteads to ports to divert merchant traffic, as occurred during the 1995-96 missile firings and live-fire exercises.

Chinese doctrine also includes activities such as air blockades, missile attacks, and mining or otherwise obstructing harbours and approaches. More traditional blockades would have greater impact on Taiwan, but tax PLA Navy capabilities. Any attempt to limit maritime traffic to and from Taiwan would likely trigger countervailing international pressure, and risk military escalation. Such restrictions would have immediate economic effects, but would take time to realize decisive political results, diminishing the ultimate effectiveness and inviting international reaction.

Amphibious Invasion. Publicly available Chinese writings offer different strategies for an amphibious invasion of Taiwan, the most prominent being the Joint Island Landing Campaign. The Joint Island Landing Campaign envisions a complex operation relying on supporting sub-campaigns for logistics, electronic warfare, and air and naval support, to break through or circumvent shore defences, establish and build a beachhead, and then launch an attack to split, seize, and occupy the entire island or key targets.

Amphibious operations are logistics-intensive, and their success depends upon air and sea superiority in the vicinity of the operation, the rapid buildup of supplies and sustainment on shore, and an uninterrupted flow of support thereafter. An amphibious campaign of the scale outlined in the Joint Island Landing Campaign would tax the capabilities of China's armed forces and almost certainly invite international intervention. Add to these strains the combat attrition of China's forces, and the complex tasks of urban warfare and counterinsurgency – assuming a successful landing and breakout – and an amphibious invasion of Taiwan would be a significant political and military risk for China's leaders.

4

India's Security and China Policy

Earlier sections of this book explain changes in India's post-Cold War security concept and adjustments to its China policy. In the process of this discussion, we have distinguished two phases of adjustment to both the post-Cold War India security concept and China policy, and established that these changes were more or less simultaneous. We have also found that India's China policy reflects its security concept; in other words that adjustments to the content of India's China policy correspond to continuities and discontinuities in India's security concept. It may be said that this consistency demonstrates the important influence India's security concept has had on its China policy.

Policy-making, in any event, is the linking of concepts and policy; in other words, concepts, through government policy-making, crystallize into policy. Exploring the evolution of the Indian policy-making class and mechanisms, therefore, also benefits understanding of the manner in which security concepts of different eras and phases have influenced India's China policy.

India's foreign policy behaviour during the Cold War was largely determined by a few predominant personalities, both its foreign and security policies having long been dominated by Nehru and Indira Gandhi. The two leader's views on China had decisive influence on India's China policy. When considering India's defeat in the 1962 Sino–Indian Border Conflict and the open wound it represented to both the Nehru family and the INC, their adoption of an unyielding tack toward China was the sole political means of saving face. Sino–Indian relations consequently remained in stalemate for nearly 30 years. When Rajiv Gandhi replaced his mother in 1985, he seemed at first to follow her line on foreign policy. The rapidly changing international situation, however, forced him to veer from it, and specific improvements in Sino–Soviet relations compelled his adjustments to India's China policy. Soviet leader Mikhail Gorbachev urged Rajiv Gandhi during a visit to India in 1986 to improve relations with China, saying it would suit Soviet interests, and hinting at a press conference that the USSR would no longer be willing to provide support to India in the event of Sino–Indian conflict. In this situation, Rajiv Gandhi considered that India on its own would be powerless against a threat on two fronts. He was hence forced to change his preparations for a two-front war, as it was apparent that dispelling tensions along the eastern front through reconciliation with China would allow him to concentrate India's energies on the western front with Pakistan.

The Nehru family's stately bearing was absent after the Cold War, and the INC's power had declined. The insularity that had characterized India's foreign policy-making process since independence, however, did not change. The nation's foreign and security policy stayed in the hands of the prime minister and cabinet from 1991 to 1996, during which time the views of Prime Minister Rao and leaders of the INC government on security and foreign policy matters were decisive, and the influence of parliament, think tanks and academic institutions was negligible. It is notable, however, that Rao's background as home minister, defence minister and external affairs minister throughout the 1980s, as well as his status as the Congress Party's elder statesman, signified that he was a loyal adherent of Nehruvianism, and unrepresentative of any new type of thinking. The transformation of India's security concept during the Rao administration, therefore, can be understood as entirely the result of external forces.

As earlier mentioned, changes in the international and domestic situation compelled Rao to change his understanding of national strength. He began emphasizing the strategic influence of economic strength and promoting restoration of the economy as a matter of urgency in withstanding security threats in the aftermath of the Cold War. This passive reaction to a complex situation gave the impression of India's overall foreign policy as passive and defensive. India adopted a focused approach to diplomacy during this period, directing its energies towards restoring the economy but maintaining a low profile in international affairs, as expressed in its China policy. Rao continued and furthered Rajiv Gandhi's adjustments by focusing on stabilization of Sino–Indian political relations and establishing tranquil borders as means to ensuring the recovery of India's domestic economy.

Two major changes occurred in India's foreign policy-making process during 1998. The first was the BJP's assumption of office that ended the long-standing INC power monopoly, and established foundations for a clean break with the traditional security concept. Although the BJP's domestic policies had a relatively ideological slant and promoted a Hinduist revival, the party was pragmatic as regards foreign policy. In contrast to the Congress Party, it dared to confront history, criticise India's previous foreign policy and introduce new thinking. Jaswant Singh, successively the Vajpayee government's External Affairs Minister and Finance Minister, published early in 1999 a book entitled *Defending India* in which he systematically describes his new security concept. Various views were thereafter expressed in government-issued articles. The BJP was obviously preparing to move on from the passive security concept of the Rao era. The second major change was India's refinement of its foreign policy-making mechanism. The November 1998 establishment of the National Security Council symbolized India's casting off of the influence and control of personality-based policy-making in favour of scientific research, inquiry and decision-making, and comprehensive long-term planning. The introduction by National

Security Advisory Board subordinated to the National Security Council of scholarly authorities, reporters and former government and military officials demonstrated how much more open India's foreign policy-making process had become.

The BJP differed in its approach to China policy from both that of the Cold War era Nehru family, with its 1962 complex, and the early 1990s Rao government, which had been wearied and bound hand and foot by domestic and international pressure. The BJP's seizing of this historic opportunity confirmed India's rise as the nation's long-term strategic goal and placed its relationship with China on the strategic level.

In other words, the BJP saw the Sino–Indian relationship as an important influence on India's rise. Although the two nations would be dealing with historically significant problems, they could be seen as a starting point.

The gradual opening of India's foreign policy-making process, moreover, made way for a vibrant exchange of ideas regarding China policy, which fell roughly into three groups: the first held that Sino–Indian cooperation suits both sides' interests and that post-Cold War China has no intention of making an enemy of India, desiring instead friendly relations and strategic partnership; the second that China is a long-term strategic threat to India because China's strategic objectives lie in establishing hegemony over Asia, which necessitates India's containment and, therefore, limitation of Indian influence. India, therefore, should adopt diametrically opposed policies; and the third group, situated between the two, held that the two nations could simultaneously rise to become main Asian powers and that competition and cooperation could coexist. Discussions on how to evaluate and understand China by Indian scholars and strategic circles are ongoing. After frequent debates among Indian National Security Council groups, the third, middle-ground viewpoint seems to be gaining acceptance.

When the INC regained power in 2004, a variety of factors led the new government to carry on with the previous administration's security concept. The new INC government's China policy was its predecessor's legacy, because the rise of India's international status during the BJP coalition government left the INC powerless to dispute the success of the previous government's foreign policy. The INC's democratized and more youthful leadership team was also willing to jettison historical baggage and look to the future. Although the Nehru family's leadership role within the Congress Party remained uncontested, the influence of Prime Minister Manmohan Singh and Foreign Minister Mukherjee on foreign and security policy could not be disregarded. Moreover, the liberalization of India's foreign policy-making process was superimposed against a long-standing civil service system which ensured continuity of policy. In other words, many masterminds of BJP foreign policy still active in the external affairs ministry, defence ministry and other relevant functional departments under the INC, as well as in consultative committees, the media, think tanks and other non-functional departments, continued to exert influence.

Substantial changes occurred in India's China policy after the end of the Cold War whereby the nation's long-standing (1962–1988) antagonistic approach became one of reconciliation and engagement. These adjustments originated to a great extent in changes in the sub-continent's post-Cold War security concept, manifest in two major shifts which effected two major phases of adjustment in India's China policy. The new post-Cold War China policy nonetheless retained traces of the former, programme, imbuing it with a duality that reflected the overlap of India's old and new security concepts.

A change in India's security concept first became apparent during the period from the end of the Cold War to 1998. The first phase of adjustments this change triggered in India's China policy was evident in the sub-continent's extended concept of military might as national strength to one encompassing economic factors, and acknowledgement of the strategic value of economic strength in countering what it perceived as the looming threat of marginalization within the international community. Restoration of the domestic economy hence became a main measure through which to resist security threats in the post-Cold War era. Having made this shift in foreign policy objectives towards economic recovery, India set about creating a favourable environment within which to achieve this goal. Overall implementation of a China policy of preserving stable Sino–Indian relations by guaranteeing border tranquillity was vital to achieving this strategic objective. India consequently focused on the feasibility of reconciliation and, in view of China's reflective, inward-looking mood, no longer viewed China as an enemy. As regards India's specific policies, while focusing on the establishment of a progressive means to guaranteeing tranquil borders, thereby stabilizing Sino–Indian relations, India at the same time sought communication and cooperation in other areas. To avoid provoking China, the Indian government made tactical adjustments to its approach to Tibet from that of exploiting the issue and causing uproar to handling the matter in a low-key manner.

The new developments apparent in India's security concept in 1999 brought with it the second phase of adjustments to India's China policy. Indian leaders considered that the nation's security environment had improved to the extent that it constituted a strategic opportunity for India to rise to global-power status. This change in thinking and understanding caused the second shift of objective in India's foreign policy from that of improving the economy to the grand goal of global-power status. It corresponded to India's acknowledgement of the crucial nature of the Sino–Indian relationship and change of focus from border tranquillity and stable political relations to comprehensive considerations of how the two nations' relationship would strategically affect India's; rise. These insights compelled a shift of objective in India's China policy towards making China a positive factor in the sub-continent's rise; also recognition that this objective could be accomplished only by maintaining a stable basis for Sino–Indian relations. Official introduction during this phase of a comprehensive security concept signalled India's adoption of a more pragmatic, comprehensive handling of its relations with China. The specific steps it adopted were: increasing economic cooperation with China, thus benefiting India's economic development and stabilizing bilateral political relations; strengthening military communication and security dialogue, thus deepening understanding of China's strategic intentions towards India, increasing mutual trust, minimizing misunderstandings and avoiding conflict; and seeking Chinese support in its quest for a permanent seat on the UN Security Council, which would expand India's political power and international prestige.

In the course of research, however, it became apparent to the author that India's security concept did not undergo a thoroughgoing change after the Cold War ended, as elements of the Cold War approach remained in place. Although India's security concept extended after 1988 to include both military and economic security, the ultimate purpose of national defence as regards a fundamental guarantee of security nonetheless remained that of increased military strength to safeguard national unity and territorial integrity. India abandoned its strategy of pursuing security through alliances, yet still viewed parity and the principle of checks and balances as hallmarks of its national defence. Influenced as it was by traditional concepts, post-Cold War India's China policy was imbued with vigilance. Even though India did not perceive China as a threat in the short term, it was nevertheless concerned that the swing in balance of power between the two was not in its favour, and that China constituted a potential obstacle to India's rise. Indian leaders consequently embarked on a race against China to expand comprehensive national strength, particularly military force, including India's nuclear capability, as the means to a balance of power. India at the same time sought to offset Chinese influence both regionally and globally through development of strategic relationships with the United States, Japan and other nations. The sub-continent also remained vigilant in the long-standing issues of border disputes and Sino–Pakistani relations, and maintained pressure on China in this regard.

Changes in post-Cold War India's security concept were thus the result of both domestic and foreign factors. The first change during the early post-Cold War period was triggered by passive reactions to transformations in the nation's domestic and international situation that, in turn, prompted a passive transformation of thinking and understanding, manifest in passive defensiveness of India's foreign policy, specifically its China policy. The security concept that appeared during the late 1990s was comparatively proactive. The expanded strength of India's domestic economy and improvement of its external environment compelled a new understanding of security issues, as expressed in the proactive change in its security concept. This assertiveness was manifest in strategy and in an active, enterprising foreign policy. Seizing the historic opportunity to realize India's rise had become the common security objective of both major Indian political parties. Decentralization of political power and expanded openness of the foreign policy-making process, however, caused India's old and new security concepts to bind into one, and the resultant duality of India's hybrid security concept since the Cold War's end is reflected in its China policy. As India's dual security concept will continue into the foreseeable future, the duality of its China policy will be difficult to change.

NATIONAL SECURITY POLICY AND STRATEGY

The concept of national security rests mainly on the proposition that many foreign and domestic political, economic and military issues are inter-related, each with implications on the other. In India's case, this has been highlighted by insurgencies and other political events, particularly in border-states, and other outside pressures, which are brought to bear on the country's economy and technological progress from time to time. A response to this type of environment calls for a highly focussed national security policy and strategy. Effective guidance on national security and defence policy objectives is fundamental to the defence planning process. National security is a relative matter without a firm criteria but unless firm national security objectives are set and a defence policy evolved, there can be no military doctrine or balancing of defence effort with other national objectives and priorities such as maintaining a viable economy and supporting development of society.

The lack of a cohesive national security strategy and defence policy has many implications. First, it results in the absence of clear political direction regarding politico-military objectives, which is the very basis of sound defence planning. Secondly, there is inadequate coordination of defence plans and economic development. Finally, science and technology policies for defence, general industrialisation and other development programmes are not coordinated properly to achieve security goals and objectives.

Perspective Planning

A Defence Plan has to be prepared on the basis of a 15-year long perspective planning system, such that the first five years of the plan are very firm (Definitive Plan), the second five years less firm (Indicative Plan) and the third five-year term tentative (Vision Plan). There has to be a reasonably firm allocation of financial resources for the first five years and an indicative allocation for the subsequent period. Perspective planning needs to be done in the Integrated Defence Headquarters, where military, technical and R&D experts take an integrated view of future threats and challenges. This has to be based on future battlefield scenarios, and array of forecasts, evaluation of strategic options and force mixes, and analysis of potential technical and industrial capabilities. Based on this, the respective Service should work on their perspective plans and the R&D and Defence Production/Supplies experts should spell out their requirements in terms of effort, technology and indigenous production.

Integrated Planning

As stated earlier, the CDS, who would be the cornerstone of integrated operational planning for defence, has not been appointed. India's defence planning, therefore, continues to be Service based. Often, the threat perception of one Service is at variance with that of another Service. What emerges is essentially a sum of total of Service or department wise programmes. The focus is not on overall goals or priorities but on what is required by a particular Service. In its endeavour to lay the groundwork for an increased share of the budget, each Service tends to exercise its own priorities, favouring its own plans to the detriment of joint plans.

Subjects like surveillance, air defence, electronic warfare, and amphibious operations, which relate to more than one Service, do not get adequate attention. Integrated planning for defence is essential for creating balanced force structures and for the successful execution of all military missions. In fact, it is the most effective manner of ensuring effective defence. According to Charles Hitch, "the revolution in military technology has not only changed the character of our military programmes, it has also to a significant degree blurred the lines of demarcation among various Services". Most major military missions today require the participation of more than one military service. Therefore, the principal concern now must be centred on what is required by the defence establishment as a whole to perform a particular mission—not what is required by a particular Service to perform its individual part of that 'mission'. The areas of commonality in modern weapon systems are immense and growing rapidly. Communications, guidance systems, missiles, radars, lasers—even traditional equipment such as guns, fuses, ammunition and vehicles are common. Integrated defence planning is necessary in view of escalating costs of these weapons and equipment.

Self-reliance in Defence Technology

The DRDO has a network of 51 laboratories and establishments. The Scientific Advisor (SA) to the Raksha Mantri (RM) is the Secretary of this Department. The DRDO has a staff of 30,000, including 6,800 scientists and engineers. It receives approximately four to six per cent of the defence budget annually.

The DRDO is engaged in the pursuit of self-reliance in critical technologies relevant to defence. It formulates and executes a programme of scientific research, design and development for the induction into the Armed Forces of state-of-the-art weapons and other equipments. In April 1984, the DRDO envisaged a programme "to transform the Department into a leader of international class with the mission to capture and retain commanding heights in critical technologies". A 'mission mode' organisational structure and approach was approved by the Government with a view to increasing the element of self-reliance from the current 30 per cent to 70 per cent by 2005. This goal, however, is nowhere in sight.

The Department has developed more than 1,100 items of weapon systems and equipment with a production value of over Rs 6,000 crore. But it has not been able to make any major contribution to the state-of-art weapons and equipment. Most of its programmes, like Prithvi (sea borne version), Trishul (short-range surface to air missile), Akash (medium-range surface to air missile), Nag (anti-tank missile), Light Combat Aircraft with Kaveri engine, Pinaka (multiple-barrel rocket system), MBT Arjun, Electronic Warfare equipment, new radio sets for the Army, Sonar system for Navy, and many other items, are way behind schedule.

Despite the media hype, the costs have been heavy. MBT Arjun, when it goes into production mode, will have more than 60 per cent imported components, including several crucial components like the engine and gun control system. It will cost over Rs 25 crore a piece whereas the cost of a T-90 tank, which is as superior (if not more), is less than Rs 10 crore along with technology transfer. Matters have come to such a pass that the Armed Forces have stopped believing media reports about the so-called 'successful trials' of weapons and equipment.

Because of the failure to deliver the required weapons and equipment, defence planning and Force structuring by the Services has suffered continuously. The DRDO's inability to deliver in time has caused a crisis of confidence and constant dissatisfaction in the Services. In order to ensure smooth progress towards self-reliance in defence technology, the Government must undertake a periodic performance audit of DRDO projects to reinforce efforts in areas of success and weed out projects that are unproductive.

EXTERNAL SECURITY THREATS TO INDIA

India has the disadvantage of being situated in close proximity to what is being described as "the epicenter of global terrorism". Tribal region near the Afghanistan-Pakistan border is constantly drawing attention of America's Global War on Terror (GWOT) since 2001. India's increasing relevance to the US strategic canvas, troubled relationship with Pakistan since the independence of the country, deteriorating and unpredictable relationship with China, unstable political climate in Nepal along with Maoist insurgency, mistrustful relationship with Bangladesh, civil-war ravaged and still-healing Sri Lanka, authoritarian Myanmar have rendered any fair estimation of Indian preparedness to deal with these security challenges an onerous task. We will now analyse capabilities and interests of each of these players and then asses their influence on India's strategic calculations.

The United States of America

India's relationship with the sole military and economic superpower of the world has been on the rise during the previous decade. A new shift in Indo-US relations was witnessed during President Clinton's visit in 2000, fortified by Presidents Bush and Obama's visit to the country. That said, although India remains ideologically non-committal to signing the CTBT and NPT regime; there has been tremendous improvement in the nuclear energy field through singing the Indo-US Nuclear Treaty in 2006.

The US has always been a practitioner of hard real-politick, its policies have always been defined by its own interests in the region. The US support to Pakistan's military through CEATO arrangements in 1960s, later President Nixon's visit to China in Feb 1972 which was secretly facilitated by Pakistan and resulted in melting the ice between the two nations, support to Pakistan's defense apparatus and Taliban through 1980s and now military offensive in the Af-Pak tribal region have all been calibrated on the US self-interests. All these steps have had a profound impact on India's external security environment. The continued US presence in our North-West border is cited to be one of the main reasons behind Pakistan's belligerent attitude in the aftermath of the Parliament attack in 2001 and 26/11mayhem in 2008. The Pakistani Army knows Indian options are severely limited to strike across Pakistani territory owing to military assistance she is providing to GWOT. Apart from limiting India's punitive capability against Pakistan for its sponsoring terrorist attacks and their infrastructure in India, the US has also provided substantial financial and military to Pakistan which have adverse consequences to our strategic calculations.

Nonetheless the US is likely to dominate world affairs for at least another two decades. India has to work towards minimizing adverse impact of the US-Pak assistance on our external security. On a lighter note, India should emphasize to the US that for fighting tribal insurgents in its North-Western region; Pakistan does not need F-16s and nuclear submarines!

People's Republic of China

Indo-China relations have been marked with distrust and fear on both sides after 1962 border clash which resulted in China usurping Aksai Chin area in J&K giving it easy road access from the Tibetan plateau to remote Xinxiang region in the West. Additionally China's rise in the past three decades has given it tremendous weight in international political and security circles. China has patiently been working towards building military-economic and political alliances around India's periphery – termed as "strings of pearl strategy". China remains India's number one security threat. It has provided consistent military assistance to Pakistan for use against India, funded armed rebels in the North-East and has continued to up the ante in diplomatic circles through stapled visas, visa denials and spying on Tibetan Diaspora in

India. Although India needs to be sensitive towards Chinese sensitivities towards Tibet, India has failed to play an assertive role in communicating its interests to the Chinese side. On the other hand, China has built up superior civilian and military infrastructure along Indo-Tibet border. Our defense preparedness vis-à-vis China leaves much to be desired. As has rightly been enunciated by one of our Army Chiefs, the possibility of Two-Front War scenario with both Pakistan and China should be factored in while preparing our doctrine of war and operational readiness.

To match China's might and thwart any misadventure from our Northern neighbour, we should invest heavily in our infrastructure in border areas, phase out obsolete military hardware, raise at least 3 mountain divisions for the Eastern sector and shore up anti-ballistic missile capability through expedited Agni programs. Fortunately Indian economy's healthy growth in the past decade has ensured greater defense outlay but even now our defense budget at 2.1% is way below 4.5% and 4.7% of Pakistani and Chinese budgets as % of their respective GDP and even the allocated funds do not get fully utilized for modernizing the forces but for the lack of speedy and transparent procurement procedures.

A look at the following chart shows the yawning gap between the defense expenditures of China and India. China is widely known to have unders tated its publicly announced defense budgets. The defense expenditure for Pakistan does not include capital outlay hence actual spending should be higher than shown here. Hence the need to selectively utilize our limited defense outlay for maximizing lethality of our forces.

To that end recent successful trial of indigenously designed and developed Light Combat Aircraft (LCA) Tejas is a welcome development. Similarly other big-ticket purchases for example C130s and Medium Multi-Role Combat Aircraft (MMRCAs) should also be expedited for induction into the Indian Air Force. Indian Navy's recent announcement of forming an Andaman specific command is a right step towards influencing Malacca strait area which can be one of the pressure points on the Chinese Navy in the event of a prolonged conflict. But our Navy needs much awaited aircraft career to project military power away from the shores. Unfortunately Russian aircraft carrier Gorshkov is waiting for about a decade for acquisition. Other steps should be towards economically integrating countries in our immediate neighbourhood to balance strategic Chinese investment in these countries. A strong political will is required to transform the forces and provide them necessary resources to successfully face the challenges on the external front.

Pakistan

The perennial challenge before Indian defense apparatus to manage external covert and overt threat from Pakistan does not need any emphasis. Since the birth of that country, we have fought them four times in war - 1948, 1965, 1971 and 1998. Besides the country is facing low intensity conflict in J&K abetted and sponsored by Pakistani military, in the North-East and through support to various fringe extremist group within the country. The country also faces huge challenge before its economy in the form of fake rackets being operated from Karachi and Dubai and widely believed to have blessings of Pakistan's infamous Inter-Services Intelligence – its external spy agency.

Thus Pakistan remains one of our principle worries at both external and internal security fronts. Besides on the basis of its long-standing strategic partnership with China, it can stretch our armed forces capabilities in the Eastern sector.

The modernization plans of Karakoram highway, the development of Gwadar as an aval port by the Chinese Navy and covert assistance to Pakistan's nuclear and missile program are on the anvil; these two countries should be watched very carefully in our defense planning. Rapid implementation of the mooted Cold-Start Strategy should be pursued by the forces to neutralize Pakistani threat quickly in a two-front war scenario and deny the bigger neighbour to our North an advantage from the Western sector.

Immediate Neighbourhood

Unfortunately our other neighbours with the exception of Bhutan also don't provide any succour to military planners and political leaders and are equally as challenging as China and Pakistan. While Nepal is in the grip of political turmoil since the ouster of unpopular King Gyanendra, India has to play its cards carefully lest it be seen with a big brother agenda. India and Nepal share an open boundary with free exchange of people and currency across the borders. Although few contentious points remain in the Indo-Nepalese relations; they should not be allowed to obstruct our efforts in ensuring political stability in this strategically important neighbour of hours. Perhaps Indian leftist parties can be utilized by the Central government to persuade Maoist leadership in Nepal to desist from mollycoddling too much with the Chinese to our and Nepal's detriment.

Bangladesh on the other hand is showing signs of delivering on the stated policy of the Government of Prime Minister Sheikh Hasina of not letting her country's soil for anti-India activities. Bangladesh has recently handed over many high profile terrorist leaders hiding in their country. India has also reciprocated with huge USD 1 billion economic assistance in the form of line of credit to Bangladesh. But India should actively continue to manage her somewhat uneasy relationship with the Opposition leader in Bangladesh former PM Mrs. Begum Khalida Zia. Seeking active Bangladeshi cooperation in destroying the terrorist infrastructure of Harkat-ul-Jihad-al Islami (HuJI) remains a challenge for Indian security agencies.

Although India at first neglected their relationship with Burmese military rulers, there have been improvements in the past few years in our bilateral relations. China has been investing in Kyaukryu and Sittwe as commercial ports on the west coast close to our NE states. Both of these ports can be used as a naval base and should be a cause of concern. India also needs to co-opt Myanmar for curbing the North Eastern rebel groups e.g. NSCN, ULFA and Manipur rebels which find shelter in dense forests along the international border. For that increased economic and military cooperation without inviting international limelight is a challenge as recently the US has started objecting to our strengthening relationship with the junta. India also faces competition from China in keeping Sri Lanka attuned to our interests. The recently finished Civil War in the North-East Sri Lanka has incurred huge emotional and economic costs for the Indian Tamils. Thus encouraging cordial linguistic relations in Sri Lanka through persuading Lankan government towards equitable distribution of resources and fair treatment of ethnic minorities is a priority for Indian foreign policy mandarins. Bhutan has demonstrated sensibilities to our concerns by wiping off ULFA rebels in their territory in 2003 and India rightly assists in their economic, social and defense developments. Similarly India should also manage our closest ally during the Cold War era – Russia – to counterbalance China and procuring critical defense supplies.

CHINA'S NATIONAL DEFENCE AND SECURITY SITUATION

With the advent of the new century, the world is undergoing tremendous changes and adjustments. Peace and development remain the principal themes of the times, and the pursuit of peace, development and cooperation has become an irresistible trend of the times. However, global challenges are on the increase, and new security threats keep emerging.

Economic globalization and world multi-polarization are gaining momentum. The progress toward industrialization and informationization throughout the globe is accelerating and economic cooperation is in full swing, leading to increasing economic interdependence, inter-connectivity and interactivity among countries. The rise and decline of international strategic forces is quickening, major powers are stepping up their efforts to cooperate with each other and draw on each other's strengths. They continue to compete with and hold each other in check, and groups of new emerging developing powers are arising. Therefore, a profound readjustment is brewing in the international system. In addition, factors conducive to maintaining peace and containing war are on the rise, and the common interests of countries in the security field have increased, and their willingness to cooperate is enhanced, thereby keeping low the risk of worldwide, all-out and large-scale wars for a relatively long period of time.

World peace and development are faced with multiple difficulties and challenges. Struggles for strategic resources, strategic locations and strategic dominance have intensified. Meanwhile, hegemonism and power politics still exist, regional turmoil keeps spilling over, hot-spot issues are increasing, and local conflicts and wars keep emerging. The impact of the financial crisis triggered by the U.S. subprime mortgage crisis is snowballing. In the aspect of world economic development, issues such as energy and food are becoming more serious, highlighting deep-seated contradictions. Economic risks are manifesting a more interconnected, systematic and global nature. Issues such as terrorism, environmental disasters, climate change, serious epidemics, transnational crime and pirates are becoming increasingly prominent.

The influence of military security factors on international relations is mounting. Driven by competition in overall national strength and the development of science and technology, international military competition is becoming increasingly intense, and the worldwide revolution in military affairs (RMA) is reaching a new stage of development. Some major powers are realigning their security and military strategies, increasing their defence investment, speeding up the transformation of armed forces, and developing advanced military technology, weapons and equipment. Strategic nuclear forces, military astronautics, missile defence systems, and global and battlefield reconnaissance and surveillance have become top priorities in their efforts to strengthen armed forces. Some developing countries are also actively seeking to acquire advanced weapons and equipment to increase their military power. All countries are attaching more importance to supporting diplomatic struggles with military means. As a result, arms races in some regions are heating up, posing grave challenges to the international arms control and nonproliferation regime.

The Asia-Pacific security situation is stable on the whole. The regional economy is brimming with vigor, mechanisms for regional and sub-regional economic and security cooperation maintain their development momentum, and it has become the policy orientation of all countries to settle differences and hotspot issues peacefully through dialogue. The member states of the Shanghai Cooperation Organization (SCO) have signed the Treaty on Long-Term Good-Neighborly Relations, Friendship and Cooperation, and practical cooperation has made progress in such fields as security and economy. The conclusion of the ASEAN Charter has enabled a new step to be taken toward ASEAN integration. Remarkable achievements have been made in cooperation between China and ASEAN, as well as between ASEAN and China, Japan and the Republic of Korea. Cooperation within the framework of the East Asia Summit (EAS) and the South Asian Association for Regional Cooperation (SAARC) continues to make progress. The Six-Party Talks on the Korean nuclear issue have scored successive achievements, and the tension in Northeast Asia is much released.

However, there still exist many factors of uncertainty in Asia-Pacific security. The drastic fluctuations in the world economy impact heavily on regional economic development, and political turbulence persists in some countries undergoing economic and social transition. Ethnic and religious discords, and conflicting claims over territorial and maritime rights and interests remain serious, regional hotspots are complex. At the same time, the U.S. has increased its strategic attention to and input in the Asia-Pacific region, further consolidating its military alliances, adjusting its military deployment and enhancing its military capabilities. In addition, terrorist, separatist and extremist forces are running rampant, and non-traditional security issues such as serious natural disasters crop up frequently. The mechanisms for security cooperation between countries and regions are yet to be enhanced, and the capability for coping with regional security threats in a coordinated way has to be improved.

China's security situation has improved steadily. The achievements made in China's modernization drive have drawn worldwide attention. China's overall national strength has increased substantially, its people's living standards have kept improving, the society remains stable and unified, and the capability for upholding national security has been further enhanced. The attempts of the separatist forces for "Taiwan independence" to seek "de jure Taiwan independence" have been thwarted, and the situation across the Taiwan Straits has taken a significantly positive turn. The two sides have resumed and made progress in consultations on the common political basis of the "1992 Consensus," and consequently cross-Straits relations have improved. Meanwhile, China has made steady progress in its relations with the developed countries, strengthened in all respects the good-neighborly friendship with its neighbouring countries, and kept deepening its traditional friendship with the developing countries. China is playing an active and constructive role in multilateral affairs, thus notably elevating its international position and influence. China is still confronted with long-term, complicated, and diverse security threats and challenges. Issues of existence security and development security, traditional security threats and non-traditional security threats, and domestic security and international security are interwoven and interactive. China is faced with the superiority of the developed countries in economy, science and technology, as well as military affairs. It also faces strategic maneuvers and containment from the outside while having to face disruption and sabotage by separatist and hostile forces from the inside. Being in a stage of economic and social transition, China is encountering many new circumstances and new issues in maintaining social stability. Separatist forces working for "Taiwan independence," "East Turkistan independence" and "Tibet independence" pose threats to China's unity and security. Damages caused by non-traditional security threats like terrorism, natural disasters, economic insecurity, and information insecurity are on the rise. Impact of uncertainties and destabilizing factors in China's outside security environment on national security and development is growing. In particular, the United States continues to sell arms to Taiwan in violation of the principles established in the three Sino-U.S. joint communiques, causing serious harm to Sino-U.S. relations as well as peace and stability across the Taiwan Straits.

In the face of unprecedented opportunities and challenges, China will hold high the banner of peace, development and cooperation, persist in taking the road of peaceful development, pursue the opening-up strategy of mutual benefit, and promote the building of a harmonious world with enduring peace and common prosperity; and it will persist in implementing the Scientific Outlook on Development in a bid to achieve integration of development with security, persist in giving due consideration to both traditional and non-traditional security issues, enhancing national strategic capabilities, and perfecting the national emergency management system. At the same time, it will persist in pursuing the new security concept featuring mutual trust, mutual benefit, equality and coordination, and advocating the settlement of international disputes and hotspot issues by peaceful means. It will encourage the advancement of security dialogues and cooperation with other countries, oppose the enlargement of military alliances, and acts of aggression and expansion. China will never seek hegemony or engage in military expansion now or in the future, no matter how developed it becomes.

National Defence Policy

China pursues a national defence policy which is purely defensive in nature. China places the protection of national sovereignty, security, territorial integrity, safeguarding of the interests of national development, and the interests of the Chinese people above all else. China endeavors to build a fortified national defence and strong military forces compatible with national security and development interests, and enrich the country and strengthen the military while building a moderately prosperous society in all aspects. China's national defence policy for the new stage in the new century basically includes: upholding national security and unity, and ensuring the interests of national development; achieving the all-round, coordinated and sustainable development of China's national defence and armed forces; enhancing the performance of the armed forces with informationization as the major measuring criterion; implementing the military strategy of active defence; pursuing a self-defensive nuclear strategy; and fostering a security environment conducive to China's peaceful development.

According to the requirements of national security and the level of economic and social development, China pursues a three-step development strategy to modernize its national defence and armed forces step by step in a well-planned way. This strategic framework is defined as follows: Promoting the informationization of China's national defence and armed forces. Taking informationization as the goal of modernization of its national defence and armed forces and in light of its national and military conditions, China actively pushes forward the RMA with Chinese characteristics. It has formulated in a scientific way strategic plans for national defence and armed forces building and strategies for the development of the services and arms, according to which it will lay a solid foundation by 2010, basically accomplish mechanization and make major progress in informationization by 2020, and by and large reach the goal of modernization of national defence and armed forces by the mid-21st century.

Overall planning of economic development and national defence building. Sticking to the principle of coordinated development of economy and national defence, China makes overall plans for the use of its national resources and strikes a balance between enriching the country and strengthening the military, so as to ensure that its strategy for national defence and armed forces building is compatible with its strategy for national development. It makes national defence building an organic part of its social and economic development, endeavors to establish scientific mechanisms for the coordinated development of economy and national defence, and thus provides rich resources and sustainable driving force for the modernization of its national defence and armed forces. In national defence building, China makes it a point to take into consideration the needs of economic and social development and insists on having military and civilian purposes compatible with and beneficial to each other, so as to achieve more social benefits in the use of national defence resources in peacetime.

Deepening the reform of national defence and armed forces. China is working to adjust and reform the organization, structure and policies of the armed forces, and will advance step by step the modernization of the organizational form and pattern of the armed forces in order to develop by 2020 a complete set of scientific modes of organization, institutions and ways of operation both with Chinese characteristics and in conformity with the laws governing the building of modern armed forces. China strives to adjust and reform the systems of defence-related industry of science and technology and the procurement of weapons and equipment, and enhance its capacity for independent innovation in R&D of weapons and equipment with better quality and cost-effectiveness. China endeavors to establish and improve the systems of weaponry and equipment research and manufacturing, military personnel training and logistical support that integrate military with civilian purposes and combine military efforts with civilian support. In addition, China makes an effort to establish and improve a national defence mobilization system that is centralized and unified, well structured, rapid in reaction, and authoritative and efficient.

Taking the road of leapfrog development. Persisting in taking mechanization as the foundation and informationization as focus, China is stepping up the composite development of mechanization and informationization. Persisting in strengthening the military by means of science and technology, China is working to develop new and high-tech weaponry and equipment, carry out the strategic project of training talented people, conduct military training in conditions of informationization, and build a modern logistics system in an all-round way, so as to change the mode of formation of war-fighting capabilities. Persisting in laying stress on priorities, China distinguishes between the primary and the secondary, and refrains from doing certain things, striving to achieve leapfrog development in key areas. China persists in building the armed forces through diligence and thrift, attaching importance to scientific management, in order to make the fullest use of its limited defence resources.

China implements a military strategy of active defence. Strategically, it adheres to the principle of featuring defensive operations, self-defence and striking and getting the better of the enemy only after the enemy has started an attack. In response to the new trends in world military developments and the requirements of the national security and development strategy, China has formulated a military strategic guideline of active defence for the new period.

This guideline aims at winning local wars in conditions of informationization. It takes into overall consideration the evolution of modern warfare and the major security threats facing China, and prepares for defensive operations under the most difficult and complex circumstances.

Meeting the requirements of confrontation between war systems in modern warfare and taking integrated joint operations as the basic approach, it is designed to bring the operational strengths of different services and arms into full play, combine offensive operations with defensive operations, give priority to the flexible application of strategies and tactics, seek advantages and avoid disadvantages, and make the best use of our strong points to attack the enemy's weak points.

It endeavours to refine the command system for joint operations, the joint training system and the joint support system, optimize the structure and composition of forces, and speed up the building of a combat force structure suitable for winning local wars in conditions of informationization.

This guideline lays stress on deterring crises and wars. It works for close coordination between military struggle and political, diplomatic, economic, cultural and legal endeavours, strives to foster a favourable security environment, and takes the initiative to prevent and defuse crises, and deter conflicts and wars. It strictly adheres to a position of self-defence, exercises prudence in the use of force, seeks to effectively control war situations, and strives to reduce the risks and costs of war. It calls for the building of a lean and effective deterrent force and the flexible use of different means of deterrence. China remains committed to the policy of no first use of nuclear weapons, pursues a self-defensive nuclear strategy, and will never enter into a nuclear arms race with any other country.

This guideline focuses on enhancing the capabilities of the armed forces in countering various security threats and accomplishing diversified military tasks. With the focus of attention on performing the historical missions of the armed forces for the new stage in the new century and with raising the capability to win local wars in conditions of informationization at the core, it works to increase the country's capabilities to maintain maritime, space and electromagnetic space security and to carry out the tasks of counter-terrorism, stability maintenance, emergency rescue and international peacekeeping. It takes military operations other than war (MOOTW) as an important form of applying national military forces, and scientifically makes and executes plans for the development of MOOTW capabilities. China participates in international security cooperation, conducts various forms of military exchanges and promotes the establishment of military confidence-building mechanisms in accordance with this guideline.

This guideline adheres to and carries forward the strategic concept of people's war. In accordance with this guideline, China always relies on the people to build national defence and the armed forces, combines a lean standing force with a powerful reserve force, and endeavours to reinforce its national war potential and defence strength. China is working to set up a mechanism for unified and efficient national defence mobilization, stepping up the mobilization of economy, science and technology, information and transportation, and making improvements in the building of the reserve force. China is striving to make innovations in the content and forms of people's war, exploring new approaches of the people in participating in warfare and support for the front, and developing new strategies and tactics for people's war in conditions of informationization. Moreover, the People's Liberation Army (PLA) subordinates its development to the overall national construction, supports local economic and social development, and consolidates the unity between the PLA and the government, and between the PLA and the people.

China and India Today: Diplomats Jostle, Militaries Prepare

Just as the Indian subcontinental plate has a tendency to constantly rub and push against the Eurasian tectonic plate, causing friction and volatility in the entire Himalayan mountain range, India's bilateral relationship with China is also a subtle, unseen, but ongoing and deeply felt collision, the affects of which have left a convoluted lineage. Tensions between the two powers have come to influence everything from their military and security decisionmaking to their economic and diplomatic maneuvering, with implications for wary neighbours and faraway allies alike. The relationship is complicated by layers of rivalry, mistrust, and occasional cooperation, not to mention actual geographical disputes.

Distant neighbours buffered by Tibet and the Himalayas for millennia, China and India became next-door neighbours with contested frontiers and disputed histories in 1950, following the occupation of Tibet by Mao's People's Liberation Army (PLA). While the rest of the world started taking note of China's rise during the last decade of the twentieth century, India has been warily watching China's rise ever since a territorial dispute erupted in a brief but full-scale war in 1962, followed by skirmishes in 1967 and 1987.

Several rounds of talks held since 1981 have failed to resolve the disputed claims. During his last visit to India, in 2010, Chinese Premier Wen Jiabao dashed any hopes of early border settlement, stating that it would take a very long time to settle the boundary issue—a situation that in many ways works to Beijing's advantage. An unsettled border provides China the strategic leverage to keep India uncertain about its intentions, and nervous about its capabilities, while exposing India's vulnerabilities and weaknesses, and encouraging New Delhi's "good behavior" on issues of vital concern. Besides, as the ongoing unrest and growing incidents of self-immolations by Buddhist monks in Tibet show, Beijing has not yet succeeded in pacifying and Sinicizing Tibet, as it has Inner Mongolia. The net result is that the 2,520-mile Sino-Indian frontier, one of the longest inter-state boundaries in the world, remains China's only undefined land border. It is also becoming heavily militarized, as tensions rise over China's aggressive patrolling on the line of actual control (LAC) and its military drills, using live ammunition, for a potential air and land campaign to capture high-altitude mountain passes in Tibet.

Over the last decade, the Chinese have put in place a sophisticated military infrastructure in the Tibet Autonomous Region (TAR) adjoining India: five fully operational air bases, several helipads, an extensive rail network, and thirty thousand miles of roads—giving them the ability to rapidly deploy thirty divisions (fifteen thousand soldiers each) along the border, a three-to-one advantage over India. China has not only increased its military presence in Tibet but is also ramping up its nuclear arsenal. In addition, the PLA's strategic options against India are set to multiply as Chinese land and rail links with Pakistan, Nepal, Burma, and Bangladesh improve.

Developments on the disputed Himalayan borders are central to India's internal debate about the credibility of its strategic deterrent and whether to test nuclear weapons again. Being the weaker power, India is far more concerned about the overall military balance tilting to its disadvantage. India sees China everywhere because of Beijing's "hexiao gongda" policy in South Asia: "uniting with the small" — Pakistan, Bangladesh, Nepal, Burma, and Sri Lanka — "to counter the big" — India. When combined with Chinese nuclear and missile transfers to Pakistan and building of port facilities around India's periphery, and a dramatic increase in the PLA's incursions and transgressions across the LAC, the official Indian perception of China has undergone a dramatic shift since 2006, with China now being widely seen as posing a major security threat in the short to medium term rather than over the long term. The Indian military, long preoccupied with war-fighting scenarios against Pakistan, has consequently turned its attention to the China border, and unveiled a massive force modernization program, to cost $100 billion over the next decade, that includes the construction of several strategic roads and the expansion of rail networks, helipads, and airfields all along the LAC. Other measures range from raising a new mountain strike corps and doubling force levels in the eastern sector by one hundred thousand troops to the deployment of Sukhoi Su-30MKI aircraft, spy drones, helicopters, and ballistic and cruise missile squadrons to defend its northeastern state of Arunachal Pradesh, territory three times the size of Taiwan that the Chinese invaded in 1962 and now claim sovereignty over as "Southern Tibet."

Propelled by incidents related to border disputes, Chinese opposition to the US-India nuclear energy deal, India's angst over the growing trade deficit due to perceived Chinese unfair trade practices, potential Chinese plans to dam the Brahmaputra River, and the "war talk" in the official Chinese media in the 2007 to 2009 period (reminding India not to forget "the lessons of 1962"), mutual distrust between the Indian and Chinese peoples is growing. Clearly, China's extraordinary economic performance over the last three decades has changed the dynamics of the relationship. China and India had similar average incomes in the late 1970s, but thirty years later they find themselves at completely different stages of development. China's economic reforms — launched in 1978, nearly thirteen years before India's in 1991 — changed their subsequent growth trajectories by putting China far ahead of India in all socioeconomic indices. Both China's gross domestic product and military expenditure are now three times the size of India's; recent surveys conducted by Pew Global Research show a growth in popular distrust, with just twenty-five percent of Indians holding a favorable view of China in 2011, down from thirty-four percent in 2010 and fifty-seven percent in 2005. Likewise, just twenty-seven percent of Chinese hold a favorable view of India in 2011, down from thirty-two percent in 2010, with studies of Internet content showing a large degree of "hostility and contempt for India."

Nor is there much effort to keep these emotions submerged. Reacting to the test launch in mid-April of a long-range Agni-V ballistic missile, dubbed the "China killer" by India's news media, a Chinese daily wryly noted that "India stands no chance in an overall arms race with China," because "China's nuclear power is stronger and more reliable." The unequal strategic equation, in particular the Chinese perception of India as a land of irreconcilable socioreligious cleavages with an inherently unstable polity and weak leadership that is easily contained through proxies, aggravates tensions between the two. In 2008, an official reassessment of China's capabilities and intentions led the Indian military to adopt a "two-front war" doctrine against what is identified as a "collusive threat" posed by two closely aligned nuclear-armed neighbours, Pakistan and China. This doctrine validates the long-held belief of India's strategic community that China is following a protracted strategy of containing India's rise.

India is also responding by strengthening its strategic links with Afghanistan, Tajikistan, Mongolia, Vietnam, and Burma — countries on China's periphery. In testimony to the US Senate in February, James Clapper, the director of national intelligence, noted that "the Indian military is strengthening its forces in preparation to fight a limited conflict along the disputed border, and is working to balance Chinese power projection in the Indian Ocean." That "balance" includes a strategic tilt toward the United

States that has also had a damaging effect on Sino-Indian relations. Although leaders from both countries often repeat the ritualized denials of conflict and emphasize burgeoning trade ties, such platitudes cannot obliterate the trust deficit. Few if any of China's strategic thinkers seem to hold positive views of India for China's future, and vice versa. Chinese strategists keep a wary eye on India's "great power dreams," its military spending and weapons acquisitions, and the developments in India's naval and nuclear doctrines. A dominant theme in Chinese commentary in the last decade is that India's growing strength—backed by the United States—could tip Asia's balance of power away from Beijing.

Not surprisingly, bilateral relations between Asia's giants remain, in the words of Zhang Yan, China's ambassador to India, "very fragile, very easy to be damaged, and very difficult to repair." Both have massive manpower resources, a scientific and industrial base, and million-plus militaries. For the first time in more than fifty years, both are moving upward simultaneously on their relative power trajectories. As the pivotal power in South Asia, India perceives itself much as China has traditionally perceived itself in relation to East Asia. Both desire a peaceful security environment to focus on economic development and avoid overt rivalry or conflict. Still, the volatile agents of nationalism, history, ambition, strength, and size produce a mysterious chemistry. Neither power is comfortable with the rise of the other. Both seek to envelop neighbours with their national economies. Both are nuclear and space powers with growing ambitions. Both yearn for a multipolar world that will provide them the space for growth and freedom of action. Both vie for leadership positions in global and regional organizations and have attempted to establish a sort of Monroe Doctrine in their respective neighbourhoods— without much success.

And both remain suspicious of each other's long-term agenda and intentions. Each perceives the other as pursuing hegemony and entertaining imperial ambitions. Both are non–status quo powers: China in terms of *territory*, power, and influence; India in terms of *status*, power, and influence. Both seek to expand their power and influence in and beyond their regions at each other's expense. China's "Malacca paranoia" is matched by India's "Hormuz dilemma." If China's navy is going south to the Indian Ocean, India's navy is going east to the Pacific Ocean. Both suffer from a siege mentality born out of their elites' acute consciousness of the divisive tendencies that make their countries' present political unity so fragile. After all, much of Chinese and Indian history is made up of long periods of internal disunity and turmoil, when centrifugal forces brought down even the most powerful empires. Each has its vulnerabilities—regional conflicts, poverty, and religious divisions for India; the contradiction between a market economy and Leninist politics for China. Both are plagued with domestic linguistic, ethno-religious, and politico-economic fault lines that could be their undoing if not managed properly.

In other words, China and India are locked in a classic security dilemma: one country sees its actions as defensive, but the same actions appear aggressive to the other. Beijing fears that an unrestrained Indian power—particularly one that is backed by the West and Japan—would not only threaten China's security along its restive southwestern frontiers (Tibet and Xinjiang) but also obstruct China's expansion southwards. Faced with exponential growth in China's power and influence, India feels the need to take counterbalancing measures and launch strategic initiatives to emerge as a great power, but these are perceived as challenging and threatening in China.

China's use of regional and international organizations to institutionalize its power while either denying India access to these organizations or marginalizing India within them has added a new competitive dynamic to the relationship. In the past decade, India has found itself ranged against China at the UN Security Council, East Asia Summit, the Asia-Pacific Economic Cooperation, the Nuclear Suppliers Group, and the Asian Development Bank. In 2009, China vetoed a development plan for India by the latter in the disputed Arunachal Pradesh, thereby internationalizing a bilateral territorial dispute. In a tit-for-tat response, New Delhi has kept Beijing out of India-led multilateral frameworks such as the Bay of Bengal Initiative for Multi-Sectoral Technical and Economic Cooperation, the India-Brazil-South Africa Dialogue, and the Mekong–Ganga Cooperation forums, and rejected China's request to be included as observer or associate member into the 33-member Indian Ocean Naval Symposium, started by India in 2008.

Resource scarcity has added a maritime dimension to this geopolitical rivalry. As China's and India's energy dependence on the Middle East and Africa increases, both are actively seeking to forge closer defence and security ties with resource supplier nations (e.g., Saudi Arabia and Iran), and to develop appropriate naval capabilities to dominate the sea lanes through which the bulk of their commerce flows. Since seventy-seven percent of China's oil comes from the Middle East and Africa, Beijing has increased its activities in the Indian Ocean region by investing in littoral states' economies, building ports and infrastructure, providing weaponry, and acquiring energy resources. Nearly ninety percent of Chinese arms sales go to countries located in the Indian Ocean region. Beijing is investing heavily in developing the Gwadar deep-sea port in Pakistan, and naval bases in Sri Lanka, Bangladesh, and Myanmar. Whether one calls it a "string of pearls" or a series of places at which China's navy can base or simply be resupplied, that navy is setting up support infrastructure in strategic locations along the same sea lanes of communication that could neutralize India's geographical advantage in the Indian Ocean region. A recent commentary from the official Xinhua news outlet called for setting up three lines of navy supply bases in the northern Indian Ocean, the western Indian Ocean, and the southern Indian Ocean. It stated: "China needs to establish overseas strategic support stations for adding ship fuel, re-supply of necessities, staff break time, repairs of equipment, and weapons in Pakistan, Sri Lanka, and Myanmar, which will be the core support bases in the North Indian Ocean supply line; Djibouti, Yemen, Oman, Kenya, Tanzania, and Mozambique, which will be the core support bases in the West Indian Ocean supply line; and Seychelles and Madagascar, which will be the core support bases in the South Indian Ocean supply line."

For its part, New Delhi is pursuing the same strategy as Beijing and creating its own web of relationships with the littoral states, both bilaterally and multilaterally, through the Indian Ocean Naval Symposium, to ensure that if the military need arises, the necessary support infrastructure and network will be in place. India has also stepped up defence cooperation with Oman and Israel in the west, while upgrading military ties with the Maldives, Madagascar, and Myanmar in the Indian Ocean, and with Singapore, Indonesia, Thailand, Vietnam, Taiwan, the Philippines, Australia, Japan, and the United States in the east. In December 2006, Admiral Sureesh Mehta, then India's naval chief, expanded the conceptual construct of India's "greater strategic neighborhood" to include potential sources of oil and gas imports located across the globe — from Venezuela to the Sakhalin Islands in Russia. The Indian navy currently has a stronger naval presence on the Indian Ocean than does China. It is strengthening its port infrastructure with new southern ports, which allow greater projection into the ocean. Taking a leaf out of China's book, the new focus is to develop anti-access and area-denial capabilities that will thwart any Chinese attempt at encirclement or sea-access denial.

In short, maritime competition is intensifying as Indian and Chinese navies show the flag in the Pacific and Indian oceans with greater frequency. This rivalry could spill into the open after a couple of decades, when one Indian aircraft carrier will be deployed in the Pacific Ocean and one Chinese aircraft carrier in the Indian Ocean — ostensibly to safeguard their respective trade and energy routes.

In turn, India's "Look East" policy is a manifestation of its own strategic intent to compete for influence in the wider Asia-Pacific region. Just as China will not concede India's primacy in South Asia and the Indian Ocean region, India seems unwilling to accept Southeast and East Asia as China's sphere of influence.

Just as China's rise is viewed positively in the South Asian region among the small countries surrounding India with which New Delhi has had difficult relations, India's rise is viewed in positive-sum terms among China's neighbours throughout East and Southeast Asia. Over the last two decades, India has sought to enhance its economic and security ties with those Northeast and Southeast Asian nations (Mongolia, South Korea, Japan, Taiwan, Vietnam, Singapore, Thailand, Indonesia, and Australia) that worry about China more than any other major power. As China's growing strength creates uneasiness in the region, India's balancing role is welcome within the Association of Southeast Asian Nations (ASEAN) in order to influence China's behavior in cooperative directions. While the Southeast Asian leaders seek to deter China from utilizing its growing strength for coercive purposes and to maintain regional autonomy, Indian strategic analysts favour an Indian naval presence in the South China Sea and the Pacific Ocean to counter Chinese naval presence in the Indian Ocean. On maritime security, Southeast Asians seem more willing to cooperate with India than China, especially in the Strait of Malacca.

A key element of India's Pacific outreach has been regular naval exercises, port calls, security dialogues, and more than a dozen defence cooperation agreements. India has welcomed Vietnam's offer of berthing rights in Na Trang Port in the South China Sea, and news reports suggest that India might offer BrahMos cruise missiles and other military hardware at "friendship prices" to Vietnam. The conclusion of free-trade agreements with Singapore, South Korea, Malaysia, Japan, and the ASEAN, coupled with New Delhi's participation in multilateral forums such as the East Asia Summit and the ASEAN Plus Eight defence ministers' meetings, have also reinforced strategic ties. India's determination to strengthen its strategic partnership with Japan and Vietnam, commitment to pursue joint oil exploration with Hanoi in the South China Sea waters in the face of Chinese opposition, and an emphasis on the freedom of navigation are signs of India maneuvering to be seen as a counterweight to Chinese power in

East Asia. New Delhi is also scaling up defence ties with Tokyo, Seoul, and Canberra.

The US-India partnership is also emerging as an important component of India's strategy to balance China's power. India seeks US economic and technological assistance. It helps this relationship that India's longtime security concerns — China and Pakistan — also now happen to be the United States' long-term and immediate strategic concerns as well. Both the Bush and Obama administrations have encouraged India's involvement in a wider Asian security system to balance a rising China and declining Japan. Apparently, US weakness — real or perceived — invites Chinese assertiveness. Since the United States does not wish to see Asia dominated by a single hegemonic power or a coalition of states, India's economic rise is seen as serving Washington's long-term interests by ensuring that there be countervailing powers in Asia — China, Japan, and India, with the United States continuing to act as an "engaged offshore power balancer."

The "India factor" is increasingly entering the ongoing US policy debate over China. Asia-Pacific is now the Indo-Pacific, a term underlining the centrality of India in the new calculus of regional power. The 2010 US Quadrennial Defence Review talked of India's positive role as a "net security provider in the Indian Ocean and beyond." India's "Look East" policy, which envisions high-level engagement with "China-wary" nations (South Korea, Japan, Taiwan, Vietnam, Thailand, Indonesia, and Australia), dovetails with the US policy of establishing closer ties with countries beyond Washington's traditional treaty partners to maintain US predominance. The US-Indian strategic engagement, coupled with India's expanding naval and nuclear capabilities and huge economic potential, have made India loom larger on China's radar screen. An editorial in a Shanghai daily last November lamented the fact that "India will not allow itself to stay quietly between the US and China. It wants to play triangle affairs with the duo, and will do anything it can to maximize its benefit out of it. Therefore, China will find it hard to buy India over." The Chinese fear that the Indian-American cooperation in defence, high-tech R&D, nuclear, space, and maritime spheres would prolong US hegemony and prevent the establishment of a post-American, Sino-centric hierarchical regional order in Asia. This tightening relationship, and the possibility that what is presently a tilt on India's part could turn into a full-fledged alignment, is a major reason for recent deterioration in Chinese-Indian relations.

Although these relations remain unstable and competitive, both have sought to reduce tensions. Despite border disputes, denial of market access, and harsh words against the Dalai Lama, leaders in both countries understand the dangers of allowing problems to overwhelm the relationship. Burgeoning economic ties between the world's two fastest-growing economies have become the most salient aspect of their bilateral relationship.

Trade flows have risen rapidly, from a paltry $350 million in 1993 to $70 billion in 2012, and could surpass $100 billion by 2015. Several joint ventures in power generation, consumer goods, steel, chemicals, minerals, mining, transport, infrastructure, info-tech, and telecommunication are in the works. Intensifying trade, commerce, and tourism could eventually raise the stakes for China in its relationship with India. On the positive side, both share common interests in maintaining regional stability (for example, combating Islamist fundamentalists), exploiting economic opportunities, and maintaining access to energy sources, capital, and markets.

Despite ever-increasing trade volumes, however, there is as yet no strategic congruence between China and India. As in the case of Sino-US and Sino-Japanese ties, Sino-Indian competitive tendencies, rooted in geopolitics and nationalism, are unlikely to be easily offset even by growing economic and trade links. In fact, the economic relationship is heavily skewed. The bulk of Indian exports to China consist of iron ore and other raw materials, while India imports mostly manufactured goods from China—a classic example of the dependency model. Most Indians see China as predatory in trade. New Delhi has lodged the largest number of anti-dumping cases against Beijing in the World Trade Organization. India is keener on pursuing mutual economic dependencies with Japan, South Korea, and Southeast Asian nations through increased trade, investment, infrastructure development, and aid to bolster economic and political ties across Asia that will counter Chinese power.

Even as a range of economic and transnational issues draw them closer together, the combination of internal issues of stability (Tibet and Kashmir), disputes over territory, competition over resources (oil, gas, and water), overseas markets and bases, external overlapping spheres of influence, rival alliance relationships, and ever-widening geopolitical horizons forestall the chances for a genuine Sino-Indian accommodation. Given the broad range of negative attitudes and perceptions each country has for the other, it is indeed remarkable that China and India have been able to keep diplomatic relations from fraying. How long this situation can last is more and more uncertain as each country is increasingly active in what would once have been seen as the other's "backyard" and both engage in strategic maneuvers to checkmate each other.

Just as China has become more assertive vis-à-vis the United States, Indian policy toward China is becoming tougher. India's evolving Asia strategy reflects the desire for an arc of partnerships with China's key neighbours — in Southeast Asia and further east along the Asia-Pacific rim — and the United States that would help neutralize the continuing Chinese military assistance and activity around its own territory and develop counter-leverages of its own vis-à-vis China to keep Beijing sober.

DEFENCE PRODUCTION AND SUPPLY

The Defence Production Department created in 1962 and the Department of Defence Supply set up in 1965 were merged in 1984 to constitute the Department of Defence Production and Supplies. Presently, 39 Ordnance factories and eight Defence Public Sector Undertakings (DPSUs) come under this department. The Directorate of Quality Assurance, Air Technical Development and

Production (Air), Standardisation, and Exhibition Organisation also form part of this Department.

The Ordnance Factories produce more than 1,500 items of arms, ammunition, equipment and components. Most of these products constitute relatively low to medium technology items. Twenty per cent of the output goes to non-defence customers. Due to the very high cost of production, delivery delays and suspect quality, it has not been possible to meet export targets and, sometimes, even orders given by the Services. Ordnance factories as well as DPSUs need to shed the manufacture of low technology items to the private sector and focus on hi-tech products. They should also be in a position to take up substantial product improvement themselves and not be dependent on DRDO.

Defence Planning Tools

In recent years, defence economics and management techniques have made an important contribution to defence planning. A number of techniques such as Operational Research and Systems Analysis (ORSA), Planning Programming and Budgeting System have been developed to make the planning process more systematic and to maximise the benefits obtained from the given amount of resources. Systems Analysis can assist in developing rational procedures for procurement of new weapons systems. Systems performance at design stage can be evaluated through computer simulation. Planners all over the world are using computerised war-gaming techniques and structure analysis. Prospects exist for a more enlightened approach that can bring together military officers, historians, technologists and quantitative analysts.

In many countries, there is a growing interest in analytical realism, operational relevance and integrated defence planning. In India the Services are far behind in introducing these aids in our defence planning system. The planning directorates in Service Headquarters do not even have data banks which can provide relevant information on a specified subject. Most of the planners have high combat and command qualifications but little clue of the modern techniques. There is an urgent need to introduce modern planning aids into our planning system. Defence planners should also learn the basic principles and techniques of economic analysis and not leave it to their 'Finance' colleagues.

Management of Defence Budget

A major lacuna in defence planning and implementation has been lack of financial commitment for the Plan period. Financially, the defence plans are treated more as annual plans rather than composite five years plan. There is a rush to spend the annual capital budget by the end of the financial year since the amount not spent has to be surrendered. In FY 2004-05, the previous government had proposed to institute a non-lapsable Defence Modernisation Fund of Rs 25,000 crore. This was a long awaited reform in the defence-finance mechanism as budgeted capital expenditure worth thousands of crores was surrendered year after year. However, the new government, being of the view that there are no provisions in the budgetary rules and regulations to carry forward unspent funds for three years, has done away with this reform.

It needs to be pointed out that a similar procedure was being followed in the 1930s and 1940s. The provisions invoked at that time need to be studied carefully and could be used as a precedent. Action should be taken expeditiously to revive the Defence Modernization Fund.

Otherwise, funds earmarked for capital expenditure on an annual basis will continue to lapse, leading to lack of systematic defence preparedness.

In the Revenue Budget, there is a need to include incentives to save and reduce annual maintenance expenditure without adversely affecting operational efficiency. It is also necessary to exploit the increasing domestic industrial capability to support the existing infrastructure and thus reduce maintenance costs and enhance the quality of maintenance.

Human Resources Management

The development of human resources must keep pace with the modernisation of the armed forces so that new, state-of-the-art equipment can be optimally exploited by well trained and motivated soldiers, sailors and airmen. The age profile of military personnel, particularly in the Army, and the age of commanders at battalion and brigade levels needs to be looked into. Currently, a soldier has to serve for 15 to 17 years to earn his pension. When he retires, besides the lifelong pension that has to be paid, a trained individual is lost to the nation. Similarly, while there is a shortage of approximately 14,000 officers, most officers retire in rank of Lieutenant Colonel or Colonel at the age of 52-54 years when they still have years of productive life ahead though they are no longer fit for active combat.

Innovative measures need to be adopted to reduce the effects of the current national loss on this account. The best method would be to institute a procedure of 'lateral induction" under which both officers and personnel below officer rank can be transferred to central police and paramilitary forces(CPMFs). The colour (active) service of jawans should be reduced to 7-10 years with no pension liability after which the volunteers are transferred to the BSF, CRPF, ITBP, CISF and other such forces. Similarly, the Shipping Corporation of India, National Port Trust and other such maritime organisations can fruitfully employ Naval personnel. Ex-servicemen will be expected to serve in these organisations till superannuation, after which they would be entitled to pension. This will improve the age profile of the Services, provide trained manpower to the CPMFs, ensure productive long-term employment for a large number of trained men till superannuation, and also reduce the pension bill of the Central Government.

The Army should increase the recruitment of Short Service Officers to make up its shortfall. Induction of these officers to the CPMFs after five years of service will improve junior leadership and effectiveness of these forces in internal security and counter insurgency operations.

CHINA'S CURRENT SECURITY POLICY

In response to the attacks in Africa during the last five years, China has confronted the problem of nontraditional security threats in several ways.

The PRC's initial reaction is to work with local governments. "China will cooperate closely with immigration departments of African countries in tackling the problem of illegal migration, improve exchange of immigration control information, and set up an unimpeded and efficient channel for intelligence and information exchange," China's 2006 *Africa Policy* stated.

"In order to enhance the ability of both sides to address nontraditional security threats, it is necessary to increase intelligence exchange, explore more effective ways and means for closer cooperation in combating terrorism, small-arms smuggling, drug trafficking, transnational economic crimes, etc." Beijing has instructed its embassies in Africa to keep a close watch on local security. The swift and successful evacuation of Chinese citizens from Chad also demonstrated that China has developed operational scenarios to deal with these emergencies. The Chinese government has also started issuing travel advisories.

In Sudan and Kenya, state-owned companies receive protection from local armed forces against attacks by rebels. Beijing has signed an agreement with South Africa to prevent the Chinese diaspora from turning into a target for armed gangs. Such measures are designed to help Chinese citizens and companies avoid some of the risks related to operating in Africa, but they do not provide any guarantee for safeguarding China's economic activities if the situation keeps deteriorating. In the case of Sudan, China learned the hard way that prodding instable governments can have drastic consequences. If problems start to occur at the regional level, supporting these emerging states might prove even riskier.

Nor does this narrow security response address China's uncertainty about the military capability of African nations. The dilemma reverts back to the realistic supposition of self-help. Is the PRC trying to safeguard its interests by building up its own military presence in Africa?

Bilateral military exchanges are a first indicator to test whether this assumption holds true. According to the Chinese government, interaction with other armed forces expanded significantly, with 174 high-level visits in 2001 and more than 210 in 2006. This upward trend was not maintained in Africa, however, where such bilateral exchanges have remained stable at an annual average of 26. Beijing has established a permanent military dialogue only with South Africa. Interviews with European diplomats in ten randomly chosen African countries also reveal that the number of accredited military officers in Chinese embassies, i.e., military attachés and their support staff, has barely or not expanded at all in the last few years. In fact, only in 15 countries are Chinese military attachés assigned on a permanent basis. China's military diplomacy in Africa remains modest, and it has not kept up with the impressive number of Chinese trade officials posted in African nations to strengthen economic ties in the last few years.

Military aid is another indicator. Providing military hardware to partner nations can serve various objectives. In a context of competition, it helps to thwart defence cooperation with other states or to prevent other powers' attempts to alter the regional military balance. Defence aid might help a privileged political partner to safeguard economic interests. Whereas these three objectives are motivated by security issues and long-term economic interests, defence aid may well be the result of more short-sighted aspirations. There is no evidence that China's military aid successfully counterbalances other powers, such as the United States.

Apart from Sudan and Zimbabwe, most countries that have received Chinese military aid in the last few years are also supplied by Washington. In 2007, Beijing temporarily froze the supply of heavy arms to Khartoum after pressure from the West. When Nigeria's Vice President, Atiku Abubakar, announced that his nation would turn to China instead of the United States for arms,

Beijing's response was reluctant, and no major supply operations materialized. China's military aid programs should not be considered as support for its forays into the mining industry. For instance, between 2004 and 2008, resource-rich Nigeria received only half as much military aid as Ghana or Uganda. During this period, China provided more military assistance to Angola than to Sudan, even though the security challenges in the latter were much greater.

Although violence in Somalia has threatened China's oil exploration activities in both Ethiopia and Kenya, China only made a commitment to Kenya to help in protecting its border. China has, at times, provided military aid, but such assistance does not seem to be part of any coherent strategy related to protecting its security interests.

Finally, self-help would imply the deployment of military forces whenever China's interests are threatened, possibly in an attempt to train friendly armed forces and dissuade any challengers. Yet, such a Chinese military presence is negligible. China has no bases in Africa, as does the United States and France, nor has it trained African soldiers to counter threats to its national interests.

In Sudan, Zimbabwe, Cameroon, and Gabon, China has employed teams of three to ten instructors, but they are assisting in the maintenance of equipment, rather than providing training for combat missions. In Zambia and Algeria, similar examples of cooperation exist but are limited to medical activities. Other major powers deployed naval vessels in an effort to combat piracy and to maintain the maritime supply lines surrounding Africa. During such operations, the Chinese Navy has rarely shown its flag.

In 2000, China sent its newest *Luhai*-class guided missile destroyer and a supply ship to Tanzania and South Africa. A 2002 fleet composed of a guided missile destroyer, the *Qingdao*, and a supply ship, the *Taicang*, visited Egypt. These voyages were gestures of courtesy rather than a reaction to security challenges. They were limited in duration, and no actions were attempted against pirates or poachers. In December 2008, however, the Chinese government did deploy two destroyers and a replenishment ship in the Gulf of Aden to participate in the United Nations-backed mission against piracy. A mission that was only undertaken after receiving a positive signal from US Pacific Command chief Admiral Timothy Keating.

Instead of dealing with security threats unilaterally, China has resorted to bandwagoning. Although in the 1980s and early 1990s, Beijing opposed attempts by the international community to intervene in African security issues, nowadays it tends to join them. Beijing is increasingly recognizing the United Nations' role in resolving the numerous conflicts and safeguarding the sovereignty of developing nations. In the 1990s, China began supporting United Nations (UN) missions designed to implement peace agreements between rivalling parties, on the condition that a well-defined and restricted mandate was included. Traditional peacekeeping operations such as those in Somalia (UNSOM I), Mozambique, Rwanda, and Sierra Leone all were supported. When the UN Security Council decided to dispatch forces to Liberia in 2003, China offered to support the mission and gradually increased the number of its peacekeepers to 1,300 in 2007.

At the same time, however, failed states and national governments that had actively participated in atrocities challenged the efficacy of many of the traditional UN operations. China's focus on the primacy of sovereignty, requiring at a minimum the state's consent, collided with the willingness of other nations to intervene aggressively under the UN Charter's Chapter VII mandate.

Beijing loudly opposed the move by European countries to push for Operation Turquoise in Rwanda, Washington's call to broaden the UNSOM mandate, or France's demand for a troop increase in the 2004 UN operation in Ivory Coast. Despite its strong concerns, China did not veto these interventions at the UN Security Council, but rather abstained and remained aloof from implementation. Sudan was the first instance where China actively lobbied an African government to permit a UN mission on its soil.

Via active brokering and indirect pressure, China succeeded in neutralizing the incompatibility between its economic interests and the principle of noninterference on the one hand, and western appeals for intervening in Darfur and the need for long-term stability on the other.

That Beijing recognizes the importance of collective security became apparent in 2006, when China was the first nation to ask the UN Security Council for a peacekeeping mission in Somalia. In June that year, at a Security Council meeting in Addis Ababa, China's Permanent Representative to the UN, Wang Guangya, scolded other diplomats for neglecting Somalia and urged them to support the deployment of peacekeepers. "I was reluctant to take on this role," said Wang, explaining that African governments had been pushing China to raise the issue in the Council, "but there was a lack of interest by the other major powers."

Initially, the proposal was tentatively received by Great Britain and the United States, but after various talks in New York, Beijing and Washington jointly sponsored a resolution for the deployment of a UN mission. In 2007, in early consultations with France, China supported a French draft resolution on Chad calling for the dispatch of mainly European peacekeepers under the auspices of Chapter VII. It was significant that China approved the "close liaising" with the Hybrid Operation in Darfur (UNAMID), where earlier it had objected to the development of links between UNAMID and UN missions. "Our support for the resolution on Chad shows that we are prepared to cooperate to tackle security issues at a regional level and that our awareness on the increasing complexity of violent conflicts in Africa grows," a Chinese diplomat explained.

China is also turning to African regional organizations to collaborate on security issues. In the China-Africa Action Plan, approved in November 2006, Beijing vowed "to support Africa in the areas of logistics" as well as "to continue its active participation in the peacekeeping operations and demining process in Africa and provide, within the limits of its capabilities, financial and material assistance as well as relevant training to the Peace and

Security Council of the African Union." In June 2006, the Chinese government granted the African Union's Mission in Sudan $3.5 million in budgetary support and humanitarian aid. Earlier, it provided financial and technical support to the Association for West African States.

Slowly but surely, China is showing itself ready to participate in international efforts to prevent conflicts, fueled by the easy availability of small arms and illegally exported natural resources. In 2002, for instance, Beijing revised its regulation on the control of military products for export and published the "Military Products Export Control List" supplying guidelines for the export of military-related products. In the same year, it signed the "Protocol Against the Illicit Manufacturing of and Trafficking in Firearms," which committed the People's Republic to control the manufacturing, marking, import, and export of firearms, and to confiscate and destroy all illicit firearms. In 2005, the government launched a national information management system for the production, possession, and trade of light arms, and it introduced a system to monitor end-users of Chinese-made weapons to prevent the arms from finding their way to "sensitive regions" around the world via third parties. In 2006, China supported a draft UN resolution on the illicit trade of small arms and light weapons, in contrast to the United States. In 2002, China joined the Kimberley Process, a joint government, international diamond industry, and civil initiative designed to stem the flow of conflict diamonds originating from Africa. In 2005, China allowed a voluntary peer review of its support for the Kimberly Process. Although these actions still have many flaws, they seem to prove that China wishes to do more than just put "boots on the ground" in response to Africa's internal conflicts.

Despite the strategic importance of Africa, China does not try to safeguard its foothold in the region by unilaterally projecting military power. In Africa, its military diplomacy remains limited when compared with defence initiatives in other regions. If the PRC does pursue bilateral cooperation programs, these are more likely to be a part of its diplomatic charm offensive, rather than addressing threats to China's economic and security interests. Instead of relying on a military presence to counterbalance other powers, the PRC tends to join collective security efforts within the framework of the United Nations and African regional organizations. Over the past few years, this strategy of joint ventures has evolved from passive support to active cooperation. Beijing has softened its devotion to noninterference. While maintaining the primacy of sovereignty, it has become willing to support interventions whenever regional stability is at stake.

Although China has become a revisionist power in terms of its economic aspirations on the continent, it is acting as a status-quo power in terms of security objectives. There are several explanations for this stance. First, China only recently began its economic focus on the African continent. For the past two decades, China concentrated on curbing the military and diplomatic influence of Taiwan; the focus on "economization" of its Africa policy only began in the late 1990s. Hence, the security challenges it is facing now are a recent phenomena, and solutions to these challenges are just starting to be explored. The PRC is going through the early stage of resecuritization of its Africa strategy, and joining with other nations in an allied strategy can be considered the easiest immediate response. Second, and related to this point, China has not developed sufficient means to back up its security policy with military power. This is a matter of budgetary constraints. Building an independent and sustained military presence is a costly affair and would, at present, overstretch the PLA's capabilities, while Asia remains its primary focus. The PLA does not possess the logistical capacity to support sustained region wide deployment in Africa. Its long-range airlift and sealift, as well as its intelligence and command capabilities, are not up to the task. Third, the Chinese government wants to avoid the People's Republic being perceived as a hegemonic power.

In the initial stage of its economic charm offensive, the PRC tried to pursue a business-as-usual approach, maintaining a low profile and steering clear of political entanglements. That approach is no longer possible now that China stands at the forefront of Africa's political scene, actively altering the economic balance of power. Beijing is well aware of the dichotomy between its weak and strong identities and is reluctant to demonstrate any independent military capacity. Such a show of strength might reduce its diplomatic maneuverability, increase resistance from African nations-just as Washington is now experiencing-and raise suspicions elsewhere regarding Chinese intentions. Yet, as interests, perceptions, and capacities are susceptible to change, the question remains whether China will stay on this track of cooperative security.

China's interests in Africa have changed over the past decades and will undoubtedly continue to evolve. The concept for its security policy in the region will depend on the role that Africa plays as a supplier of natural resources. Africa currently supplies approximately 30 percent of China's oil imports. Beijing and its African partners announced that they are preparing to increase bilateral trade to $100 billion by the year 2010. Most of this increase will come from the import of raw commodities. In recent years, Chinese companies have laid the foundation for a substantial increase in the production of resource industries. Exploration in the Gulf of Guinea, Angola, and the Horn of Africa have the potential for an increase in oil exports to China of more than 80 percent in the next ten years. Chinese companies are just starting to tap the large mines that were recently acquired in Gabon, the Democratic Republic of Congo, Namibia, and elsewhere on the continent. Given the fact that other emerging markets such as India and Brazil are shifting the use of their raw materials from export to domestic consumption, the economic relevance of Africa to China cannot be overstated.

How necessary it is to back up these Chinese economic ventures with more overt security measures is yet to be seen. The incidents described in the first section of this article, the persistent instability in nations, as well as the weak position of amicable political leaders will undoubtedly position Africa higher on Beijing's foreign security agenda and require a more complete approach. The question again arises whether it is in China's best interest to apply its African policy independently or in synergy with other nations. The short-term costs of any unilateral action would certainly exceed those of collective action, but long-term uncertainty about the intentions of other major players might influence any concerns related to cost-effectiveness. If Washington or Delhi decides to change course and contain China's expanding influence in Africa by pursing a strategy of counterbalancing and sea denial, the repercussions for the People's Republic will be dramatic. The concerns of the national security establishments in India and the United States and their expanding military presence in Africa are not unnoticed in China, and they highlight the necessity for the PRC to build a legitimate capacity to deal with crises unilaterally.

China's diplomatic identity will help shape policy decisions in support of a more active and autonomous security strategy. Beijing is realizing that the comfortable cloak of frailty it previously presented to the world no longer fits. African partners do not attach much value to China's diplomatic schizophrenia and the complex image of an economic giant, political dwarf, and minor military player it projects. When mayhem erupts, China automatically ends up on the frontline, finding itself hounded by African governments asking it to exercise its leverage. The cases of Chad and Somalia are not the only examples of this. South Africa has accosted China regarding illegal immigrants from Zimbabwe. Central Africa has carefully examined the violent incursions from Sudan. The African Union has called upon China several times to play a more active role in promoting security. The possibility exists that individual countries may be compelled to form a closer alliance with China in order to reduce their current reliance on the European Union and United States for security. Nigeria's announcement that it would rely on China instead of the United States for military support hints at this direction. The ability of the PRC to keep a low military profile is diminishing.

On the other hand, China's self-perception is also in transition. The "Century of Humiliation" is far behind and is being replaced by a national attitude of confidence and assertiveness. Chinese leaders have built on the success of their policy of good neighbour diplomacy that resulted in fewer frictions and more influence in Asia. The People's Republic has drawn confidence from the successful launch of a number of new defence systems. As China sees its diplomatic leverage expanding geographically from the Strait of Formosa, via Asia to the rest of the developing world, its ability to deal with emerging security issues is likely to follow suit.

Finally, there is the factor of capacity. China is gearing its military for a greater deployment capability. Its large immobile army is gradually being converted into a highly specialized and flexible organization. Simultaneously, the PLA is launching new military systems that will enhance its capacity to transport these forces. In 2007, the Chinese government approved the development of large passenger jets, including military transport variants similar to the American C-17 Globemaster III.

Beijing has also ordered several new ships in an effort to enhance its naval transport capacity. In 2006, the hull of the first T-071 vessel was laid.

This landing-platform dock has a range that goes far beyond Taiwan, with the aim of providing sea-based support to operations on land, humanitarian aid, and assisting in evacuations and disaster management. These vessels will be supported by a new generation of large replenishment ships and could be escorted by advanced frigates and destroyers.

The Chinese flotilla that was sent to Somalia demonstrates China's new blue-water capacity. The type 052C *Lanzhou*, for instance, is a showcase of the advanced detection capacity for China's Navy. Its multifunction, active phased-array radar has a detection range of 450 kilometers and is complemented with a long-range, two-dimensional air search radar that has a 350-kilometer range and three additional systems to detect incoming missiles and aircraft. China is advancing its ability to pursue a more confident and independent security policy in Africa.

Will all this newfound military activity be sufficient to offset the antagonistic response it is likely to provoke? Probably not. If China decides to go solo and to pursue a more aggressive security policy in Africa, it is improbable that it will be able to overcome countermoves by India and the United States. It will be difficult for China to safeguard maritime trade with Africa if India exercises its naval dominance in the Indian Ocean. The sheer geographical divide between the PRC and the African continent makes it extremely difficult to support military activities if the United States or India opposes them. Contrary to China's revolutionary phase of the 1950s and 1960s when trade and economic interests only played a small part, China's increasing reliance on Africa renders it highly vulnerable to sea denial operations or a *guerre de course*. The fragile Cold War balance between the United States and the Soviet Union that allowed Mao to meddle with America's interests in Africa without having to fear political or economic reprisals can no longer be counted on. These days China has much to lose if it provokes Washington or Delhi.

CHINA, INDIA, SOUTHEAST ASIA AND GLOBAL POLICY REFORM

The opening wide of China's door to trade and FDI has not occurred in isolation. Trade policy around the world has become progressively more liberal as part of wider packages of market-based reforms. A veritable trade policy revolution has spread across the developing world, especially since the early 1980s, though it has been patchy and uneven. The Asian financial crisis, followed by crises in Russia, Brazil and Argentina, raised strong doubts about further liberalisation. This has centred on financial liberalisation, especially of short-term capital flows, but it has had a knock-on effect on trade and FDI. Broadly speaking, previous liberalisation has not been reversed, but its forward momentum has slowed.

Southeast Asia fits this pattern. The real burst of trade-and-investment liberalisation took place in the 1980s and first half of the 1990s, particularly in Malaysia, Thailand and Indonesia. Singapore and the Philippines were exceptions: in the former, export-led industrialisation and the return to liberal trade policies took place earlier; in the latter, substantial trade-and-investment liberalisation had to wait until the 1990s. Vietnam started opening its borders as part of its transition from Plan to Market from the late 1980s. Cambodia has seen liberalising reforms only more recently. Laos remains largely closed; and Myanmar even more so. Tiny Brunei is a largely unreformed economy and polity based on oil-revenue windfalls.

The Asian crisis changed matters somewhat. True, trade, FDI and other liberalisation measures were not reversed. Indeed, Singapore, Thailand and Indonesia went further in a liberalising direction – in the latter two countries induced by IMF structural-adjustment programmes. But, with the exception of Singapore, government enthusiasm for further liberalisation declined markedly. This was reinforced by powerful interests keen to protect their markets against foreign competition, and a populist backlash of sorts against globalisation in general.

How does China fit in? Its first decade of reforms centred on internal liberalisation, especially in agriculture. Then followed a brief period of uncertainty and suspense after the Tienanmen massacre. The last decade, however, has seen the biggest trade-and-investment liberalisation programme the world has ever seen. In short time, China has swung from extreme protection to rather liberal trade policies, indeed very liberal by developing-country standards. This was crowned by its accession to the WTO, with by far the strongest commitments of any developing country. The pace of internal and external liberalisation has not let up since.

This recent episode is all the more remarkable in that it has happened in the world's most populous country. In contrast, most episodes of radical external liberalisation have occurred in quite small countries (e.g. most of the east-Asian Tigers, Chile, and the east- European transition economies). While many others slowed down after the Asian crisis, China continued to race ahead.

India has had a rather different trajectory. Its retreat from the "licence raj" – its equivalent of Soviet-style central planning – began half-heartedly in the 1980s; but it was a foreign-exchange crisis in 1991 that provided the window of opportunity for more thoroughgoing market-based reforms. These were radical by Indian standards, though less so compared with policy reforms elsewhere. They covered macroeconomic stabilisation, trade liberalisation, relaxation of FDI restrictions, privatisation and, not least, the dismantling of domestic licensing arrangements that had governed most formal economic activity. Since the initial burst in 1991-93, reforms have proceeded in a stop-go manner. They have not been reversed; but they have moved ahead more slowly and fitfully compared with southeast Asia (pre-Asian crisis) and China (pre- and post-Asian crisis). Democratic politics, including the complications of multi-party governing coalitions and the federal division of powers between the Union government and the states, has made faster, more decisive reforms elusive.

The above account is admittedly impressionistic; the following sections will go into relevant detail on trade-policy developments. Before getting into that detail, it is worth flagging four big lessons from recent policy-reform experience.

First, there are sceptics who play down external liberalisation and its link to growth. In China, other parts of east Asia and India, liberalisation has been gradual, partial and controlled, they say, and it has been mixed judiciously with industrial-policy interventions and capital controls. That is (more or less) true. But, as Martin Wolf argues, "it mistakes the trees for the forest." Of course none of these countries has adopted full-blown free trade like Britain in the nineteenth century or Hong Kong in the twentieth century. Rather – this is the central point – they have, to varying degrees, moved in the direction of a market economy, with better protection of property rights, freer enterprise and competition in place of state ownership and planning, and more exposure to foreign trade and investment. To argue otherwise would be absurd.

Second, one is accustomed to dry social-scientific talk about liberalisation, followed by large numbers on growth and poverty reduction. That should not obscure the biggest boon of all. The market economy, not least through trade-policy reform, has opened up personal freedoms and life-chances that were unimaginable even a generation ago. That is the product of increasing wealth and the institutions that accompany it. In short, market-based reforms are about prosperity *and* economic freedom – though not necessarily civic and political freedom, at least in the short term.

Third, trade-policy reforms can only be understood as part of broad market-based reforms, and in conjunction with "second-generation" institutional reforms. External liberalisation delivers abundant, long-term gains only *in interaction with* the build-up of domestic market-supporting institutions. Opening to the world creates the spontaneous stimulus for institutional upgrading to better exploit trade-and-investment opportunities, e.g. through better currency and banking practices, and the development of ports and inland communications. Reciprocally, better enforcement of private-property rights and contracts, cleaner, more efficient public administration, and more investment in education and infrastructure, maximise the gains for importers, exporters, and domestic and foreign investors. Openness, therefore, is a *handmaiden* of growth, not a quick fix.

The link to institutions also points to big and enduring gaps in Chinese, Indian and southeast-Asian reforms. Liberalisation of tariffs and quotas at the border can be done relatively quickly and easily, in technical if not political terms. But trade-related institutional reforms "behind the border" are full of local particularities, technically complicated, administratively demanding, politically very sensitive and inevitably gradual. This applies to the legal system and public administration, and to domestic regulations concerning intellectual property, services, competition and investment rules, public procurement, customs administration, food-safety and other product- and process-related standards. Taken together, this involves nothing less than restructuring the state to make it support, not hinder, a complex, globally integrated market economy.

The World Bank and other sources now pay much more attention to the quality of institutions and how they shape the business climate. China and India do very badly on "investment-climate" indicators such as the number of legal and administrative procedures involved in starting a business, the time taken during this process, bankruptcy procedures, corruption and contract enforcement. Southeast Asia presents a mixed picture: Singapore regularly comes out at the top end of these indicators; the new ASEAN members include some of the worst-governed countries in the world; Indonesia and Philippines also do poorly; Malaysia and Thailand fare better, but still with much room for improvement.

Fourth, one cannot escape the link between economic-policy reform and political systems. In China, centralised authoritarian politics has maintained political stability and driven economic reforms at a frenetic pace. Decentralised democratic politics slows down Indian reforms. That widens the policy and performance gap with China. Southeast Asia again presents a mixed picture: pluralist democratic politics in Indonesia, Philippines and Thailand (all relatively recent developments) exists alongside authoritarian, semi-authoritarian and semi-democratic politics in other ASEAN countries.

The long-term picture might well look different. In China, there is bound to be increasing tension between centralised authoritarian politics and decentralised market-economy reforms. Widening economic freedoms and a burgeoning middle class will create new demands not just for better-quality governance, but also for civic and political freedoms. How that tension will be resolved remains to be seen; but it is a question mark hanging over the future of a sustainable, flourishing market economy in China.

As for India, while democratic politics slows things down in the short term, it is progressively *legitimating* market-based reforms along the way. A decentralised political and civic culture, with in-built checks and balances, allows for multiple experiments at state and local levels. It is no accident that the more innovative policy reforms tend to come less from the Union government and more from forward-looking state governments in the south and east of India. That sets up a demonstration effect for others to emulate. Finally, a free-breathing society is best suited to a sophisticated services-based market economy full of individualistic, risk-taking entrepreneurs. These are the "open-society" characteristics of the West, and particularly of the USA. India's open society – its combination of Western-style democracy, constitutional liberalism and supporting institutions — is its long-term insurance policy for a flourishing market economy. That is less the case in China or southeast Asia.

CHINA'S, INDIA'S AND SOUTHEAST ASIA'S TRADE-POLICY FRAMEWORKS

Trade-and-economic policy reforms

In China, since 1978, economic-policy reform has been incremental and ultra-pragmatic. The more comprehensive transformation of the Chinese economy and society belongs to the post-Tienanmen phase. A headline reform package was introduced in 1994, covering banking, finance, taxation, investment, foreign exchange and foreign trade. It included the unification of the exchange rate and a new Foreign Trade Law. Currency convertibility, privatisation, the formal recognition of private-property rights and a host of other market-based reforms have followed.

China's integration into the world economy, particularly through its trade reforms, is also more a product of the latter phase, following more gradual opening in earlier phases. Liberalisation has whittled down licensing coverage (down to 5 per cent of imports in 2000 from two-thirds of the total in 1988), and the use of plan prices (to less than 5 per cent of retail commodities by 2000). Even in agriculture, where state pricing is more important, over 80 per cent of sales are at market prices. The overall coverage of non-tariff barriers (NTBs) (licenses, quotas, tendering requirements, state trading and designated trading) had come down to 21.6 per cent of imports and less than 10 per cent of tariff lines by 2001. NTBs fell by about 80 per cent during the 1990s. At a rough estimate, the protective impact of NTBs has fallen from 9.3 per cent in the mid 1990s to 5 per cent today.

Tariffs have come down sharply in tandem with the decline in NTBs. The simple average statutory tariff was 43 per cent in 1992. Waves of tariff reform, particularly one in 1996, had brought it down to 17.5 per cent by 1998 and 16.6 per cent by 2001. Extensive duty exemptions almost completely liberalised imports of intermediate inputs and of investment goods used for export processing.

In sum, as Nicholas Lardy argues, China had undertaken enormous unilateral liberalisation of trade and FDI, and with it sweeping industrial and agricultural restructuring, in the decade *before* WTO accession. That still left significant knots of up-front protection: declining state-run industries; oil and sensitive agricultural commodities subject to monopolistic state-trading arrangements; high-tech industries targeted for industrial-policy promotion; and, most important, services sectors.

China's accession to the WTO and subsequent initiatives have taken reforms even further. That will be discussed later. But it is now clear that the main obstacles to doing business in China have less to do with formal border barriers and more with (formal and informal) non-border barriers. These concern the unpredictability and arbitrariness that come with large regulatory discretion; the lack of a rule of law in terms of impartial judicial oversight and enforcement of property rights and contracts; and the anti-competitive drag of state-owned industrial enterprises and state-owned banks. All this gets deep into domestic economic policies and institutions. It concerns the long-term restructuring of the Chinese state, away from pervasive interference and in the direction of a smaller, more limited operation that can perform fewer functions better. This is a vast trade-related reform agenda; but it has as much to do with the liberalisation of internal trade and the integration of domestic markets as with further external liberalisation. Growth and more widely shared prosperity can only improve if there is a better interaction between external openness and the internal market, mediated by market-supporting institutions.

Indian trade-policy reforms have not been as dramatic or breathtaking, but still considerable by Indian standards. In 1991, the average unweighted tariff was 125 per cent, with peak tariffs on agricultural products going up to 300 per cent. The tariff structure was extremely complicated, with high tariff escalation (higher tariffs on processed goods compared with semi-processed and unprocessed production inputs). This was accompanied by extremely high NTBs (quotas, licensing arrangements and outright bans). Inward investment was either banned or severely restricted. Exchange controls and the internal restrictions of the licence raj (almost) completed the picture.

Much has changed almost fifteen years on. Most border NTBs have been removed, as have internal licensing restrictions. Applied tariffs have come down to an average of about 20 per cent. The maximum tariff on manufactures was lowered to 20 per cent in 2004, and then to 15 per cent in the 2005 budget. Manufacturing tariffs will be rationalised into three bands (0-5-15 per cent); and the intention is to bring average tariffs down to ASEAN levels (around 10 per cent) soon. However, agricultural tariffs remain very high, averaging over 50 per cent. Most restrictions on manufacturing FDI have been removed. Executive orders are being used to relax FDI restrictions in services (given the difficulty of securing a parliamentary majority for such measures).

Hence Indian trade-policy reforms have come far, especially in manufactures. This leaves much to do on tariffs and NTBs in agriculture; and on FDI as well as domestic-regulatory restrictions on foreign services providers. These are much tougher nuts to crack, as are domestic labour-market regulations, privatisation of

SOEs, domestic agricultural policies, and a bloated public administration.

What about southeast Asia? Overall, largely as a result of reforms in the 1980s and 90s (earlier in Singapore), the old ASEAN members have average tariffs in the 10-per-cent range or lower, with correspondingly low NTBs. FDI restrictions have been progressively lowered. Tariffs, NTBs and FDI restrictions are particularly low in manufacturing – hence in large part the integration of the region into east-Asian and global manufacturing supply chains, especially in IT products. But agricultural protection is much higher; tariff escalation is not insignificant; and services markets are subject to high FDI and domestic-regulatory restrictions. Dual-economy structures have resulted: relatively open and efficient manufacturing sectors driven by FDI and exposed to global competition coexist with protected, inefficient domestic sectors. The new ASEAN members, either stuck with planned economies or in transition from Plan to Market, have much higher tariff and especially non-tariff barriers.

Singapore is the regional exception. After Hong Kong, it has the world's most liberal trade policies and is the world's most globalised economy. It is a free port with zero tariffs on all imports except four tariff lines (on alcoholic beverages). It is fully open to FDI except for a few services sectors. Unilateral liberalisation and domestic regulatory reform, especially since the Asian crisis, have reduced protectionist barriers in some services sectors.

Malaysia is one of the world's most globalised economies with relatively liberal trade policies by developing-country standards. However, there are peak tariffs, tariff escalation and assorted NTBs in politically sensitive goods sectors; and protection in services remains high. Protection must also be seen in the context of *bumiputera* policies to discriminate in favour of the Malay majority.

Thailand retains relatively high protection by the standards of other old ASEAN members, but its average tariff has come down closer to their levels. However, it still has greater tariff dispersion and escalation; NTBs are not insignificant; and protectionism in services is considerable. No meaningful liberalisation of the economy has occurred under the present Thaksin administration.

Indonesian trade policies have swung from high protection to openness in a comparatively short period. Its average tariff has come down to under 10 per cent. The IMF Structural Adjustment Programme agreed with the Indonesian government in 1998 significantly accelerated trade-and-FDI liberalisation and domestic regulatory reform in goods and services sectors. However, there are higher tariffs and tariff escalation, particularly in agriculture. There is also recent evidence of creeping protectionism through higher NTBs, particularly on agricultural products, textiles and steel. Overall, government enthusiasm for further liberalisation has clearly waned in recent years.

The situation in the Philippines is rather similar to that in Indonesia. Trade policies have swung from high protection to openness in the past decade. The average tariff has come down to well under 10 per cent. But this coexists with peak tariffs and tariff escalation in sensitive sectors, particularly in agriculture. There is recent evidence of creeping protection through higher NTBs, again concentrated on agricultural products. Protectionism is much higher on FDI and trade in services than it is on trade in goods. Restrictions on foreign ownership written into the Philippine constitution remain the most visible market-access hurdle. Overall, the government has displayed little enthusiasm for further liberalisation since the Asian crisis, and domestic protectionist pressures have increased.

Vietnam's transition from Plan to Market has proceeded in stops and starts since 1986, but it has come far cumulatively – though not nearly as far as China. Liberalisation, including trade, has picked up since 2000, though domestic institutional reforms have lagged behind. Foreign trading rights have been liberalised extensively; quantitative restrictions and other NTBs have come down; and the average nominal tariff now stands at about 18 per cent, though the tariff structure contains higher tariffs on many products and high tariff dispersion. Protection in services remains very high. The government continues to discriminate heavily in favour of state-owned industrial enterprises and state-owned banks. Overall, Vietnamese protection in terms of tariffs, NTBs and FDI restrictions remains much higher than it is in the old ASEAN members. It also compares unfavourably with China, given the latter's huge external and internal liberalisation measures before and after WTO accession.

Cambodia has progressed with trade-policy reforms, crowned by its accession to the WTO in 2004. Laos and Myanmar are much further behind.

The foreign-policy dimension

Trade policy stands at the junction of domestic economic and foreign policies, with tight links to both. The imperatives of China's modern foreign policy are steady integration into the global economy and political stability in the east Asian neighbourhood. These objectives have driven fundamental change in China's relations with other major powers, and its participation in international institutions. The Beijing leadership sees China as an emerging great power, indeed part of a concert of great powers, with shared global interests and responsibilities. That is one new frame in which to view Chinese foreign policy.

"Constructive engagement" characterises China's key bilateral relationships, especially the central one with the USA, but also with the EU, India, ASEAN and others. The overriding objective is to forge stronger commercial bonds, contain protectionist pressures directed against Chinese exports, and prevent geopolitical tensions from getting out of hand.

Constructive engagement in international institutions proceeds alongside closer relations with major powers. China joined a host of international organisations through the 1980s. It has participated actively in the IMF, World Bank, WIPO and other international economic agencies, tapping into technical expertise and policy advice in addition to financial aid. It has also been active in the UN. In all these forums, China has acquired the good-citizenship credentials of a "system maintainer", not a "system wrecker". Its approach to international law is the same: it wants to join existing arrangements, make them work better, and play its part in future rule-making.

The rapid professionalisation of the leadership and higher levels of public administration reinforces these trends. Since the 1980s, a new technocratic and outward-looking generation of officials and diplomats has emerged, many with significant foreign exposure.

In sum, Chinese foreign policy has evolved a pragmatic mix of nurturing big-power relationships and active participation in international institutions. The former is a *Realpolitik* calculus; the latter an expression of multilateral credentials. The two approaches are seen as complementary. Their common denominator is much less confrontational, more flexible, sophisticated and nuanced diplomacy, low on megaphone rhetoric and high on patient, behind-the-scenes cooperation to achieve practical results. Trade diplomacy, multilaterally in the WTO and on bilateral and regional tracks, is perhaps the most visible sign of this foreign-policy transformation.

However, this foreign-policy story, on its own, would be Panglossian. Set against the very real trends mentioned above are occasional tendencies of aggressive nationalism. This seems to be directed at Taiwan and Japan, notwithstanding ever-closer commercial ties with them. Finally, the Chinese government seems happy to maintain cosy relations with some of the most repulsive regimes around the world. An optimist would argue that foreign policy will ultimately be swayed by the imperatives of global economic integration. Optimism, however, should always be tinged with realism.

India's foreign policy has undergone a parallel transformation since the end of the Cold War. It has switched from leadership of the "non-aligned" Third World and support for the Soviet

Union to constructive engagement with other powers in the developed and developing worlds. Its relations with the USA are blossoming, both on the "high politics" of security and the "low politics" of commercial relations. It is trying to cement parallel alliances with China, ASEAN, Brazil and South Africa. It is playing a more forward-looking, system-maintaining rather than system-wrecking game in international institutions. However, this has not yet translated into much more pragmatic and flexible diplomacy in the WTO – one key difference with China.

Generalisations about ASEAN are difficult in that its members have different foreign policies with few common denominators, despite ASEAN rhetoric to the contrary. Hence there are substantial intra-ASEAN differences in bilateral relations with external powers; and ASEAN cooperation in international institutions, including the WTO, is lacking. However, security concerns and global economic integration have given ASEAN countries one common denominator: nearly all want to have good relations with the USA and the rising powers of China and India. But this is mostly a matter of bilateral (country-to-country) cooperation rather than cooperation involving ASEAN as a group.

5

China and India: The Great Asian Power

A shifting global power balance from West to East has become a much remarked upon phenomenon of recent years, but it has antecedents in earlier decades. The first country to present a modern "Asian challenge" was Japan, one of the defeated powers of World War II. In 1960, Japan was still considered to be a struggling developing country, poorer than Argentina. By the 1970s it had emerged as the leading Asian economy, welcomed as a founding member of the elite club of the Group of Seven industrialized nations (G7) and en route to global great-power status. On a lesser scale, South Korea was also being recognized as a low-income nation that was lifting itself up mightily and moving to the head of the class of the newly industrializing countries.

What is different about the current attention to rising Asia is the sheer magnitude of the transformational processes occurring simultaneously in the world's two most populous countries. Much of the globalization with which we are familiar has been led by the G7 and OECD countries. In the future, globalization could have more of an Asian face. In the words of the U.S. National Intelligence Council study, "Asia will alter the rules of the globalizing process. By having the fastest-growing consumer markets, more firms becoming world-class multinationals, and greater S&T [science and technology] stature, Asia looks set to displace Western countries as the focus for international economic dynamism – provided Asia's rapid economic growth continues." Asian powers are also expected to dominate global politics later in this century. The ability of Western countries, notably the United States, to accommodate that fact could therefore be crucial to the future of world order.

Within Asia, the most attention is clearly focused on its preeminent emerging global players China and India, both of which are adding enormous numbers of new workers and consumers to the global economy while developing huge middle classes larger than the entire populations of most G7 countries. As a recent business article surveyed the prospect:

The postwar era witnessed economic miracles in Japan and South Korea. But neither was populous enough to power worldwide growth or change the game in a complete spectrum of industries. China and India, by contrast, possess the weight and dynamism to transform the 21st-century global economy. ... even America's rise falls short in comparison to what's happening now. Never has the world seen the simultaneous, sustained takeoffs of two nations that together account for one-third of the planet's population.

For the past two decades, China has been growing at an astounding 9.5% a year, and India by 6%. Given their young populations, high savings, and the sheer amount of catching up they still have to do, most economists figure China and India possess the fundamentals to keep growing in the 7%-to-8% range for decades. (...) In the coming decades, China and India will disrupt workforces, industries, companies, and markets in ways that we can barely begin to imagine.

Other projections have come to similarly dramatic conclusions about the impacts of these two emerging powers on both the geo-economic and geo-political global landscape. The NIC study suggests that a combination of sustained high economic growth, active promotion of high technologies, population size, expanding military capabilities and international policy ambitions will fuel their rising power on the world stage. Among the expected manifestations are the following:

- The demographic weight of China and India will be such that they will not need to approach Western standards of living to achieve great-power standing.
- China will become the leading centre of world manufacturing and exports. ("Competition from 'the China price' already powerfully restrains manufactures prices worldwide.")
- "China's and India's perceived need to secure access to energy supplies will propel these countries to become more global rather than just regional powers ...."
- "China's desire to gain 'great power' status on the world stage will be reflected in its greater economic leverage over countries in the region and elsewhere as well as its steps to strengthen its military. East Asian states are adapting to the advent of a more powerful China by forging closer economic and political ties with Beijing, potentially accommodating themselves to its preferences, particularly on sensitive issues like Taiwan."
- "China will overtake Russia and others as the second largest defence spender after the United States over the next two decades and will be, by any measure, a first-rate military power."
- "The rise of India also will present strategic complications for the region. Like China, India will be an economic magnet for the region, and its rise will have an impact not only in Asia but also to the north – Central Asia, Iran, and other countries of the Middle East."
- The China-India relationship will be one to watch. Some may see India as a potential "counterweight" to China's influence. But their trade with each other will rise rapidly and they could form a potent strategic alliance.
- "The United States and China have strong incentives to avoid confrontation, but rising nationalism in China and fears in the US of China as an emerging strategic competitor could fuel an increasingly antagonistic relationship."

- Since "China's ability to sustain its current pace is probably more at risk than is India's ... India could emerge as the world's fastest-growing economy as we head towards 2020."

So far there is little sign that China's torrid economic pace is slowing, with the latest figures showing an expansion of 9.9% in 2005, recently overtaking the United Kingdom and France in economic size, and likely Germany in 2008. However, there are a number of downside risks and disruptions that accompany this extraordinary rise: massive internal migration from the countryside to the cities, fragile financial systems and state-owned enterprises, pervasive corruption, rising socio-economic inequalities, inadequate social safety nets and health-care systems in the face of an ageing population and epidemic diseases, growing levels of unemployment and civil unrest, demands for political as well as economic liberalization, for democracy and rights as well as market freedoms, and the spectre of conflicts involving Taiwan or North Korea.

Indeed, some argue that China's combination of a neo-Leninist state and rampant crony capitalism is not sustainable and is more likely to lead to decay than democratic transition. As one sceptic puts it: "For the moment, China's strong economic fundamentals and the boundless energy of its people have concealed and offset its poor governance, but they will carry China only so far. Someday soon, we will know whether such a flawed system can pass a stress test: a severe economic shock, political upheaval, a public health crisis, or an ecological catastrophe. China may be rising, but no one really knows whether it can fly." About 800 million people, 70% of the population, still live in the countryside, and the gap between the rural poor and urban elites is larger than at any time since the 1949 revolution. As a recent *Economist* article put it: "A spectre is haunting China – the spectre of rural unrest."

How well, or badly, China is able to manage multiple transitions and surmount potential internal challenges will be critical to its role in shaping world politics in the coming years.

At the same time, it is undeniable that China's growing weight in political and military as well as economic terms is already reshaping the strategic balance in Asia and globally. Much of the attention has focused on China's aggressive diplomacy, an uneasy United States-China relationship and closer United States-India relations.

A report prepared for members of the U.S. Congress prior to the first East Asia Summit in mid-December 2005 – a new formation that excludes the United States, unlike broader forums such as APEC (Asia Pacific Economic Cooperation) – suggests that: "Fundamental shifts underway in Asia could constrain the U.S. role in the multilateral affairs of Asia. The centrality of the United States is now being challenged by renewed regionalism in Asia and by China's rising influence."

According to James Hoge: "Suspicious Americans have interpreted larger Chinese military budgets as signs of Beijing's intention to roll back America's presence in East Asia.

Washington is thus eager to use India, which appears set to grow in economic and military strength, as a counterbalance to China as well as a strong proponent of democracy in its own right." That in turn feeds Chinese suspicions of current United States-India military cooperation (which also raises sensitive nuclear nonproliferation issues) as part of a policy of "soft containment of China."

An article on the eve of President Bush's March 2006 visit to India refers to "China's fear that America's grand strategic design is to encircle it and block its rise as a great power."

Military historian and journalist Gwynne Dyer goes so far as to suggest that "Washington and New Delhi are laying the foundations for a new Cold War in Asia." But other analysts point out that "India is far too canny, and cares too much about its own China relationship, to be drawn into such a game." (Interestingly, India has also been improving relations with Taiwan, with the launching of a Taiwan-India Cooperation Council in February 2006.)

CHANGE OF POWER ST ATUS AND THE SPEED OF CHINA'S RISE

Entering the 21st century, there are more and more predictions about when China will become a superpower. Some guess that China will be as strong as the United States in the coming decade, some bet that in 20 years and some predict its rise in year 2040. h spite of those disagreements among scholars, the forecasts were all based on the speed at which China's total power has been growing in recent years, without any consideration of the influences of the other powers' growth. As we are aware that China's power status is related to that of the other states, when forecasting China's future power status, we should not only take account of the speed of China's power growth but also the growth of the other states' power. To foresee the future change of China's power status, we should clarify the conditions for ascent and descent of international power status.

Conditions for Ascent and Descent of Power Status

As a state's power status is determined by quantitative comparisons of powers among states, the change in power status of a state depends on the difference in power growth rates between two states in a given period of time. Based on the afore-mentioned formula of a state's power status, the expression for the change of a state's power status should be $Sc = A(1 + Ra)/B(1 + Rb)$ " A/B, (here Sc refers to the result of a change in power status of two states A and B; where A and B indicate the original power for State A and State B respectively; while Ra and Rb indicate the actual growth rates of the two states, respectively). The expression shows that the change of a state's power status depends entirely upon the power growth rates (Ra and Rb) of the two states over a certain period of time. That is, the state with a faster power growth rate will rise, and the other will fall, and the statuses remain unchanged if the growth rates of the two state powers are the same. Over a fixed time period, the difference in power growth rates for the two states may result in three possibilities for change of a side's power status: rising, falling or unchanged. The three scenarios may result from 13 different situations, in which there are five for ascent, five for descent and three for no change.

It will be a political issue if a state is able to rise to a superpower in a few decades, but only an historical issue if a state rises to a hegemon over hundreds of years. As the atrophy of a state's power is a significant factor for the rapid rise of other states' power statuses, it creates an important scenario for a shift of power between two states. Therefore, power atrophy is an important political issue deserving more attention than power growth. A state's power increases in most years, decreases occasionally and very rarely has zero growth. Thus, the probability of the 10 scenarios of power-status change varies. Often both states enjoy positive power growth simultaneously; it is less common for one state to have a positive power growth while the other has a negative one; it is rare for both states to have negative power growth and is even less common that one state incurs zero power growth. When two states simultaneously have positive or negative power growth, it takes a longer time for their power gap to change and their power statuses to shift, and the probability of power-status shift is small. If one of the two states incurs zero power growth, their power gap will change relatively rapidly and there will be a higher probability for their power status to shift. However, the fastest change in the two states' power gap or their power statuses will occur when the two states have opposite power growths, i.e. one state's power increases and the other's decreases $(Ra > 0 > Rb$ or $Ra < 0 < Rb)$. Because national power grows in most years and opposite power growths of two states tend to shift power statuses easily, the factors leading to power atrophy are more significant than the factors enhancing national power in terms of changing the power gap and power status between states.

Political turbulence can cause a state's comprehensive power to diminish severely and rapidly, and it alters a state's power status at a faster rate than does economic development. Being defeated in a war, state disintegration, civil war, social turmoil and political movements all work effectively in shifting power status. The shift of power status between China and the Soviet Union after the Cold War serves as a typical example. In 1991, prior to collapse, the Soviet Union was the only competing superpower in the world rivalling the United States, and its power status drastically differed from that of China. However, as the succeeding state of the former Soviet Union after its collapse, Russia's comprehensive power endured a drastic fall and as a result its geographical area was reduced by about 24%, its population reduced by 48%, its economy decreased by 11%, and the size of its military was cut by 33.7%. At that time Russian comprehensive power was still greater than China's, however, its power status fell into the same class that China belonged to. The power gap between them was only in degree and no longer in character. Thereafter, Russia's economy declined for years, its military capability was severely weakened, and its political power was diminished internationally. Even though it is hard for us to figure out in which specific year the power-status shift occurred, we are quite certain that China's comprehensive power surpassed that of Russia during the 1990s. Up to 1999, sustaining only military superiority over China, Russia fell far behind China in aspects of political power and economic power. In 1999, Russia's GDP accounted for only one-fourth or one-third of China's GDP of $1 trillion.

Economic crisis can cause a nation's power to decrease rapidly and it works as a faster agent than economic development in changing the power gap or power status between two states. The East Asian Financial Crisis during 1997–98 widened the power gap between China and the Southeast Asian countries and meanwhile reduced the disparity of economic power between China and Japan. The East Asian Financial Crisis decreased China's annual economic growth rate to 7% from 9% prior to the crisis while it caused negative and zero economic growth, respectively, for Indonesia and Japan. Indonesian GDP fell to $50 billion in

1998 from $190.3 billion in 1995 (in 1998 its currency exchange rate fell to US$1:IDR7500 from $1:IDR2321 in 1996) and it recovered to $208.3 billion in 2003, with only a 9.5% increase from its GDP in 1995. In that period, Japan's GDP reduced from $5083.1 billion in 1995 to $4326.4 billion in 2003, a total reduction of 15%. During the same period, China's GDP (by currency exchange rate) doubled from $704.1 billion in 1995 to $1409.9 billion in 2003. Therefore, in the eight years from 1995 to 2003, the economic gap between Indonesia and China had been widened from 3.7 times to 6.8 times, while the economic gap between China and Japan narrowed from 7.2 to 3.0 times. In terms of PPP, China's economy even surpassed Japan's, causing a shift in their economic power rankings.

Political Factors Determining the Fluctuation of China's Power Status

According to the principle that opposite power growths among states tend to change power status between states easily, we come to realize that in 10 years (by 2015) whether China can sustain the existing power status will be determined mainly by the likelihood of political crisis that may cause China's power status to descend. Since its foundation in 1949, China's power status has undergone a spell of four rising and three falling periods.

During 1950–58 China's power status had been rising. During that period, the Korean War tremendously raised both China's military power status and her domestic and international capabilities of political mobilization. Between 1952 and 1958, China's GDP increased by as much as 1.9 times. During 1959–63 China's comprehensive power atrophied severely. The Anti-Rightwing Movement led the Chinese government to adopt the policies of 'Great Leap' and 'People's Commune', which resulted in an overall economic crisis. It was not until 1964 that China's economy recovered to the same level of 1960. In 1959, Sino–Soviet relations began to deteriorate and China was facing joint pressures from both the United States and the Soviet Union. During 1964 and 1965, China's national power enjoyed a brief rising period but fell again during 1966–76. In May 1966, the Cultural Revolution occurred and the country was immersed in turbulence and chaos when the government's ability to maintain order was severely hampered, economic activities stagnated, and the military weakened. However, in the same period of time, many Asian states such as Japan, South Korea and Singapore had industrialized their countries and their power status was rising rapidly in relation to China's. From 1978 to 1988 was a period when China restored its social order, increased its domestic mobilization capability and normalized relations with the United States and the Soviet Union. Consequently, China had again enhanced its international political capability, and its economy sustained an average annual growth as high as 10.2%. The political events of 1989–93 slowed China's economic growth, and dramatically reduced its domestic and international political mobilization capabilities. Thus, China's power status fell as her political power diminished in such a drastic manner. From 1993 to 2004 was the third period when China's power status ascended. During this interval, China gradually emerged from the international isolation which had started in 1989 and its capabilities of domestic and international mobilization once again increased. During 1993–2004, China's economy sustained an annual growth of 9.2% and the 1997 East Asian Financial Crisis accelerated the ascendance of China's economic power status. Ever since the founding of the People's Republic of China, each of the three major descents of China's power status was traced back to a political crisis rather than wars or economic difficulties. Therefore, we can believe that as long as there is no future political crisis, China will be able to avoid a fall in its power status.

Based on the principle that national power usually sustains growth in the majority of years, the author argues that the major external elements affecting the speed of rise of China's power status will be: (1) US military commitments and an increase or decrease of its international mobilization capabilities, and (2) the pace of political integration of the European Union (EU). According to the current growth of the comprehensive strengths of major powers, the author assumes that no other single nation, except the United States, could have larger comprehensive power than China in the next 10 years. Although each individual European state has smaller comprehensive power than China, the EU as a unified power will have a superior status to China's. If the political integration of the EU results in an international player with national character in the next 10 years, our references for judging China's future power status should include both the United States and the EU. Some people suppose that China's future power status would fundamentally depend upon China's economic growth. They obviously have neglected the political and military powers of the United States and the EU. China possesses a huge supply of low-paid labour, therefore in the next 10 years China's economic growth will be faster than that of the United States and the EU. It is also quite possible for China to narrow its economic gap with the United States and the EU. Nevertheless, there is uncertainty with regard to the development of the military and political powers of China, the United States and the EU in next 10 years.

In 10 years from now, China may narrow its military gap with the EU but the change of its military gap with the United States will depend on its military containment against Taiwanese secessionists. A favourable security environment will constrain the EU from large military expenditure.

Therefore, in the next 10 years, China's military strength will grow faster than that of the EU and will reduce the military gap between the two. Nevertheless, the change of military disparity between China and the Unites States will be determined by the rates of military investment of the two sides. As a result of the pro-independence group introducing a timetable for Taiwan to achieve legitimate independence by 2008, the Chinese government will inevitably enhance its military capability to contain Taiwanese secessionists. If the Chinese government was to launch a military attack against Taiwan's independence, it would be possible for China to narrow its military gap with the United States. If the

United States continues to wage wars against smaller states while China has no need to attack Taiwanese secessionists militarily, the US military budget will increase faster than that of China's, thus the military power gap between China and the United States would be enlarged.

In the coming decade, China will probably reduce the disparity of its political power with that of the United States, but in the meantime her advantageous political power with relevance to the EU may diminish. In the 1990s, global democratization and marketization increased the US international mobilization capability to a historical peak. With little resistance from the UN Security Council, the United States obtained UN authorizations on waging the Gulf War in 1991, the Somali War in 1996, the war in Kosovo in 1999 as well as the war in Afghanistan in 2001.

Many countries provided military and economic support to the United States during these wars. However, the United States current unilateral policy caused its international political mobilizing capability to fall sharply from 2003. Without any UN authorization, the United States waged war in Iraq under the excuse of alleged Iraqi possession of weapons of mass destruction. The US action encountered strenuous objections from many traditional European allies, headed by France and Germany.

As no weapons of mass destruction have been discovered in Iraq, US international influence has been seriously weakened. In the next 10 years, hegemonic position will drive the United States to continue its unilateralist foreign policy. Meanwhile, China will maintain its multilateral diplomacy to harmonize relationships with her neighbours, the EU and the developing countries of other regions.

Their opposite foreign policies will reduce the political power disparity between China and the United States. Presently, China has greater political power than the EU because China is a single state while the EU is a regional organization with inconsistent foreign policies adopted by its member states. In 1999, the EU introduced the Euro which entered circulation in 2002 and finally established a single currency system on the EU market. In the year 2004, the political leaders of EU member states signed the European Constitution laying a legislative foundation for the EU to become a single state entity. If the EU constitution is approved by its member states, it will establish its own three-in-one entity of administrative institutions including a council, a committee and a foreign ministry. Future political integration of the EU will enhance its character as a large national state, which may help it to narrow its political power disparity with China.

Based on the above analysis, if we assume that both the United States and the EU act as single states, the comprehensive national power gap between either China and the United States or the EU and China will probably be narrowed by the year 2015. China's comprehensive power status may rank third in the world. In 10 years and beyond, it may be possible for China to reduce its economic power disparity with the United States and the EU even though its economic power may still be smaller than theirs. China will narrow its military power gap with the EU but its overall military strength will still be weaker than that of the United States or the EU. In terms of political power, China will narrow the gap but still cannot catch up with the United States. China may maintain her political power superiority over the EU but the disparity between the two may be reduced by further political integration of the EU if all its member states ratify the EU Constitution before 2015.

We have discussed why China enjoys the leading power status among the major powers with the exception of the United States. Based on the principle that a nation's power status ascends in accordance with a faster growth rate, we may presume that China will strengthen its power superiority over Japan, Russia and India within the next 10 years. If the EU becomes a single state entity by 2015, Britain, France and Germany will no longer be regarded as individual international players. Thus, we only assess here the power status between China and three other states: Japan, Russia and India.

With regards to economic power, low-cost labour and a rapidly expanding domestic market will ensure China a faster economic growth than Japan and Russia in the next 10 years. According to World Bank data based on PPP calculations, Japan, Russia and China have GDP per capita in 2001 of $26,940, $8230 and $4580, respectively. This indicates that China's labour wage level was less than 18% of Japan's and 56% of Russia's. Low-cost labour guarantees foreign investors long-term high profits in China. At the end of 2005, China adopted a floating exchange rate according to World Trade Organization regulations and the Renmenbi (RMB) will appreciate continuously over the next 10 years. The increase in RMB exchange rate will make China's economic growth appear even faster. Although it enjoys the same advantage of low-cost labour as China, India is far behind China in aspects of opening-up to foreign investment as well as other economic reforms. Therefore, the Indian economy will continue to grow at a slower pace than that of China.

In terms of military power, it is anticipated over the next decade none of the three states, namely Japan, Russia and India, will be involved in military conflict with the United States. Therefore, the military spending of these states will increase slower than China's. Even though India and Russia are both faced with the threat of separatism in Kashmir and Chechnya, respectively, they do not face direct military protection of these separatists by the United States. As a result, the threat to Russia and India, from the separatists in these two regions, will not be comparable to that caused by the Taiwanese secessionists. Japan is under US military protection, hence its military investment will not increase as fast as that of China. The Japanese government has decided to reduce its 2005–09 military expenditures to $233 billion, i.e. 3.7% less than its average annual military spending in the previous five years.

As a result of the danger of Taiwanese independence, China is faced with potential military clashes with the United States in the Taiwan Straight. China's military spending in the next 10 years will increase much faster than that of Japan, Russia and India. This will in turn reduce the military disparity between China and Russia and at the same time make its military superior to Japan and India.

In terms of political power, China's endeavours in East Asian regionalization will effectively enhance its ability for political mobilization over the next 10 years. China will have the opportunity to further improve its relations with the EU and that will strengthen China's influence on global affairs. India, Russia and Japan, however, will have few chances to further enhance political influence in their own regions. Although India has already been a leading nation in South Asia, the South Asian regionalization has much less momentum than the East Asian. The Eastern expansion of the EU is constraining Russian political influence in East Europe and the former Soviet Republics. To sustain its special relationship with the United States, Japan has adopted a policy undermining the establishment of the East Asian Community. This policy is similar to that adopted by Great Britain with regard to the EU. Japan's policy against East Asian regionalization may ultimately weaken its political influence in East Asia. In terms of global affairs, both India and Japan may have the opportunity to become permanent members of the UN Security Council but they will have little chance of obtaining the power of veto. What they actually obtain may only be a position of permanent/non-permanent membership without substantially increased power. Russian political impact on global affairs will further diminish as it is still trapped in a regressive inertia following the collapse of the Soviet Union.

CHINA GROWTH STEAL TH FIGHTER MILIT ARY TECHNOLOGY

The aircraft in the above photo looks at first sight as a complete prototype, but it actually is a very detailed full-scale engineering mock-up. It can be speculated that, after having been used to study the aircraft's internal installations, the mock-up has also received an external finish for presentation purposes. Its real function at this point, however, is probably to buttist in the definition of the required logistic support (i.e., access to the various avionics boxes and on-board systems, ground support equipment like the various ladders and the external power source units, air conditioning units and so on) as well as to study the engines' removal-installation procedures.

Since some time now it has been known that the rapidly-developing Chinese aeronautical industry is studying a new and technologically very advanced combat aircraft, also boasting significant low signature characteristics. This programme is a logical step in China's "Long March" towards full independence in designing, developing and producing combat airplanes of a technological level in line with China's status as the "other" world superpower, on an equal footing as Russia and eventually even the USA.

The scarce information available about this new advanced combat aircraft indicates that two, possibly competing, study groups (both part of the AVIC I Group of aeronautical industries) are or have been working on the subject. One of these groups (601 Insbreastute) originates from Shenyang Airplane Corporation (SAC) which is in charge of the large, twin-engine J-8 fighters in service with the PLAAF (People's Liberation Army Air Force) as well as of licence production of the Su-27SK under the local designation of J-11. The overall configuration of SAC's preliminary design, apparently designated J-13, owes significantly to the American F-A-22, being a tailed delta but with wing and horizontal tailplanes more in line with those of the F-16. The other study group (611 Insbreastute) from Chengdu Airplane Corporation (CAC), has developed the J-12, a concept which follows the less conventional canard layout used with success in the company's J-10.

While previous information (albeit admittedly unconfirmed), gave to the SAC concept the edge, perhaps as a result of the company's experience in large twin-engine fighters, this seems to have since been reversed in favour of the Chengdu design. It is however still not clear whether the designation of J-14 is intended to suggest a successor design to both the J-12 and the J-13, and whether the existence of the J-14 engineering mock-up (clearly based on the J-12) indicates that the type has been selected for development, or the compebreastion is still going on with parallel activities underway on another such mock-up based on the J-13.

While no data is available about the J-14, some speculation can be done in the attempt to extrapolate the aircraft's characteristics and thus the roles it is called to perform. The following considerations are based on what can be seen in the photo, but also involve making some buttumptions on the basis of what is known of the Chinese armed forces' perceived priorities in operational requirements, the domestic industry's approach to combat aircraft design and, finally, the well-know Chinese weaknesses in some technological fields. In addition, the well-developed cooperation with Russian companies, particularly in areas such as powerplant, avionics and possibly computer-based fly-by-wire flight control systems is also taken into consideration.

General Configuration

The J-14 will surely be fitted with a fly-by-wire flight control system and be designed for artificial stability. The Chinese should by now have matured an adequate experience in this field through a number of experimental programmes and application to actual in-service types.

The general configuration of the aircraft is clearly born out from CAC's experience in developing the J-10, with its canard layout and ventral air intake. But while the J-10 is known to be related to the Israeli LAVI, this new and much more ambitious design rather appears to have a definite relationship with the ill-fated Russian 5th generation fighter studied a few years ago, the MiG 1.44 MFI and in fact it shares a number of elements which can doubtless be traced back to the Russian demonstrator. It is thus very probable not to say certain that an agreement has been reached between the Russian and Chinese governments allowing for the transfer of information and technological data as well as consultancy services being provided by RSK MiG and Russian research centres (arguably including the TsAGI aerodynamic research insbreastute) to develop the new Chinese fighter.

The J-14's planform closely matches that of the MiG 1.44, i.e. a canard layout (the canard surface are fully movable) with mid-positioned wing and widely separated twin-vertical surfaces canted outward, which continue under the wing in twin ventral fins, these too being canted outward à la J-10. While not visible in the photo, wind tunnel models show that the 1.44 configuration has been maintained also in the booms protruding from the wing and contributing to support the vertical tailplanes and ventral fins. These booms probably end with radomes covering electronic warfare antennas and possibly also a rearward facing radar, similar to the installation experimented in the Su-37 a few years ago. In the MiG 1.44, the portion of wing between the fuselage-engine pods and the booms is extended rearward past the wing trailing edge and includes a couple of moving surfaces contributing, together with the all-moving canard surfaces, to the longitudinal control of the airplane. It is not yet possible to buttess whether this solution, too has been maintained for the J-14.

But while the overall aerodynamic configuration of the J-14 follows that of the MiG 1.44 demonstrator, a radical redesign has been implemented in the pursuit of a significant reduction in the radar cross-section value. In particular, the aircraft incorporates a pronounced wing-body blending, which was totally lacking in the original Russian design. Further, the air intake, while in the same ventral position under the forward fuselage, has a completely new shape, and by the same token the upper part of the airplane is also completely different and shows towards the rear the protuberances of the engine "pods" which blend with the fuselage and wing roots in a curious reminiscence of the Northrop YF-23. Also, the front fuselage merges down into the upper wing, blending with the separated engine bay bulges while maintaining some relation with the "clbuttical" Su-27 forward fuselage shape. The search for enhanced stealth performance is also apparent in the "flattened" profile of the entire front fuselage section (nearly identical to the Su-32), as well as in the generalised use of serrated doors to cover the landing gear and missile bays.

On the other hand, it remains clear that a canard configuration is hardly the ideal solution from the point of view of a reduced radar signature. Summing up, it would thus seem safe to buttume that the J-14 is a "stealth-optimised" aircraft rather than un uncompromising stealth design à la F-A-22 or (in a different clbutt) the F-35 JSF.

Above the raised front fuselage is located the single-seat pilot chickenpit. This is closed by a single-piece frameless bubble-type transparent canopy which appears technological very demanding under various aspects such as manufacturing process, adequate optical qualities and bird-impact resistance, yet allowing through-ejection. On the other hand, the pilot is provided with superb all-around visibility also due to the position of the chickenpit above the forward fuselage "hump", again a reminiscence of the Su-27.

After Chinese visit Ships, U.S. Officials Hope for Reciprocation

After Chinese visit ships, U.S. officials hope for reciprocation {EXCERPT}, by Allison Batdorff, Stars and Stripes Pacific edition, Friday, June 23, 2006 ANDERSEN AIR FORCE BASE, Guam ˜...

The main landing gear, with single wheels mounted on telescopic legs, retracts outward, with the legs being accommodated in the fuselage side blending into the wing bottom and the wheels into the wing (a similar geometry has been selected for the F-A-22). In order to minimise the volume of the bay occupied by the gear in the retracted position, the telescopic main gear legs are shortened via a pulling bar acting on a lever, similarly to what has been introduced in the Eurofighter TYPHOON. While not clear in the photo, it is possible that the same landing gear leg shortening design has also been selected for the nose twin-wheel element.

Powerplant Installation

In view of the twin-engine layout of the J-14 and its estimated TO weight in air combat configuration (some 25-28 tons with full internal fuel, gun ammunition, 2 x SRAAM and 4 x MRAAM), its engines should give a thrust in the range of 13-14 tons in afterburning mode, so achieving a thrust-to-weight ratio in the order of 1:1. Now it seems difficult to envisage a stateof-the-art Chinese engine, particularly in this thrust clbutt, achieving full production status by the mid of the next decade when the J-14 could reasonably be expected to enter service. Even for the J-10 a Russian engine has been at last preferred. It can thus be buttumed that a Russian engine has been selected for the J-14 as well, and indeed the model which can be seen in the picture to the rear of the right wing of the mock-up has the accessory gearbox mounted above the engine in the traditional Russian style. If, as it is highly probable, this engine is a member of the Saturn-Lyulka AL-31-41 family (but it could also be a prototype of the Chinese Liming LM WS10A in the same thrust clbutt), this would make the type not fully interchangeable with the version selected for the J-10, which has the accessory gearbox located on the engine bottom, Western-style. It is also possible to speculate that the idea is to have the prototypes powered by the lower-thrust AL-31 as used in the J-11-Su-27SK-Su-30MKK, with either an evolved higher-thrust version of AL-31 or a series-production version of the AL-41 being then adopted for the series aircraft.

Coming to the engine-airframe installation, the air intake located in the bottom part of the front fuselage is of the fixed geometry type with no moving ramp, unlike the case with the J-10. This solution has made it possible to eliminate the sharp angles and slots between the moving ramp and in general to provide smooth shapes which reduce radar reflectivity.

The pronounced bulging up of the air intake inner duct helps avoid a direct presentation of the critically reflective engine fan-compressor face to enemy illuminating radar from the forward emisphere. In addition, the bulge is needed to make room for the nose landing gear bay and, even more, for the bottom fuselage weapons bay.

Notwithstanding its fixed geometry, the air intake shows elements which should generate a couple of oblique shock waves before the normal one, thus guaranteeing an adequately efficient dynamic pressure recovery in the supersonic flight regime. The well-shaped bulge along the bottom of the centre fuselage entering the air intake, which forms the upper part of the air intake duct, seems reminiscent of the latest Lockheed Martin's vaunted design for a fixed-ramp, multi-shock air intake planned for use on the production F-35 and already experimented on an F-16. This peculiar layout, together with the forward-raked air intake lip (already seen in the late 1950s on the F8U-3 CRUSADER III) is clearly intended to generate the oblique shock waves mentioned above.

The location of the air intake under the fuselage is well suited to provide a smooth distortion-free airflow to the engines. From this particular point of view, the hinged bottom lip present in the TYPHOON works even better at extreme angles of attack, but it implies the penalty of a higher radar signature. In more general terms, the choice of a single air intake configuration in a twin-engine airplane may be open to some criticism, in that it is less than ideal to maintain correct working conditions (i.e., smooth undistorted airflow to the remaining engine) in the event of an engine flaming out for whatever reason. The air intake thus establishes a potential single point failure in an otherwise completely redundant twin-engine installation.

It can be expected that Thrust Vector Control (TVC) nozzles, probably of the axisymmetric type (despite their not insignificant contribution to overall nuclear signature), will be a standard feature of the J-14 to both enhance manoeuvrability and reduce trim drag in cruise flight.

Armament

Chinese design derived from a Russian model such as the GSh-6-23 23mm installed in the MiG-31 and the Su-24. The gun is installed in the upper right fuselage side, just above the canard surface. The firing port, unlike the F-A-22 is left permanently open, hence generating a not so negligible radar reflection.

The main armament is carried in three weapons bays, whose arrangement looks like virtually a clone of the F-A-22. Two smaller bays are located on the fuselage sides and appear to be tailored to each accommodate a single short-range air-to-air missile, while the large underfuselage bay, closed by twin doors, will probably accept at least four medium-range AAMs. It may be speculated that the J-14 is intended to carry "compressed carriage" clipped-wing versions of the AAMs already in use with the PLAAF, i.e. the PL-8 and the Russian R-73 for short-range dogfights and the R-77 and the indigenous PL-12 for medium-range work. The R-77 is already suitable for carriage in an internal bay in its standard version, being equipped with very small span wings while the lattice tail control fins can be fold forward flush with the missile body.

Underwing store stations are surely foreseen to carry additional weapons and fuel tanks, when there is no need to maintain a high level of stealthness.

Combat Avionics

J-14 is already in full-scale development, the main choices related to the avionics systems should have already been made, at least at the conceptual level. However, the Chinese domestic industry is almost certainly not in a position to supply the advanced avionics required in a sophisticated aircraft like the J-14, and contributions from abroad will be required-from Russia, Israel and arguably even Europe.

The J-14 being intended to enter service in around 2012-2015, it may be expected that the Chinese are aiming at equipping it with a radar with electronically scanning (ASEA) antenna, capable of multiple targets engagements-provided that a source for such a radar could be identified. In the Russian tradition, a pbuttive search and track system based on optronic devices (FLIR with integrated laser rangefinder) is expected to be also installed in a retractable or faired turret. As already mentioned, the dual rear booms could carry, in addition to various pbuttive and-or active defensive systems also a rear-facing radar.

Finally, it can be expected that the chickenpit instrumentation for the production version will be based on an Helmet Mounted Display-Sight (HMD-S) totally replacing the HUD, although the latter instrument is clearly visible in the photo. The head-down displays would probably include three or four large Multi Function Displays (MFD), which should have the possibility to present a digital map and a complete tactical situation. A real-time data link is also an expected addition to the fully integrated avionics system to enhance the situation awareness of the pilot, particularly when operating in multiships combat groups to make the most use of the commonly available information from the various platforms.

INDIA AS A RISING MILITARY POWER

China has taken serious note of India's growing military power over the last decade. India, which has traditionally talked of the power of argument began to talk of the argument of power. In fact, the 1998 nuclear tests themselves were indicative of the fact that India had begun to realize the role of hard power in securing its national interests and also in making her voice heard in international politics. India's growing military profile is especially evident in the maritime domain. The Indian navy has emerged as the net security provider in the Indian Ocean over the last decade. In 2004, it unveiled its first-ever naval doctrine that defined India's legitimate areas of interest stretching from the Persian Gulf to the Malacca Straits. It released its updated version in 2009, incorporating the rapid changes in the geo-strategic environment involving India. India's defense ties with the US have developed at a frenetic pace, which has played the central role in India's military modernization. For example, recent defense contracts signed with the US include US$ 1.1 billion for C-130J Super Hercules transport planes and US$2.4 billion for 10 Globemasters airlifters.

In January 2009, the Indian Navy signed an agreement with the U. S. to buy eight P-8I planes worth nearly US$2.1 billion, so as to replace the aging long range aerial reconnaissance fleet of eight Russian-made Tu-142s and five IL-38 planes. The tests of its China-centric Agni series missile systems and the development of a Ballistic Missile Defense system. India's future military plans are even more ambitious, which further complicates China's strategic calculations. For example, the Indian Ministry of Defense in late 2011 announced its biggest expansion package to date, a US$13 billion military modernization plan. Under this plan within next five years, the Indian army is set to deploy 90,000 more soldiers and raise four new divisions along India's border with China, the largest such mobilization since the Sino-Indian border clashes of 1962.

India's Po ly/Multi-aligned Diplo macy

The India that China defeated in 1962 was guided by a foreign policy doctrine called *non-alignment* vis-à-vis the superpower rivalry, and it remained the cornerstone of India's international diplomacy for more than four decades. However, this foreign policy paradigm underwent a U-turn when it metamorphosed into *poly/multi-alignment* under the new leadership in New Delhi in 1998. The new foreign policy outlook broadly had two components, namely, *improving relations with the US* and its *Look East Policy-II*.

The turnaround in India-US relations from being "estranged democracies" during the Cold War to "engaged democracies" in the 2000s has played a central role in bringing out a shift in China's India posture over the last decade. The anti-China element in the dramatically improving Indo-US relations was not very difficult to discern. Chinese scholar Jing-Dong Yuan notes that the warming of US-Indian relations took place at a time when China-US relations were undergoing serious setbacks in the late 1990s. In 1999, NATO bombed the Chinese embassy in the former Yugoslavia (the only embassy that it targeted); in May of that year, the Cox Report charged Chinese nationals with nuclear espionage and accused China of proliferation activities. hostile attitude toward the PRC further exacerbated tensions in early 2001. Also, the revised Nuclear Posture Review (NPR) included China as a nuclear target.

Meanwhile, in a diametrically opposite turn of events, India-US relations suddenly displayed signs of dramatic improvement. US President Bill Clinton visited India in March 2000 (the first presidential visit since Carter's visit in 1978). The US' National Security Strategy Report of 2002 released by the White House redefined India-US relations, stating that because of "India's potential to become one of the great democratic powers of the twenty-first century," the United States would "invest time and resources [for] building strong bilateral relations with India," and "work hard to transform our relationship accordingly." Consequently, the years 2002-03 witnessed a series of high-level meetings and substantial cooperation between the two democracies. Yet another contrast was the U.S.'s approval of Israel's sale of the Phalcon airborne warning and control systems to India in 2003 after the blockage of a similar sale to China in 2000.

Another Chinese security analyst Du Youkang argues that the US strategy of maintaining the balance of power in South Asia during the Cold War has gone beyond the balance of power and has tilted toward India. He cites the Clinton administration's pro-India attitude during the Kargil conflict, and his subsequent official tour to South Asia, where he spent six days in India compared to five hours in Pakistan. The growing strategic ties between the two countries provides a dangerous historical precedent for Beijing. During the Cold War, China perceived India-USSR relations in terms of an anti-China alliance in South Asia. So the strategic partnership between India and the US in the 2000s is, from China's perspective, the revival of the same anti-China alliance – the only difference being that the US has replaced the Soviet Union. Zhang Guihong compared the US-India Western Pacific.

The other pedestal of India's multi-aligned diplomacy included its *Look East Policy-II*. India's Look East Policy-I was officially initiated in 1992. Like most of the previous Indian policies it was reactionary and an outcome of ad hoc-ism. The main driver behind this policy was the economic doldrums of early 1990s, and India saw Southeast Asia as a springboard to join unfolding globalization. However, India displayed an uncharacteristic proactiveness in projecting the Look East policy in its second incarnation in the first-ever India ASEAN summit in Phnom Penh, Cambodia in 2002. India added a politico-security dimension to this policy. It developed security ties with the ASEAN group. From ASEAN's perspective, developing such ties with India (apart from the US presence in the region) provided them a sense of strategic reassurance given their territorial disputes in the South China Sea with a rapidly growing, authoritarian China.

An important highlight of India's Look East Policy-II, from China's viewpoint, has been a transformational improvement in India-Japan relations. Although the ice between their relations was broken with the visit of Prime Minister Mori Yoshiro to India in August 2000, their relations broadened and deepened in the second phase. The April 2005 joint statement issued during Koizumi Junichiro's visit to India introduced a "strategic" dimension to the partnership. The establishment of the Strategic and Global Partnership between India and Japan in December 2006 elevated relations to a new level. In 2006 Japan became only the second country with which India had a bilateral annual summit apart from Russia. When then Prime Minister Shinzo Abe visited India in August 2007, the joint statement sought to provide a roadmap for new dimensions to the strategic and global partnership. The October 2008 joint statement during Prime Minister Manmohan Singh's visit to Japan mentioned the advancement of the strategic and global partnership, making Japan the only country Partnership Agreement (CEPA) which came into force in August of the same year. In late December 2011 India's External Affairs minister visited Japan in October 2011 for the Fifth round of the India-Japan Strategic Dialogue. Japanese PM Yoshihiko Noda visited India for the sixth annual meeting of the leaders of India and Japan. It was the success of India's Look East Policy-II (and not Look East Policy I) that made China remark that India's Look East Policy is "look to encircle China."

India Emerging as an Economic Giant

India and China had similar per capita income by 1974. However, China surged well ahead of India thanks to its deep economic engagement with the US after the Policy of Reform and Open Up (*gaige kaifang*) by Deng Xiaoping in 1978. While China's Open Door policy was a well-thought-out initiative, India, following its legacy of taking radical initiatives only while in crisis, embarked upon its own version of Open Door policy in 1991. The much-needed reforms removed obstacles to economic freedom, and India began to play catch-up, steadily re-integrating into the global economy. A Goldman Sachs report from 2007 found another watermark in India's economic history since 1991 when it pointed out that since 2003 India has been one of the fastest growing major economies, leading to rapid increases in per capita income, demand, and integration with the global economy.

The story of India's economic success has captivated Chinese attention over the last decade. Among Chinese scholars a new discourse has begun over India's economic success story, especially in the IT and consensus that China is a great success in exports, inside China, focusing on China's lag in information technology, Chinese researchers ask why India has become so competitive in the international software market when India has many unattractive features."

Chinese scholars now debate an "Indian Model" as an alternative to the "Chinese model" for developing countries. The Indian model, as understood by Chinese scholars, is characterized by avoiding its weaknesses and exploiting its strengths. For example, India leapfrogged from the primary sector (agriculture) to the tertiary sector (services) by exploiting its inherent advantages in the IT sector which includes a vast, young English-speaking population, the entrepreneurial genius of its private sector, computer literacy, a sound banking sector, and a culture that respects the rule of law. Chinese analysts have especially taken notice of what they call "India New Economy" which is acting like an engine to the Indian Model. Ma Jiali argues that although India is a baby elephant in the manufacturing industry, it is a "doughty tiger" in the information sector. Another set of scholars attributed India's success in this sector to its diaspora. It opined, "India's IT success is also attributed to the large cohort of educated overseas Indians who have good connections and invested heavily in their home country in recent years as a result of favourable government policies. The dynamism brought by the overseas Indians was comparable to the boost brought by the overseas Chinese since the 1978 economic reform in China."

India's Growing Soft Power

The drivers triggering a shift in China's India posture can be placed under the rubric of India's *hard power*. However, India's (re)rising *soft power* has also contributed to this shift in China's outlook a country's ability to alter the behavior of others through attraction rather than sticks or carrots. India has been a democracy right since its birth as a modern nation-state in 1947. However, its sluggish economic growth and weak military profile that led to its defeat in 1962 seriously tarnished this aspect of India's soft power. With the rising India story, its democracy as an important component of its soft power has again come into the global limelight. India has more than 1 billion people. It is linguistically, culturally, racially, and religiously diverse, and it is growing economically at an enviable pace under democratic governmental institutions (except for the emergency period of 1975-77 when civil liberties were undermined). Its culture values peaceful coexistence, nonviolence, and religious tolerance. All of these factors, combined with the largest pool of English speakers outside the US, has increased India's power of attraction without need for coercion or persuasion, a fact not lost on an envious, hard power-minded China. The country to which India has projected most of its soft power is the US, through the export of highly skilled manpower, consisting mainly of software developers, engineers, and doctors. China has been keeping a close watch on the rising influence of the Indian community in the United States, especially over the last decade. In order to improve its own soft power in the United States, China has sent far more students to the United States than India. As per the Institute of International Education's annual report in the academic year 2009-10, out of 690,932 international students in the United States nearly 128,000 of them, or more than 18 percent, were from China while India sent only 107,897 students in the same academic year. However, with Oct 2011, educational exchanges between India and the US would rise much faster in the future.

MILITARY MANPOWER AND STRATEGIC ENVIRONMENT

India's regional security environment is marked by Afghanistan's endless civil war despite US-led North Atlantic Treaty Organization (NATO) intervention and the overthrow of the despotic Taliban regime and its tense relations with Iran and the Central Asian Republics (CARs). Pakistan's half-hearted struggle against the remnants of the al Qaeda and the Taliban, the fissiparous tendencies in Balochistan and the Pushtun heartland, the continuing rise of the cancer of radical extremism and creeping Talibanisation, the unstable civilian government, the floundering economy and, consequently, the nation's gradual slide towards becoming a 'failed state', pose a major security threat to India.

The collusive nuclear weapon-cummissile development programme of China, North Korea and Pakistan and Iran's quest for nuclear weapons are issues of concern. Sri Lanka's inability to find a lasting solution to its ethnic problems despite the comprehensive defeat of the LTTE (Liberation Tigers of Tamil Eelam) has serious repercussions for India. Bangladesh's emergence as the new hub of Islamist fundamentalist terrorism even as it struggles for economic upliftment to subsistence levels, could trigger a new wave of terrorism in India.

The Maoist ascendancy in Nepal and its adverse impact on Nepal's fledgling democracy, as also Nepal's newfound inclination to seek neutrality between India and China, are a blow to what has historically been a stable relationship. Simmering discontentment in Tibet and Xingjian against China's repressive regime is gathering momentum and could result in an open revolt. The peoples' nascent movement for democracy in Myanmar and several long festering insurgencies may destabilise the military Junta. The spill over of religious extremism and terrorism from Afghanistan and political instability in the CARs (Central Asian Republics) are undermining development and governance. Other vitiating factors impacting regional stability in India's neighbourhood is unchecked proliferation of small arms which has been nurtured and encouraged by large-scale narcotics trafficking.

India's unresolved territorial and boundary dispute with China and an un-demarcated Line of Actual Control (LAC) on the India-Tibet border do not augur well for long-term peace and stability between these two Asian giants. Though the border is relatively stable, a future border war with China, though improbable, cannot be ruled out.

China's carefully orchestrated plan aimed at the strategic encirclement of India is evident from its unjustifiable opposition to India's nuclear weapons programme; its strong military support to the ruling regime in Myanmar; its diabolical assistance to the LTTE in Sri Lanka; its increasing proclivity to build and acquire ports in the Bay of Bengal and the Arabian Sea – the so-called "string of pearls" strategy; its attempts to isolate India in the ASEAN Regional Forum (ARF) and to prevent India's entry to the Shanghai Cooperation Organisation (SCO); and, its relentless efforts to increase its influence in Nepal, Bhutan and Bangladesh.

Clearly, China's growing power and influence in Asia poses a long-term strategic challenge to India as a competing regional power. The 60-year old dispute over Jammu and Kashmir (J&K) continues to bedevil India-Pakistan relations. The Line of Control

(LoC) in J&K and the Actual Ground Position Line (AGPL) at Siachen Glacier were perpetual flashpoints and witnessed active military hostilities for most of these 60 years. Violations of the LoC, such as the intrusions engineered by Pakistan in the Kargil district of J&K in the summer months of 1999, are fraught with danger and have the potential to lead to full-scale conventional conflict. Also, India accuses Pakistan of sponsoring a "proxy war" through terrorist outfits nurtured by the Inter-Services Intelligence (ISI) Directorate in J&K.

With the military continuing to drive from the backseat in Pakistan, the recurrence of such misadventures remains likely, particularly if the domestic political and security situations continue to deteriorate. Pakistan's 450,000 combatant personnel remain India's foremost military threat. Progress on the India-Pakistan Composite Dialogue process has been stalled due to Pakistan's disinclination to bring to justice the perpetrators of the Mumbai terror attacks. The only positive factor is that a mutually respected cease-fire has been in place on the LoC since November 25, 2003.

Though it is an ancient civilisation, India is a young nation state that is still engaged in the process of nation building. This process has been marked by ethnic tensions, fissiparous tendencies and socio-economic challenges. India has been saddled with a long-drawn low level insurgency in J&K due to its inability to fully integrate all parts of the state with the national mainstream.

Failure to find an amicable solution and end the alienation of the people of the Kashmir Valley, in particular, could have widespread repercussions in other parts of the country and in the region. Similarly, several of India's north-eastern states have been in turmoil for many decades due to political and economic neglect, poor governance and, consequently, inadequate socio-economic development. Left Wing Extremism or Maoist terrorism is the latest manifestation of India's internal instability. These internal security challenges are likely to continue to prevail over the next two decades. The end of the Cold War led to what could be characterised as an era of strategic uncertainty. Defence planning has become more difficult in several ways. The sources and types of conflicts for which planning must be carried out have become more diverse and less predictable even as the number of potential adversaries continues to grow. The range of missions that armed forces need to undertake is expanding to include those likely to be assigned in sub-conventional conflict, including low-intensity border wars and insurgency fuelled by foreign powers. And, the global security agenda has expanded in functional terms.

Yesterday's peripheral challenges such as the security of energy sources and the threat from mass migrations now compete with conventional threats for a share in the defence pie. Systemic changes in the structure of the global economy, communications and military technologies are likely to alter the strategic stakes. These changes in the security paradigm are changing the strategic terms in which policymakers, military leaders and defence analysts must address long-term defence planning so as to evolve defence capabilities that will be relevant to the emerging threats.

The asymmetric character of contemporary conflict challenges conventional thinking and demands fresh responses. General Rupert Smith has identified six key trends that define modern warfare:1 the growing role of non-state actors as well as multinational forces as combatants; looking for creative new uses for old weapons; emphasis on force protection rather than using force at any cost; the prolonged nature of modern wars; a new focus on winning the hearts and minds of people; and, a shift from absolute objectives to more flexible ones.

He writes that in the Clausewitzian trinity (army, state and people), the balance between the three has changed. "There was a time when armies dominated — as they still do in the country of warlords; later, states were able to command the complete obedience of their people. Now it is the people who are in charge and the strategic objective is their hearts and minds." The aim of this book is to examine the salient issues affecting the recruitment, training and retention of suitable personnel in the Indian armed forces, understanding the linkage between manpower and technology and recommending measures to reduce the cost of manpower in the light of India's strategic environment. The chapter also takes stock of similar re-structuring issues across major Western armies.

PERCEPTION OF BALANCE OF POWER

In general, there are two main theoretical schools of international relations: *realism* and *liberalism*. *Realism* identifies the entire system of state relations based on criteria such as strength, power, geopolitics, geostrategy and the correlation of forces largely among Great Powers. *Liberalism* emphasizes other factors, such as economic interdependence, "soft" sources of power, and the role of international institutions and multilateralism.

According to many scholars, while various approaches could be considered supplementary, realism is the more dominant theoretical tradition since the policies of Great Powers and their relations have so far strongly influenced international affairs. Moreover, the regional and multilateral institutions would not be able to function without the participation of Great Powers.

The theory on balance of power is associated with realism and remains the most fundamental framework for understanding international relations. The concept of balance of power has historically been used to explain the actions of states in an insecure environment. The system was first formed and operationalized among the applied though debate on it continues.

Balance of Power: Meaning

Balance of power is perceived *as the basic concept in the relations among states.* Modern theory on balance of power is connected to the Newtonian conception of an universe in equilibrium. The substance of this theory is: *Under normal circumstances, all states always seek to maximize their power and international positions through various methods and techniques, and because of the adjustments of the "invisible hand", no one gains hegemony and an equilibrium in the international relations systems is maintained.*

This definition suggests a mechanism in which any attempt by any state to expand its power and attain dominance or hegemony that would allow it to impose its will on the other states will be resisted. No state, therefore, will be in a position to determine the fate of others.

Thus, a state of equilibrium in the international relations system is one in which no state becomes an absolute dominant power; more powerful states, in spite of pursuing various strategic interests, are satisfied with the existing territorial, adjustments may take place, no powerful state (or group of states) seeks to change the system fundamentally, as it would not yield additional benefits commensurate with the anticipated costs.

Consequently, the Great Powers have frequently supported the balance of power system throughout history, because they have both greater capacity to influence outcomes and the largest stake in the established order. In effect, balance of power mirrors the Great Powers' compromises on the distribution of benefits and spheres of influence in the world on the basis of their correlation of forces.

Rules of the Diversion

The aim of countervailing power is the protection of each state's security and the system in which these states exist as a whole. Therefore, the way to ensure each state's security is to prevent the emergence of any preponderant state that would lead to an upset of the existing status of equilibrium.

As Wolfer puts it, in balance of power terms, these rules can be stated in the following manner:

(a) *Watch a potential adversary's power and match it.*

(b) *Ally oneself with a weaker state to restore the balance of power.*

(c) *Abandon such alliances when the balance has been restored and the common danger has passed.*

(d) *Regard national security interests as permanent; alliances must therefore change when a new threat rises.*

(e) *Do not treat defeated states harshly through punitive peace treaties (today's adversary may be tomorrow's ally).*

Change of Balance

An international system is not maintained in a state of stable equilibrium when important shifts in the array of forces among states occur. There are two basic elements leading to the attempts to change the balance of power system:

- Differential growth in political, military and technological power that creates a change in the array of forces among states.

- Shifts in states' domestic political coalitions may necessitate redefinition of their "national interests" and foreign policies.

An equilibrium can be altered if there is a shift in political, military and technological capabilities of states and, as a result, *the expected benefits exceed the expected costs of bringing about a change in the system.* Victorious state or states would create the new peace settlements and status quo reflecting the redistribution of power in the system. The hegemonic wars in this view included the Thirty Years War from 1618-1648, the wars of King Louis XIV from 1667-1713, the Napoleonic Wars from 1792-1814, World War I from 1914-1918 and World War II from 1939-1945. However, resolution of crises is still possible through peaceful adjustment of the systemic disequilibrium, by compromises or moderation of the ambitions of emerging Great Powers. Essentially, it is the sharing of costs and benefits in keeping the status quo among the existing Great Powers.

The determinants of whether or not to create and maintain the international balance of power are the cost-benefit calculations that a state (or states) will make in the determination to change the existing equilibrium. The material environment (e.g., economic growth, demographic change, military technologies, communications and transportation conditions), the international system structures, and "internal" factors (e.g., leadership personalities, national identities, political-economic interests of groups and others in the society) provide incentives or disincentives for a state to attempt to change the international system.

Meaning of Implement a Bal ance of Power Policy

As J. Spanier explains, all states are very concerned about their strength or power for survival. To prevent an attack, a state must be *as powerful as potential aggressors; a disproportion of power may tempt another state. A balance of power is thus a prerequisite for each state's security.* When the balance is disturbed, the tendency is to take responsive action to return to a position of equilibrium. If states disregard the operational rule that power must be counterbalanced, they place their own security in jeopardy.

As Kissinger argues, *the balance of power serves to restrict the ability of states to dominate each other and to limit the scope of conflicts.* Kissinger views the balance of power not as an automatic mechanism, but instead as one of two possible outcomes of a situation in which states are obliged to deal with each other. One state can become so powerful that it dominates the others, or else the "pretensions" of the most aggressive member of the international community are kept in check by chosen by prudent leaders.

Harman, when studying the significance of theory on balance of power, asserts that *prudent states do not amass more enemies than they can effectively counter or handle at any one time. If states must deal with two or three adversaries, it would be wiser to concentrate on the strongest one by isolating and separating it from the others.* This principle is called the "conservation of enemies".

Chessmen o n the New Strat egic Chessboard

On the international strategic chessboard, the ranks of "chessmen" are classified by geopolitical, demographic, economic, military and traditional criteria in which geopolitics has significant importance. Generally, two ranks are identified: the first rank comprises *Great Powers,* whose scope of interests and capability of intervention reaches out beyond their borders. The second rank is comprised of *Middle and Small Powers,* which do not have (or have only a very few) of these roles to act, while the Middle and Small Powers are acted upon.

The "chessmen" positioned on the strategic chessboard in the Asia-Pacific are ranked as follows:

- *First* is a group of Great Powers that includes the United States, China, Japan, Russia and India. These are the chief game players in the strategic chessboard. Their positions, however, are not necessarily equal to one another:

  - The United States is currently the single superpower having political, economic and military might, and global influence.

  - China is an emerging power with an increasingly important voice in the regional economy and greater political influence in the Asia-Pacific. -Japan is an economic power whose political and military stature are not commensurate with its economic abilities.

  - Russia's international prestige declined sharply after the collapse of the Soviet Union. In spite of this, however, Russia still has a strong military force, including nuclear weapons.

  - India is now exercising its clout mainly in the South Asian region and is also viewed as a rising power.

- *Second* is a group of Middle Powers. These countries do not have great influence on the developments in the region, but they play an important role in balancing power, as they occupy strategic geopolitical positions and are the Korea, and Vietnam.

- *Third* are Small Powers (Laos, Cambodia, Singapore) and some very small states like Brunei (with a population of 300,000 people), and the Marshall Islands (with a population of 40,000 people). Those countries can only make worthwhile stands when they are engaged in alliances or alignments with other actors.

- *In addition*, some scholars of liberalism have flirted with the idea that new transnational actors, such as international and regional organizations, NGOs and multinational corporations, are gradually playing a greater role in international affairs.

EFFECTS ON OTHER GREA T POWERS' POSITION

The United States, China, and the other Great Powers do not want to see this scenario occur, as they all will be placed in a very difficult situation in dealing with one another. However, if this case should come about, *the process of rallying forces will be followed by two blocks, with one block comprised of the United States and its allies, the other block comprised of China and its allies, and with the rest in between the two sides.* Specifically:

- Polarization is in place, with the United States and Japan on the one side (based on US-Japan Security Pact), and China and Russia on the other.
- China seeks alliances with other Asian nations (based on cultural and religious similarities), which may lead to a loose coalition between China and India and Japan (the US-Japan Security Pact to be nullified by China) to limit US influence in the region.

When China becomes more powerful and more aggressive, other Great Powers may ally with the United States to curb China's ambitions.

Regarding options taken in dealing with the United States and China, two hypotheses can be put forward:

- Russia, Japan, and India improve their relations with both the United States and China, thus making *a concert of power.* Coordination among Great Powers is formulated in solving regional and international issues in which the United States and China play leading roles.
- After the establishment of strategic partnerships, the United States and China attach less importance to their relations with other Great Powers or even compromise on each others' interests. The consequent gradual decline of the role played by Japan, Russia, and India in the strategies

of the United States and China therefore compel them to regroup to struggle for their balanced interests.

As the US-China relationship is largely driven by a mixture of cooperation and competition, both countries must attach greater importance to broadening their relations with external forces so that other countries will have more policy choices that conform to their own interests.

Effects on Middle and Small Powers' Status

The Middle and Small Powers often have less opportunity to act rather than be acted upon by the adjustments of Great Powers' strategies in complicated international relations. In Asia, the relations of neighbouring countries with China and the status of its relations with other Great Powers.

Middle and Small Powers in dealing with Great Powers:

- To ally or align with one single Great Power and rely on security, political, and economic protections from that Power.
- To participate in the games, but keep balanced relations with all Great Powers.
- To stay out of the games and keep neutral like Finland and Switzerland (the mode called "Finlandization").

Because of the widely diversified interests of all countries, there is a variety of behaviors. In view of many fundamental changes in the world today (e.g., the existence of multipower balance, growing globalization, highly interdependent conditions), *alignment is likely to be seen instead of the classical alliance, and no nation is likely to stay outside or be "neutral."*

Dibb observes that in these uncertain circumstances, Middle Powers in the region are likely to view their own interests as best served by preserving an equilibrium among Great Powers. He cites Amitav Acharya, who notes that the ASEAN states' preferred approach to regional order seems to lie in the maintenance of a regional mechanisms remain critical to the prospects for regional order in the post-Cold War era. The Middle Powers are likely to feel threatened by the domination of the Asia-Pacific region by any one Great Power, and to regard some measures of checks and balances on each by the other as the condition of their own security. According to Dibb, *all the Middle and Small Powers in the region seek ways to avoid tendencies of either a keen rivalry or confrontation or a concert of Great Powers,* because these scenarios leave them less space for maneuver.

It is anticipated therefore that whatever US-China relations develop, *Middle and Small Powers naturally opt to participate in the balance of power game, maintaining balanced relations with the Great Powers, especially with the United States and China on the one hand, and regrouping themselves to raise counterweights in dealing with those Great Powers on the other.*

6

China and India : The 'Emerging Giants' and Economy Development

Both countries have been growing fast over the last 25 years: China by 21 fold and India by 8 fold. The growth rate in China has been over 9% per annum making it possibly the fastest growing world economy while India's, too, has been impressive with over 8% per annum. The % living below the poverty line (1 $ a day) has also been appreciably reduced in both though it is more impressive in China compared to India: 12% in the former and 26% in the latter. The major effect of China's and India's economic advance is evidenced by their contribution to global output: China's and India's share being 20% and 7% respectively in 2004. Both, moreover, have rising demand for energy, raw materials and commodities. This has a positive impact on increasing the exports of developing countries, improving their terms of trade, and initiating shifts in their pattern of trade and investment.

Liberalisation policies have enhanced the economic prowess of both nations. China, moreover, as a recent member of the World Trade Organization (2001), could firmly influence global trade negotiations, possibly joining forces with India, and champion the rights of poor nations. They could establish a 'level playing field' in world trade. Indeed the combined efforts of China and India could ensure that the Uruguay Round (1986-93) to accelerate trade liberalization can be successful. They could pressurize the developed nations to fulfil their promise of opening up their markets to developing country agricultural and non agricultural exports.

Liberalisation emerged much earlier in China, in 1978, while it was initiated in India in 1991 though initial steps were taken in the 1980's. Pre-reform or pre-liberalisation forces laid the basis on which such measures were evolved. China's policies unfolded in the context of bold economic policies in the East Asia region between 1960-1990 emphasizing agricultural development, primary education, macroeconomic stability, firm public policies to support markets, and regional dynamism. China's liberalization has been embodied in market based thrusts in agriculture, industry and services, state owned enterprises, and deregulation of product prices. These have been backed by measures to induce labour mobility, and formation of Special Economic Zones.

On the domestic front, in the pre reform era in China, the savings level was high with significant capital formation (30%) and investment in infrastructure, irrigation and land development. Literacy and primary health care, too, have been impressive with virtual elimination of landlessness. It has also shed surplus labour- a move which has been inhibited in India possibly due to strong trade unions to safeguard the interest of workers. On the external front China's integration with the world economy, as mentioned earlier, has been advanced through its trade and FDI policies. This has made a significant contribution to China's growth and productivity.

India's growth rates have been relatively low in the pre-liberalisation period-4%-5% per annum compared to East Asia's 7%-8% per annum. The level of savings, too, has been lower than in China and East Asia; the levels of literacy and health care, too, have been lower, coupled with the presence of significant landlessness, and marked poverty and inequality between and within regions, sectors and socio-economic groups.

Liberalisation was initiated in India in the 1980's with a shift in attitude towards the private sector. Its momentum was increased from 1991 onwards. The high growth rate (8% per annum) in the post liberalization period and the future targets (9%-10%) are necessary but not sufficient. The structure of the economy has to be transformed. In this respect, though the % contribution of agriculture to GDP has been reduced to about 25% it still absorbs over 60% of the employed, while manufacturing and services contribute 28% and 55 % respectively to GDP. Over 62% of India's growth over 1990-2003 has been in services but it has been employment inelastic. Hence, the pace of industrialization has to be reinforced. Though poverty in India has been reduced to about 26% it is critical to widen participation by the poor in development programmes. This can ensure that high growth rates are sustained. This calls for the use of labour intensive techniques, investment in human and physical capital, and infrastructure, enhanced flexibility in labour laws, and supporting institutions to meet socio-economic goals. The state has to play an active role to fulfil such goals though market forces may guide policies. This could enable the poor to be lifted from poverty.

No doubt China has grown faster and sharply reduced the % of people below the poverty line compared to India. However, inter regional and inter group inequalities in China have increased. China and India need to persist with their integration with the international economy to sustain growth. This should encompass incorporating the poor in the process, particularly in India, and reducing regional and inter-group disparities in China. Such goals are intertwined with maintaining peace within the respective regions. This is exemplified in India by efforts to minimize conflicts with neighbouring Pakistan, curbing terrorism from within and outside the state, resolving historical border disputes between India and China, and meeting the needs of dissatisfied groups within the state. In China it is essential to respect human rights.

China-India co-operation

Enhanced economic cooperation between India and China could bolster their economic power in spite of differing positions on politics and international affairs. Thus, it emerges that the economic relationship between China and India has taken place against a backdrop of tensions.

This is exemplified by China's past political, military and economic support for Pakistan, and China's claim to Arunachal Pradesh which has been vehemently challenged by India. Leaving aside such differences China and India are seen as contributors rather than competitors to each other's development. This is welcomed by India which has adopted a 'Look East' policy to expand trade and investment links with East Asia and forge strong ties with regional institutions (eg. Association of South East Asian Nations, Asia Pacific Economic Cooperation).

The recent visit of the Chinese President Hu Jintao to Delhi (November 2006) is a significant move in initiating a platform on development, peace and stability in Asia and the world. This was underscored by the Chinese President. He perceived the relationship between China and India as being between 'old and close brothers' citing the vision of Rabindranath Tagore the Nobel Indian poet. The President's visit culminated in a pledge to double trade between the two nations to $ 40 billion by 2010. This contrasts with $ 250 million in the 1990's.

China and India have been competing for resources in Asia and Africa. China has been the winner in virtually all the sectors excepting technology. However, the two nations could devise policies to complement each other's need. Thus, India could meet China's growing appetite for raw materials (iron ore, steel and plastics) fuelling its massive manufacturing sector. China in turn could furnish manufacturing expertise and investment for Indian infrastructure. Indian critics of Chinese policies have expressed concern over the lack of transparency exemplified by their high level of subsidies. They are also anxious over the sharply increasing Indian imports from China of clothes, electronic goods and even fireworks. The Chinese have responded by highlighting India's blocking of their investments in ports and telecommunications. This has been justified by India on grounds of security. Overall, though, as the Chinese President reaffirmed, the relationship between China and India was "an opportunity and not a threat." This could pave the way for cooperation between China and India and enhance the nature and pace of globalization.

THE TRADE IMPLICATIONS OF CHINA'S EMERGENCE

China's economic development has hardly been mono-dimensional. It is not simply a creation of Western capitalists seeking to outsource labour to the lowest bidder; nor is China any longer simply a manufacturing centre of cheap plastic and simple electronic products. Chinese industry has moved rapidly up the production chain and is now producing a very large share of the world's office equipment, DVD players, digital cameras, personal computers as well as clothing and shoes and other simpler manufactured goods.

China's swift development has rerouted global supply chains forged over the last thirty years. It now runs large trade deficits with Eastern Asia while enjoying inexorably expanding trade surpluses with North America and Europe. It has become a trading nation par excellence and currently generates 70% of its national income through foreign trade. China's overall share of world trade has increased from 5% in 2000 to 10% today. (Rossi)

China is also exerting trade pressures on a range of developing and transition countries with which it is directly competing. Mexico and Turkey, for example, are losing market share in textiles to the Chinese without the kind of offsetting compensation that has proven so beneficial to much of Asia. Central and Eastern Europe now find themselves engaged in a global battle to win new investments. Hungary won important investments for basic assembly manufacturing in the mid-1990s; yet some of those plants have subsequently relocated to China. The Hungarians now recognize that in the face of serious Chinese competition, their best option is to move into ever more sophisticated production if they are to flourish in the emerging global division of labour. The net effect of China's rapid growth on the global economy has been highly positive, despite the inevitable dislocation suffered in certain sectors. Its booming economy is generating wealth worldwide. Those benefits accrue through countless channels. Yet, mercantilists and protectionists falsely argue that rising Chinese imports are invariably a bad thing and are simply sparking plant closures and job losses.

Trade economists counter that this is a misleading and partial economic interpretation of what transpires when a large country undergoes economic take-off and emerges as a major global commercial player. First of all, trading with that low cost producer invariably lowers prices for consumers as well as producers, who, as a result, are able to purchase lower cost capital goods. Price falls, in turn, check inflationary pressures in the importing economy, raise consumer welfare, and lower exporters' production costs. The resulting productivity gains help certain domestic industries win market share both domestically and internationally while rewarding workers employed in those sectors. It must also be noted that non-Chinese companies are currently generating over half of China's export earnings and 60% of import revenue. In 2000 alone, U.S corporate earnings generated in China reached $7.2 billion. (Hale and Hale) Western firms are also selling value added inputs to Chinese producers and are thus benefiting from China's place in the international division of labour. These are the winners in the game.

The losers are both the producers of import competing industries that cannot match the price/quality of imported Chinese goods and workers in those industries. Yet, those domestic import competing firms that manage to compete are likely to emerge even stronger. Most empirical work on the broad effects of expanding trade suggests that the gains of the winners in open trading systems significantly outweigh the losses of those suffering from new competition. In this process, moreover, trading countries are likely to grow more specialized in their production, leading to further productivity gains and wealth generation.

Empirical evidence tends to confirm that precisely such processes are at work in those developed and developing countries with growing trade links to China. The Economist recently estimated that if China continues to develop, and if parts of the developing world respond to its competitive challenge by adopting liberal commercial policies, the developed world could enjoy an additional 1% of growth a year, while the developing world would undergo a substantially larger rate of growth despite the dislocation which some economies would obviously undergo. (The Economist, October 2, 2004) The capacity of a single non-oil exporting developing country to have such a broad global economic impact represents an undeniable revolution in international financial and trading systems. As suggested above, it is an economic shift laden with political, diplomatic and strategic significance. Yet, in order to capture the potential gains, Western governments must ensure their economies are ever more agile and flexible. They should increase their respective capacities to shift both capital and labour into those sectors in which they are most competitive and out of those in which they are least productive.

The McKinsey Global Institute recently examined the fate of western workers who lost jobs because of firms moving production facilities to China or India. According to this study, 70% of such American workers find new work within six months, while in Germany only 40% do. This suggests that labour market rigidities can gravely complicate efforts to adapt to changing international market conditions.

China is also having a strong effect on global demand. While many casual observers see its most substantial economic impact largely in terms of its enormous exports, China is also a large and growing capital and consumer goods market. It is estimated that if current growth and income distribution were sustained until 2020, China would offer the world 100 million consumers with an average income equivalent to the current income average of Western Europe. (The Economist, October 2, 2004.) Already it has almost single-handedly revived the previously flagging economies of East Asia through high demand for a range of manufacturing inputs, high technology components and consumer goods. Australia - like a range of other commodity exporters - is enjoying a veritable economic boom thanks to burgeoning Chinese demand.

China's imports are growing at a very rapid rate - 40% in 2003 alone. Since 2001, it has accounted for one third of the increase in global import volume. China is the world's third largest importer, and in 2004 accounted for 17% of Japan's exports, 16% of the European Union's, 8.5% of the United States', 38.5% of the rest of Asia's, and 20% for the rest of the World. (Rossi) It is now Japan's leading trade partner and the second largest trade partner of the European Union behind only the United States. EU-China Trade doubled between 1999 and 2003. (Eurostat, 14/6/2004, Kihara and Takeuchi) China is also providing an important market for developing countries; 45% of China's $400 billion in annual imports comes from developing countries, and these rose by $55 billion in 2003. It is, in fact, running a significant trade deficit with the developing world. (Kharas) Some optimistic forecasts suggest that if China continues down the reform path it could be the world's largest exporter and importer within ten years.

The US trade with China deficit has reached the enormous sum of $162 billion. (Teather) Yet, imports from China do not explain the explosive growth of the US current account deficit, now at 7% of GDP and rising, partly because China has, in fact, simply replaced other suppliers to the US market. In 1988, for example, only 2% of US shoe imports came from China, while 60% came from Taiwan and South Korea. Today China has 70% of the US shoe import market, having all but displaced South Korea and Taiwan from the US market, although the Koreans and Taiwanese effectively own many of the Chinese plants selling to the United States. Many of Taiwan's electronics companies have also relocated to the Chinese mainland and are playing a pivotal role in China's electronics exports to the United States. By the end of 2003, China's deficit with Taiwan stood at $31.5 billion; $13.1 billion with South Korea; $7.6 billion with ASEAN; $5 billion with Japan; and $1.3

billion with Australia. (Hale and Hale) A similar trend can be traced in other goods markets including personal computers. While Asian countries are losing market share in the United States to China, they are being compensated by a massive increase in exports to China in higher end and more valuable products.

The Chinese economy is far more open than the Korean or Japanese economies were at similar points in their economic take-off, and the state seems to have rejected the more dirigiste model of development employed by the Japanese. China's general tariff rates have fallen precipitously from 40% in the early 1990s to 10.4% in 2004. (Beattie) It entered the WTO under highly stringent conditions that have helped to open its market even further. In 2004, exports and imports together accounted for nearly 75% of China's total GDP. This is an extraordinarily high share for such a large country, and more than double that of the United States. Part of the reason is that China's domestic non-tradable economy remains very underdeveloped.

China has also implemented exceedingly open investment rules, although foreign investors still complain about serious administrative burdens and creeping non-tariff barriers in areas like financial services and investment rules. Still, foreign investment in China accounts for some 35% of its GDP. (The Economist, October 2, 2004) It is now the world's fifth largest recipient of foreign direct investment (FDI) and is moving quickly up the list. FDI in the first ten months of 2004 reached $54 billion. These funds are fundamentally transforming China's manufacturing and transport infrastructure.

CHINA AND INDIA STRATEGIC ECONOMIC DIALOGUE (SED): PROGRESS AND PROGNOSIS

India-China Strategic Economic Dialogue (SED) an institutionalized and established process now? The third round of the SED was held in Beijing from 17-18 March 2014, in which the two sides discussed at length issues concerning international, bilateral and domestic economic conditions and deliberated on how to expand their bilateral and international cooperation. They discussed firming coordination in BRICS, G-20, UN, enhancing cooperation in trade, investment and economic fields, and forging greater cooperation among the key industries between the two countries. While some of the sentiments expressed in this round are genuine and generate a new level of India-China interactions, it needs to be seen where and how exactly this interaction can go forward. This round was conducted with the assistance of five Working Group mechanisms, namely, policy coordination; infrastructure; resource conservation and environmental protection; hi-technology; and energy. The Working Group mechanism has been key for progress and institutionalization of the SED. In May 2013 five Chinese Working Groups visited India and in September 2013 five Indian Working Groups visited China to prepare the ground for the third SED.

This essay analyses the significance of SED in India-China engagement. Besides this introductory section, it comprises four sections: *first*, it reviews the importance of SED; *second*, it delves into the areas of convergence and divergence; *third*, it explains how China's current economic and financial pre-eminence has overlooked addressing India's bilateral concerns, which creates unevenness in the SED. The essay concludes with the caveat that while the scope of the SED is relatively high today because of constant institutional engagement, it will remain limited unless the fundamental bilateral economic issues are addressed.

The SED Mechanism So Far

Usually held between the counterpart planning commissions of the two countries – the Planning Commission of India and the National Development and Reform Commission (NDRC) of China – SED is gradually becoming a mechanism of import. India and China are not only big economic powers, being the third and second largest global economies, but the panoply of their engagement has been upgraded to a new level of global and autonomous standing today. This is important when world politics has become more multipolar in nature and the two countries are engaged with each other in a range of bilateral, regional, cross-regional and global multilateral forums.

A range of dialogue mechanisms exists in India-China interactions, both at the official and non-official levels and at the political and non-political levels. The SED was first mooted in December 2010 when Premier Wen Jiabao visited India. Beijing hosted the first SED round on 26 September 2011 and New Delhi hosted the second round on 26 November 2012. The rise of emerging economies within Brazil-Russia-India-China-South Africa (BRICS) forum furthers the importance of the SED. The first SED round was led by Zhang Ping, the then Chairman of NDRC, and Montek Singh Ahluwalia, Deputy Chairman of India's Planning Commission. Some of the issues covered were the global economic condition and the macroeconomic situation at the domestic level; mid- and long-term developmental plans; energy efficiency, conservation & environmental protection; infrastructural cooperation; water use efficiency; and use of clean water technologies. The second round reiterated that the primary aim of this dialogue mechanism was to "improve macroeconomic policy coordination" between two economies. It emphasized global economic cooperation, enhancing mutual communication on macroeconomic policies, expanding trade and investment, and expanding cooperation in financial and infrastructural sectors.

It had been agreed to hold the third round in 2013, but the event was postponed. The tensions arising out of People's Liberation Army's (PLA) incursion in Ladakh in the India-China border region and Xi Jinping and Li Keqiang's assumption of power in China as new leaders may have been the reasons for this postponement. Nevertheless, the importance of SED was reiterated during the new Premier's visit to India, stressing its active role in promoting "macroeconomic policy coordination" and "pragmatic cooperation" in various fields. The two sides agreed to strengthen cooperation in issues concerning energy, environment, new and renewable energy and high technology cooperation. They also agreed to enhance collaboration in the railway sector, noted the vitality of the Doha Development Round, expressed their intention for a bilateral Regional Trade Arrangement and reviewed the state of Regional Comprehensive Economic Partnership (RCEP) negotiations. In the third SED, for cooperation in railways, three specific areas have been chosen: station development, raising the speed of passenger trains in India and for heavy haul freight. China will assist India in improving its railway tracks to enable faster movement. Besides, China is supposed to construct high-speed tracks in three sectors – Delhi-Agra, Delhi-Kanpur and Delhi-Chandigarh.

A number of factors explain the importance of SED interaction. *First*, both countries participate in various regional and global multilateral institutions and frameworks such as Russia-India-China (RIC), BRICS, BASIC and G-20. *Second*, they share a common interest in preventing protectionism in the multilateral trading system. They also share similar sentiments about reforming global financial institutions like the IMF, WTO and World Bank. Their interactions and deliberations are important not only for their individual stakes in these bodies but also for the rest of the developing world, such as improving voting rights. SED is an appropriate forum for this. *Third*, macroeconomic issues need joint deliberations, but bilateral consensus should be there in the first instance. As developing countries and two fastest emerging economies of the world, much of the global economic sustainability heavily depends upon both China and India. SED creates conditions for them to coordinate in regional and global economic dealings.

Need for Serious Global and Regional Prognosis

India and China have several dialogue mechanisms besides SED, such as India-China Financial Dialogue, India-China Defence and Security Dialogue, India-China Strategic Dialogue, and India-China Joint Economic Group (JEG) etc. On 20 August 2013, the fifth round of the India-China Strategic Dialogue was held in New Delhi. Bilateral issues like utilization of trans-border river waters, enhancing trade and investment contacts and trade imbalance and global issues such as the Bangladesh-China-India-Myanmar (BCIM) economic corridor project, possible cooperation under BRICS, emerging politics in Asia-Pacific and post-2014 Afghanistan politics were matters of discussion. In 2014, in the sixth round of India-China Defence and Security in New Delhi, the two sides discussed bilateral, regional and global security issues of strategic substance and of mutual concern, involving security conditions in South Asia, Asia-Pacific and the Indian Ocean. The two sides have also conducted six rounds of financial dialogue regarding multilateral cooperation in bodies like G 20 and Asian Development Bank (ADB). The three key issues in the dialogue have been infrastructural investments, sustaining Asia's economic growth conditions and establishing closer coordination between developed and developing economies to address the global economic situation. While most of these mechanisms overlap each other, there is no denying that India-China interaction today is more methodological: these mechanisms involve stronger global, regional cross-continental and bilateral dealings in a range of economic, security and strategic issues.

As regards the SED, this dialogue mechanism requires particular focus on two aspects: *economic multilateralism* that is linked to various geo-political issues, and *political multilateralism* that is linked with geo-economics. Greater cooperation in global financial bodies such as the IMF, WTO and the World Bank is one aspect that needs careful discussion in SED in the future. The principal outlook on forging a common perspective on "developing country" and "emerging economies" phenomenon needs serious debate, at least from India's perspective. China today is a leading country in many global financial institutions and has also emerged as a big donor in a number of international agencies. India needs to be assured by China that the "developing country" formula will continue to be common to both countries in terms of vision and strategy in the coming times. Currently, there is a question mark on this aspect, considering that the new Chinese leadership is pushing forward the idea of a "new type of major power relations", promoting China's status as a power equivalent to the USA. This is being promoted concurrently with the strong US-China Strategic and Economic Dialogue (SE&D). The India-China SED needs to discuss seriously the issue of reforming the global financial bodies. Both countries have for long advocated their reform, but common and decisive joint perspective is still missing. Besides, a solid understanding between the two is required for improving voting rights and quota in the IMF. Despite being the second and third largest economies in world ranking, their voting rights and quotas are far from impressive. Climate governance is another important issue that SED could discuss seriously in future. Climate change is not simply an issue of governance today but a macroeconomic issue that involves economic and political multilateralism. In the BASIC (Brazil-South Africa-India-China) climate grouping, the two sides have viewed climate change as a "threat and challenge" to humanity and to the goal of sustainable development. Greater deliberation is needed between the two on how to address "sustainable development" that is linked to "poverty eradication" in both India and China. Greater consensus is also needed on sustainable development where the two countries must take a lead along with other BASIC and BRICS members on the COP18/CMP8 on Doha principles, which is to be concluded by 2015. Further, working group on environment in SED must delve into where and how the two countries can cooperate in line with Rio principles of sustainable development.

Cooperation on financing projects and obtaining loans from various international banks also needs discussion and closer understanding between the two. Mr. Saumitra Chaudhuri, Member of India's Planning Commission, raised this issue during the third SED round, stating that greater cooperation is needed in multilateral forums like G-20 and ADB. The matter of the ADB is particularly significant here. In 2009, China's foreign ministry opposed strongly India's loan application in the ADB for infrastructure development in its state of Arunachal Pradesh in terms of the "Country

Partnership Strategy for India (2009-2012)". Qin Gang, the then foreign ministry spokesperson of China, expressing strong objection over the issue, stated that 'ADB as a regional development agency must not interfere in political affairs of its members'. China has enormous clout in the ADB: by 2009, it was the third largest donor to it after the USA and Japan. It has been five years after this issue raised its head, but no India-China dialogue mechanism has addressed it, including SED. It needs to be stressed that the SED mechanism loses much of its significance if it cannot de-link the security aspects from the economic aspects. The SED is the most appropriate forum to discuss this issue of ADB as it has two working mechanisms: *policy coordination* and *infrastructure*. Prime Minister Manmohan Singh in his speech on India-China relations at the Central Party School in Beijing (24 October 2013) stressed the issue, saying, "... we need to pay much greater attention to the expansion and modernization of our infrastructure. India plans to invest one trillion U.S. dollars in infrastructure in the next five years and we would welcome China's expertise and investment in this sector". The concern on both sides is on how to facilitate flow of investment from China in the Indian market and vice-versa.

The BRICS Development Bank, on which BRICS members have failed to build consensus so far despite several rounds of deliberations, is another issue that needs serious deliberation in the SED. The onus is on India and China primarily because these two are the largest economies in BRICS.

Currently, there seems to be contention regarding the location of the bank's headquarters, type of projects that this bank will finance and its source of funding. BRICS Development Bank is an idea that is linked to North-South politics, whether it will act as a plausible alternative to the Bretton Woods institutions. China, it appears, wants to hog the scenario, to have headquarters of this bank in a Chinese city, probably Shanghai. China also has a disproportionate number of billionaires, prompting it to demand a big slice of the cake in the bank. India is somewhat cagey about this possible development. Security and strategic issues need serious deliberation in SED too, especially because these issues involve economic and strategic nuances. Maritime security, China's recent "maritime Silk Road" proposal, security situation in Afghanistan, terrorism, and the geo-political implications of the recent Ukraine crisis need serious discussion in SED.

As regards China's invitation to others to join in the "maritime Silk Road" programme, before India decides to accept the offer, it is crucial to discuss in clear-cut terms Beijing's perspective on India's initiative for oil exploration in the South China Sea with the Southeast Asian countries, which China has so far opposed. SED must discuss and review the regional economic nuances that are attached to various issues that have arisen in the current international scenario that affect the region vitally.

It also needs to discuss issues such as revitalizing the Russia-India-China (RIC) forum and the RCEP. China also needs to reconsider its current opposition to India's partaking in the ASEAN+6 mechanism when it comes to the issue of regional economic integration in East Asia. A greater level of dialogue in the SED on RCEP and its negotiation process will help them to proceed much faster in terms of a possible future free trade agreement (FTA) between themselves.

Bilateral Concerns

Addressing macroeconomic issues and forging a stronger understanding in regional and global outlook can be attended better if bilateral economic grievances can be addressed easily. Trade imbalance, which in the last few years has widened in favour of China, is for India a disquieting issue.

India has regularly sought to convince China particularly to open its domestic markets in areas like Information Technology (IT), pharmaceuticals and engineering products. The Joint Economic Group (JEG) dialogue mechanism is supposed to address this issue and the SED is supposed to look after macro issues in India-China economic engagements.

This, however, creates a doubtful atmosphere for the progress of the SED. It is necessary to discuss the trade imbalance issue in SED as most of the India-China economic dealings today carry both strategic and economic ingredients. The two countries have set a target of $100 billion trade target by the year 2015, but their bilateral trade has declined in the last couple of years, from US$74 billion in 2011 to $66 billion. During the third SED, India also raised the issue of mutual investment flows to address to some extent the trade imbalance between the two countries.

Border trade is another matter that can be discussed in future India-China SED interactions.

The two countries are linked in the BCIM economic corridor project. Enhancing trade, transit and investment linkages are important aspects of the BCIM agenda. *Xinhua* reported in December 2013 that there was a sharp rise in India-China border trade in Renqinggang, which is located in Southwest China's Tibet Autonomous Region (TAR), that the trade figures there reached 86.3 million Yuan (approximately $14.3 million), a 23.3 per cent rise over the previous year. To what extent the declining value of the Indian Rupee has contributed to this rise in the border trade is not known.

These questions need serious deliberations in the SED, as these issues have strategic and economic nuances that involve greater India-China sub-regional dealings and cross-border engagements.

Summing Up

The three rounds of SED have, no doubt, built a strong momentum in the India-China institutional engagement, but the challenge is how to upgrade the level of dialogue, bring maturity to the interaction and make it a distinct and regular affair without making it just another talk shop. China has a similar dialogue mechanism with the USA. Initially started as US-China Strategic Economic Dialogue (SED), now a special "strategic track" and "economic track" has been added to this and it is known as US-

China Strategic and Economic Dialogue (SE&D). The India-China SED has not really matured as a trusted bilateral mechanism to discuss the regional and global complexities of economic and strategic substance yet. Attempts need to be made to make it much more regular and systematic and to encompass issues for open discussion of not only India-China regional and global relations but also their foreign policy objectives.

China currently has strategic dialogue mechanisms with many countries and regions, such as with the African Union (AU), European Union (EU), and with ASEAN at the think-tanks level, but the US is the only other country with which China has a SED dialogue. New Delhi needs to make a special note of this seriousness on Beijing's part where China is concerned. There is no dearth of issues that the SED can address, but the success of the mechanism will depend upon how openly and candidly the two countries discuss them. The next SED round is supposed to be held in 2015 in India. New Delhi will by then have a new government in place. For India, the challenge is not only how to give new momentum to this mechanism but also how to persuade the Chinese to address the trade deficit issue.

SINO-INDIAN CONVERGENCE: BILA TERAL AND GLOBAL

Bilateral relations between India and the People's Republic of China (PRC) have indeed come a long way after they touched their nadir in the immediate aftermath of India's nuclear tests in May 1998. China had been singled out as the "number one" security threat for India by India's Defence Minister just before the nuclear tests. After the tests, the Indian Prime Minister wrote to the US President justifying Indian nuclear tests as a response to the threat posed by China. Unsurprisingly, China reacted strongly and diplomatic relations between the two countries plummeted to an all time low.

However, some six years later, the relations between the two countries seem to be on an upswing. The visit of the Indian External

Affairs Minister to China in 1999 marked the resumption of high-level dialogue and the two sides declared that they were not threats to each other. A bilateral security dialogue was also initiated that has helped the two countries in openly expressing and sharing their security concerns with each other. India and China also decided to expedite the process of demarcation of the Line of Actual Control (LAC) and the Joint Working Group (JWG) on the boundary question, set up in 1988, has been meeting regularly. As a first step in this direction, the two countries exchanged border maps on the least controversial middle sector of the LAC.

The Indian Prime Minister visited China in June 2003, the first such visit in a decade. The joint declaration signed during the visit stated that China was not a threat to India. The two states appointed special representatives in order to impart momentum to border negotiations that have lasted twenty two years, with the Prime Minister's principal secretary becoming India's political-level negotiator, replacing the India-China JWG. India and China also decided to hold their first joint naval exercise later in the year and discussions on joint air exercise continue. India also acknowledged China's sovereignty over Tibet and pledged not to allow "anti-China" political activities in India. On its part, China has acknowledged India's 1975 annexation of the former monarchy of Sikkim by agreeing to open a trading post along the border with the former kingdom and later rectified official maps to include Sikkim as part of India.

India and China have found substantial convergence of interests at the international level. Both share similar concerns about the growing international dominance of the US, the threat of terrorism disguised as religious and ethnic movements and the need to accord primacy to economic development. India and China have both expressed concern about the US' use of military power around the world and publicly opposed the war in Iraq. This was merely a continuation of the desire of both states to oppose the US *hyperpuissance* ever since the end of the Cold War. Like other major powers in the international system, India and China favour a multi-polar world order where US unipolarity remains constrained by the other "poles" in the system. China and India zealously guard their national sovereignty and have been wary of US attempts to interfere in what they see as domestic affairs of other stares, be it Serbia, Kosovo or Iraq. Both took strong exception to the US air strikes on Iraq in 1998, the US-led air campaign against Yugoslavia in 1999, and more recently the US campaign against Saddam Hussein arguing that these violated the national sovereignty and undermined the authority of the United Nations system. Both nations also favour more democratic international economic regimes. They have strongly resisted efforts by the US and other developed nations to link global trade to labour and environmental standards, realizing clearly that this would put them at a huge disadvantage vis-a-vis the developed world, thereby hampering their drive towards economic development, a top priority. Both have committed themselves to crafting joint Sino-Indian positions in the World Trade Organization (WTO) and global trade negotiations in the hope that this might provide them greater negotiating leverage over the developed states. They would like to see further liberalization of agricultural trade in the developed countries, tightening of the rules on anti-dumping measures and ensuring that non-trade related issues such as labour and environment are not allowed to come to the WTO.

In recent years, India and China have attempted to build their bilateral relationship on the basis of their larger worldview of international politics. As they have found a distinct convergence of their interests on world stage, they have used it to strengthen their bilateral relations. They have established and maintained regular reciprocal high-level visits between political leaders. There has been a sincere attempt to improve trade relations and to compartmentalize intractable issues that make it difficult for their bilateral relationship to move forward.

India and China have strengthened their bilateral relationship in areas as distinct as cultural and educational exchanges, military exchanges, and science and technology cooperation. Bilateral trade has recorded rapid growth from a trade volume of US $265 million in 1991 to US $3596 million in 2001.

In 2001, bilateral trade saw an increase of 23.4 percent over 2000. It is expected to rise to $10 billion this year. The two nations are even evaluating the possibility of signing a comprehensive economic cooperation agreement and a free trade agreement by the end of this year, thereby building on strong complementarities between the two. Both states are also taking steps to upgrade their military-related cooperation, leading to greater understanding on the bilateral military front, something that would have been unthinkable just a few years ago. As a first step in this direction, the Chinese and Indian navies carried out joint search and rescue operations off the Shanghai coast in November 2003. Both states are also seeking to cooperate on the nuclear front with China planning to import heavy water from India to be utilized in the pressurized heavy water reactors near Shanghai. Many observers have also pointed out a subtle shift in Beijing's stance on Pakistan vis-a-vis India. China's "neutral" position during the Kargil conflict and the intense Indo-Pak crisis following the terrorist attack on the India's Parliament is seen by many as a reflection of China's sincerity in its attempts to improve ties. In keeping with China's attempts to project itself as a responsible regional player, China is seen by some as supporting peace and anti-terrorist efforts in South Asia by cooperating with the US and India. China is also seen as playing a central role in encouraging Pakistan to negotiate with India by using its leverage over Pakistan. After assuming office Prime Minister Manmohan Singh's government made it clear that it favoured closer ties with China and would continue to work towards improving bilateral relations with China. In his first address to the nation, the Prime Minister, Manmohan Singh, also emphasized the carrying forward of the process of further development and diversification of Sino-Indian relations. The late J.N. Dixit, National Security Advisor in the current government, wrote that "the Congress will continue the process of normalizing, strengthening and expanding India's relations with China, which is the most important factor affecting Asian security and stability". One of the first foreign visits of the new Indian foreign minister, Natwar Singh, was to China to attend the Asia Cooperation Dialogue in Qingdao, in East China's Shandong province and apparently had "substantive discussions" with his Chinese counterpart.

All this reflects on India continuing to build its relations with China on the convergence of interests that the two nations have achieved in recent years. Aside from the positive developments, one should not ignore the enormous obstacles that confront this bilateral relationship. There has been a dominant tendency in the Indian foreign policy establishment to focus on the strengths of its bilateral relations with China while pretending that problems confronting the relationship would somehow take care of themselves. The challenges in the Sino-Indian relationship are by no means insignificant nor will China take care of Indian interests. It is for India to recognize them for what they are and evolve a coherent strategy to tackle them.

GROWTH OF CHINA AND INDIA AND ITS INFLUENCE ON THE WORLD ECONOMY

Indicators of the Extent of Integration in World Markets for Goods and Services

An overall indicator of integration is the extent of international trade in the domestic economy as measured by the share of exports and imports in GDP and in the global economy as measured by the share of a country's exports and imports in global exports and imports.

Thus with twice as much or more share of exports and imports in GDP, more than seven times (five times) the share in World merchandise exports (imports), China is better positioned in 2004 for influencing (and also being influenced) by growth of the World economy. Interestingly, during the period 1990-2003 while the share of exports and imports in India's GDP almost doubled, the increase in share in its World merchandise exports, proportionately, was far less. Thanks to its success in the IT service sector, India's share in World exports of commercial services tripled during the same period. It would seem that in India's case, with the possible exception of services the effect of greater integration is largely one-way and domestic, in the sense of its raising the rate of GDP growth and the share of trade in domestic GDP, rather than India's more rapid GDP growth influencing global GDP growth significantly.

Shares of China and India in Global GDP and its Growth

The measures of integration in effect proxy the potential for the growth of China and India to contribute to growth in the World Economy - put another way, if these measures were zero, so that China and India were autarkic, then obviously their growth would have no effect on the growth of the other countries of the World. But on the other hand, even if positive, the measures do not necessarily imply that the growth of the two countries had or would have, significant impact on global GDP growth or on the growth of low and middle income countries (or alternatively to the growth of developing Asia). World Bank data, quantifies the impact in an accounting (not to be confused with causal) sense. Jorgenson and Vu (2005) who use purchasing power parity based exchange rates.

For purchasing power parities makes a substantial difference to the shares of the two countries in global GDP and growth. Still the two tables agree on the following:

i. The shares of the two countries (GDP levels and growth) have been increasing over time, although more so in the case of China than India. The two together accounted for more than a sixth of global growth during 1990-2003, and as high as a third during 1985-2003 once adjustment for PPP is made.

ii. The relative share of China's growth in global growth compared to India's increased from around 2.0 in 1980-90 to 3.8 in 1990-2003. Interestingly, when adjustment is made for PPP, the relative share of China decreased from about 3.0 to 2.1. This suggests that relative to India, prices in China seem to be moving closer over time to world prices, confirming once again the findings of China is integrating with the World economy faster than India. The revised GDP data for China, which raise growth rates over 1993-04 compared to old data and also show that China was poised to become the World's 6 largest economy in US$ terms strengthen this conclusion.

iii. Unsurprisingly, these two large developing economies account for a large share of GDP and growth of low and middle income countries and of developing Asia.

The IMF (2005) recognizes that policy makers in India are actively seeking to strengthen India's global linkages and to accelerate its integration with the World economy. Success in these efforts would increase the role of India in the World economy. The report explicitly refers to one of the mechanisms, India's import demand, through which this would come about. To wit,

A dynamic and open Indian economy would have an important impact on the world economy. If India continues to embrace globalization and reform, Indian imports could increasingly operate as a driver of global growth as it is one of a handful of economies forecast to have a growing working-age population over the next 40 years. Some 75-110 million will enter the labour force in the next decade, which should-provided these entrants are employed - fuel an increase in savings and investment given the higher propensity for workers to save.

SOURCES AND SUSTAINABILITY OF GROWTH

Factor Accumulation

China is already well integrated with the World economy. Indeed the share of international trade (exports and imports of good and services) in its GDP at 66% is very high for an economy of China's continental size and level of per capita income. It would be surprising indeed if the share will rise to much higher levels in the future. In China the share in population of persons in the working age (15-64), already at 65.7% in 2003, will not rise by much, if at all, and is more likely to fall in the coming decades. This reflects the effects of the draconian and coercive one-child policy instituted in 1979 and also the decline in fertility in the decade before. The dependency ratio will rise, if not in the next couple of decades, certainly soon thereafter. Its savings and investment rates at 47% and 44% of GDP respectively are also unlikely to be sustained indefinitely. These two facts suggest that from the input (labour and capital) side there will be a downward pressure on China's growth. On the other hand, as Perkins (2005) notes, China still has a large proportion of people of working age employed in agriculture and rural activities, with lower productivity than non-farm workers. He estimates that China's non-farm workforce could increase by another 70 to 100 million in the next decade depending on assumptions about expansion of senior secondary and university education. Thus, productivity gains from the intersectoral shift of labour as well as other changes that increase total factor productivity including technological improvement, could more than offset the downward pressure on growth so that aggregate GDP growth could be sustained in the ranges of 8% to 10% a year for the next couple of decades.

In India's case, demographic trends are more favorable than China's. It is true that some of the Indian states (mainly in the South but also in the West) have achieved fertility rates at or below replacement level (without the use of an abhorrent and coercive one-child policy as in China) and hence will soon experience an increasing old-age dependency ratio as in China. However in the rest, which account for more than half of India's population, fertility rates, though declining, are above replacement. Hence, India's population of working age will rise as a share of total population in the medium term. India lags behind China in the educational attainment of its workforce and hence its catch-up with China on human capital accumulation will also contribute to growth.

Moreover, with a much larger share of the workforce employed in agriculture and other low productivity activities, India has greater potential than China to experience significant productivity gains from intersectoral shift of labour. Also India's saving and investment rates around 30% in 2004-05 are likely to increase further for life-cycle as well as other reasons. In brief, India can sustain, and in fact increase, the contribution of accumulation of human and physical capital in its growth.

The GDP weighted average of the rates of gross capital formation in 1990 and 2003 were respectively 42% and 24% of GDP in China and India. Their growth rates of GDP during 1990-03 were respectively 9.6% and 5.9% in China and India (World Bank, 2005, Tables 4.1 and 4.9). China thus invested 18% more of its GDP than India, but its growth rate exceeded India's only by 2.7% per year. This implies that China's incremental capital-output ratio as measured by the ratio of differences in investment rate to the difference in growth rate i.e. $18/2.7 = 6.7$ was substantially higher than India's. Revisions of China's and India's GDP data are unlikely to change this ratio much. Although, prima facie this would lead one to conclude that China is using capital far more inefficiently, two facts suggest such a conclusion may be too facile. First, the composition of China's GDP with its far higher share of more capital intensive industry (manufacturing) at 52% (39%) compared to India's 27% (16%), and lower share of less capital intensive services at 33% compared to 51%, and second, China seems to have invested more in capital intensive infrastructure including housing. Indeed, services have been the driving force behind India's recent growth. There is some recent evidence that growth of India's manufacturing sector is accelerating. If sustained, and if growth in services (and agriculture) does not slacken, aggregate growth rate will rise.

Growth in Total Factor Productivity

It is conventional wisdom, dating back to the analysis of components of the then rapid growth in the Soviet Union in the fifties, that growth, if it depends largely on factor accumulation, is unlikely to be sustainable since factor accumulation cannot continue forever. On the other hand, growth that is driven largely by total factor productivity (TFP) growth can. There is some evidence to suggest that China may be unable to sustain its investment in physical capital and its labour force growth. It is therefore of interest to look at available evidence on TFP growth.

As is well known, TFP growth estimates are highly sensitive to the data used and above all to the methodology of estimation. Extreme caution is called for in interpreting them and using them for policy analysis. With this caveat, let me refer to available TFP growth estimates, based on different methodologies, data series and time periods for China and India. I will be selective in reporting only some, but not all, available estimates. Jorgenson and Vu (2005) focus on the possible impact on growth of the information and communication technology (ICT) revolution, by breaking up capital into ICT and non-ICT capital. They also account for human capital accumulation by distinguishing between growth in labour hours and labour quality.

A significant part of FDI inflows to China are from the Chinese Diaspora (including residents of Hong Kong and Taiwan) in contrast to India. Also, China's policy of creating special economic zones (SEZs) to attract foreign investment by exempting investors from regulations applicable elsewhere in China (particularly relating to hiring and firing and foreign ownership) and also providing excellent infrastructure (power and communications) was highly successful. India is only now creating SEZs like China's. But limits to foreign ownership apply to different entrants in different sectors and restrictive labour laws continue. Lastly, China's FDI was export oriented and also directed in part to investment in infrastructure. Given the significantly larger shares compared to India's of private capital flows in China's GDP and investment and its tilt towards exports and growth promoting infrastructure, it is clear that greater integration of China in world capital flows contributed to its faster growth and at the same time, their export orientation increased integration in goods markets as well.

To sum up the discussion of this section: taking together the likely evolution of factor accumulation and total factor productivity in the medium term, it is very likely that China would be able to sustain its average growth in the range of 8% - 10% per year. India would be able to raise its growth from around 6% of the last two and a half decades to 8% or more. China's integration with the world economy is already high. India's integration will continue to increase so that it will play a larger role in influencing the growth of the world economy than in has done until now. Also, China's policies towards external private capital flows were successful in attracting substantial flows and their use in export oriented and infrastructural activities not only contributed to growth but also increased China's integration in goods markets. This trend is likely to continue in the medium term. India is only now instituting Chinese- like policies towards capital inflows and their impact is as yet uncertain. But based on evidence from surveys of investor intentions there are reasons to be hopeful.

Let me now turn to the likely impact of greater integration of India and China with the world economy from a disaggregated perspective.

A DISAGGREGATED PERSPECTIVE

The rapid income growth in China and India, ceteris paribus, will obviously increase demand for goods and services for final and intermediate use. Part of this increase in demand will be met by imports. It is likely that increase in demand would be matched in part by increase in domestic and foreign supply and in part by increases in relative prices. The increase in supplies would itself be a response to price increases and also any induced technical changes and search for alternative sources of supply. Obviously without building and estimating a well specified, disaggregated, dynamic, multi-country global model in which policy variables are also represented, it is impossible to make projections of increases in demand, supply and their equilibrium price consequences. This understood, I will explore how export supplies currently match global import demand. This will at least given an indication of where the pressures on demand and supply are likely to emerge with global economic growth, and indirectly, the implications of rapid growth of China and India.

Several interesting facts emerge. First, China has emerged as a major exporter of manufacturers since 1990 with a global share of 8.3% in 2004. India is not yet a major exporter to the world. Within manufacturing, China has a significant share of world markets for iron and steel, office machines and telecommunications equipment and, not surprisingly, in textiles and clothing. Except for textiles and clothing, where India's share has grown modestly to 4.0% and 2.9% of global exports and less so to 1.6% in iron and steel exports, India's shares are very small and not growing. Let me now turn to a few specific industries.

Textiles and Clothing

It is well known that as quotas under the Mutifibre Arrangement (MFA) were being phased out from 1995, China took advantage of the elimination of quota markets in the USA and the EU markets and rapidly increased its share in the two markets. After the MFA was completely phased out (in fact, in anticipation of it) on January 1, 2006, Chinese exports in both markets increased rapidly leading to what is in effect, a return to the bad old bilateral quotas of MFA! India did not, and in fact could not, take full advantage of the gradual phase-out because of domestic constraints, including in particular, the reservation of garments for production by small scale enterprises (the reservation was lifted only three years ago) and restriction on textile imports. In the post MFA scenario, given appropriate policy changes, India could do better and indeed gain global market shares, although perhaps not as much as China.

A study by Nordas (2004) suggested that China and India could capture 29% and 9%, respectively, of the EU markets and

50% and 15%, respectively, of the US market. However, the simulations of Ananthakrishnan and Jain-Chandra (2005) of the effects of MFA quota elimination using an applied general equilibrium model of the Global Trade Analysis Project (GTAP Version 6), and taking into account the current safeguard restrictions of China's exports to US and EU, are not optimistic for India. While India's exports will grow, with the expiration of safeguards on Chinese exports in 2008, growth will decline. Largely because of adverse terms of trade change (i.e. falling export prices due to competition) the welfare effect of the expiration of MFA is negative for India, with the welfare loss being smaller, with safeguards on China in place. The authors note the initiation of domestic reforms in Indian textile and apparel industry in 2004 and expect their beneficial effects to emerge after a lag. They end their paper with the banal note, "India could emerge much stronger and expand its trade in textiles and apparel at a much faster pace if some of the key weaknesses are overcome" (p29)!

In an interesting review of the role of price and cost comparativeness in apparel exports in the first MFA scenario, Tewari (2005) takes note of these detailed studies of the Indian situation and concluded that with, the removal of impediments such as the high cost of imports like energy, dyes and chemicals, and by raising the scale of production and improving productivity (particularly of labour), India can compete with China. She points out, as the authors of the studies she surveyed themselves recognized, the limitation that their studies partly neglect the fundamental ways in which the structure of apparel production sourcing and trade have changed in recent years. She concludes that in the new environment, ample opportunities still exist for building lasting competitive advantage based on creativity in production, skill formation, technological innovation in marketing and distribution, and the creation of supporting institutions to help firms and workers adapt continually to volatile markets. This is a tall agenda that in principle is relevant for other industries besides textiles and apparel. However the benefits from and costs of its implementation are unknown. In any case it is not clear whether India is capable of implementing it.

Automobiles and Parts

Both China and India have tripled their share of global auto parts market between 1990 and 2004, though the shares are still small in both countries, and much smaller in India than in China. However, there are reasons to believe that both can emerge as significant players in the global market. There were only three private firms producing passenger cars in India and their capacity was heavily constrained by the government through licensing until the early eighties when a new public sector firm with Suzuki motors as collaborator was allowed entry into the market. It began a transformation of not only of India's passenger car components but also the entire auto industry including its auto parts component. As IMF's Rughuram Rajan noted, once entry barriers against foreign producers were removed and capacity licensing doubled with the reforms of 1991, not only foreign producers entered the market, but soon found out that it did not make sense for them:

... to continue sourcing their sub assemblies from outside India. Instead, they started developing local ancillary manufacturers, and gave them the technological assistance for them to become world-class. Soon India started exporting ancillary automotive products to the developed world.

The story does not end here. Telco [a domestic enterprise], capitalizing on the existence of world-class suppliers of ancillaries in India, started producing a state-of-the-art, indigenously-designed car, the Indica. The car had teething problems at first and was rejected by a now-discriminating public. But Telco engineers went back to the drawing board, fixed the flaws, and brought out a new version that swept the market in its category. From about 50,000 cars in the early 1980s, India produced over 1,200,000 in 2004, and exported 160,000 cars, many to the developed world..

Sutton (2005) examined the extent to which Chinese and Indian auto component producers have advanced towards international best practice levels of productivity and quality through a survey of nine car manufacturers in China and six in India and a range of general component suppliers in both countries with detailed bench-marking of six seat producers and six exhaust suppliers in each country. The main finding of the study is that "the development of the auto industry supply chain in both China and India has proceeded very rapidly at the level of car makers and their first-tier suppliers: here current standards of supplier quality are at, or close to, world standards. The main weakness of the supply chain lies in the fact that best practice techniques are permeating down to second tier suppliers in a very slow and uneven manner. The similarity in the pattern across both countries is striking" (Sutton, 2005, Executive Summary). It found also that "While the development of the local supply chain in both countries has in large part been driven by the presence of multinational car makers, component exports are driven equally by multinational and domestic firms. Both India and China have a substantial body of purely domestic firms that have achieved major successes in export markets; of the top ten component exporters in China, six are domestic firms; of India's top 10, half are domestic firms (and three of these belong to a single domestic industrial group" (ibid). It would seem that the prospects for both China and India to play a major role in the evolution of global auto and parts market are bright. This will intensify the competitive pressure on established auto (particularly auto parts) firms in industrial countries. This is already evident from the bankruptcy of the component makers Delphi in the US. Apparently, the Indian government has come to recognize the growth potential of the automobile industry. According to a report in The Hindu of March 11, 2006, the Finance Minister P. Chidambaram said that "We will become a global manufacturing hub for small cars in the next 3 to 5 years... we will emulate this success story in other sectors to be among the top global manufacturing centres".

It has been argued that in India employment elasticity of GDP growth in general and manufacturing in particular is low and falling (PC, 2002), which in turn implies that growth rates of output would have to be very high for demand for labour to grow significantly. Further if the source of such high output growth are to be either domestic demand or export demand, are high growth rates of either or both likely? I would argue that the employment elasticity and inferences based on it have no analytical foundations. Elementary economics would suggest that the observed employment in any period represents an equilibrium between labour supply and labour demand. In principle, both supply and demand functions could shift over time. For example, GDP growth, ceteris paribus, would shift the labour demand function outward. Similarly, growth of the number of individuals in the prime working ages due to population growth, ceteris paribus, shift the supply curve outward. Depending on the relative strengths of these shifts almost any trend (up, down or no change) in equilibrium employment is possible. In other words, the so-called "employment elasticity" is not a deep behavioral parameter and can take on any number, positive or negative. It is what econometricians would deem a "reduced form" rather than a "structural parameter".

Even if one were to treat the elasticity as economically meaningful, there is no reason to assume its past low value will prevail in the future as well. In fact, three are reasons to suggest that the elasticity will rise. First, there is evidence the rural demand for manufactured products, particularly consumer goods (durable and non-durable), has begun to grow rapidly. Second, with enabling reforms, such as elimination of reservation products for exclusive production by small scale industries, improvements in infrastructure (power, transportation and ports) India could increase its low share of exports of labour intensive manufactures as China has done. Indeed, if India were to move quickly to let FDI into retailing, not only domestic demand for various manufacture products will rise, so will export demand. There is no reason to be unduly pessimistic about growth in demand.

India's Parliament approved legislation in 2005 for establishing special economic zones (SEZs). Export processing zones established in the past had not been very successful. The creation of the SEZs was inspired by the success of similar zones in China, particularly in attacting FDI. However, some of the crucial features of China's zones, such as allowing 100% foreign ownership, freedom of enterprise managers to hire and fire workers as they see fit for due cause, and the provision of excellent transport and communications infrastructure, are missing in India's zones. There are still sectoral caps for FDI. Exemption from draconian labour laws (a state subject under India's constitution) has been left to the states. Although efficient infrastructure has been promised it remains to be seen whether it will be delivered. I would argue that the only rationale for setting up such zones would be that political and administrative constraints prevent turning the entire country into such a zone in one fell swoop. If that is indeed the case, while establishing such zones, a policy of extending them to cover the entire country soon has to be announced at the same time. This has not been done. While I do not expect the zones to be spectacularly successful, I do expect some modest success, particularly in attracting FDI to emerging manufactured exports and exports of IT services.

In China, the rapid creation of urban and infrastructure development in the coastal cities (Shanghai, and Guangzhou) and zones is reported to spurred industrial development driven by agglomeration/urbanization economies and weak labour laws. I have already mentioned the reluctance in India to reform labour laws. However, metropolitan cities, the hubs of manufacturing in the colonial era, such as Ahmedabad, Chennai, Kolkata and Mumbai are reasserting themselves as centres of industrial development. Also, other large cities (e.g. Coimbatore, Pune, the national capital region surrounding Delhi and others) are also emerging as industrial centres. Of course, because of early investment (particularly private investment) in engineering education in the states of Andhra Pradesh, Karnataka, Maharashtra and Tamil Nadu, information technology centres came to be established in their cities (respectively, Hyderabad, Bangalore, Mumbai-Pune corridor and Chennai). However, the pace of the development manufacturing hubs would be dependent on whether the reform process will be accelerated, deepened and extended. The reform agrenda has to include labour and bankruptcy laws but also land right/land market issues in urban areas. Certainly making India's court system to function more efficiently and speedily in resolving commercial disputes has to be part of the reform, although China has not been hurt particularly by its having no conventionally defined legal system. Whether in the long run the creation of a dispute settlement system outside of the traditional judicial system (e.g. special tribunals, lok adalats, etc.) will create incentives or obviate the need for reform of the judicial system is arguable. It certainly has short term benefits. But long term and substantial benefits of the reform of the judicial system should not be lost right off.

Pharmaceuticals and Chemicals

India emerged as a major producer of generics by the mid 1990s in large part because India's patent laws of the period did not offer patents to producers but only to processes. As long as the process used by the Indian generics producers differed from the process used by the producers of the corresponding branded drug under patent protection elsewhere, they were free to produce and market the generic product at home and also export it to those countries where the branded drug was not under patent protection. Alas, this has changed with India's signing of on the Uruguay Round agreement of 1994, including Trade Related Intellectual Property Rights (TRIPS). After the period of 10 years from 1995 allowed to bring its patent laws into conformity with TRIPS, India amended its law in 2005 and now has to offer product protections as well. It would take me too much afar to discuss the merits of TRIPS and its possible consequences for developing countries. Suffice here to say that the recent clarification of the compulsory licensing (and public health) provision of TRIPS has opened the door for India's highly competitive generic producers of life saving drugs, including retroviral for HIV/AIDS, to expand their markets abroad. More generally, with India emerging as an inexpensive and attractive place for trials of new drugs, and also the rising confidence of major Indian pharmaceutical companies in their ability to innovate and compete in the post TRIPS era, India could emerge as a significant pharmaceutical hub. The potential growth of China and India as suppliers of industrial chemicals is also high, with both having nearly doubled their share in global exports of chemicals.

Services

Service sector has been the most dynamic in India's economy in recent years, with a growth rate exceeding 7% per year during the last five years. This sector accounted for as high as 54% real GDP in 2005-06. Business and commercial services together with finance, insurance and real estate services accounted for 13.5% of real GP in 2005-06, trade, hotels, transport, communication and storage services accounted for another 26.2% and community, social and personal services accounting for the remaining 14.3% of GDP. In 2004-05 and 2005-06, the growth rate of services sector was 9.9% and 9.8% respectively, with the component trade, hotels, transport and communication services growing at 10.6% and 11.1% respectively in the two years. Clearly, the widely noted software services, though rapidly growing, is only a relatively small component of the vast service sector. Domestic demand is a crucial contributor of growth in transport and trade, transport, storage, community, social and personal services and to some extent in communications, hotels and financial services. Software has a dominant export demand component. Hotels, communications and financial services depend also on foreign sources of demand from tourists and foreign investors. With demand for many of these services being income elastic, it is very likely both domestic and foreign demand growth will enable India's service sector to sustain its recent rapid growth.

Labour intensive services are another potential source of growth for the two economies as well as the impact of their growth for the world economy. Realizing this potential depends to a significant extent on the outcome of service sector negotiations in the Doha round. In the unlikely scenario of considerable liberalization of service supply by Mode 4 (supply of services by temporary movement of natural persons), India and China could expand their supply of labour intensive services to the world markets.

The heated debate on outsourcing and the plethora of protective legislation that has been proposed to contain it in the United States relate to supply by Mode 1 (trade in services in which the supplies and the user remain in their respective locations). Again, the potential growth of these service sectors and their impact on growth in India have been discussed in the literature. India had a 3.1% share (one of the very few commodities or services in which China's share was smaller than India's) in the global market for other commercial services, of which the outsourced services form a large part. The export of these services from India has been growing rapidly. Net exports of software services at $16.5 billion accounted for more than half of India's total service exports (net) of $31.2 billion in 2004-05. In the first six months (April-September) of fiscal year 2005-06 software exports totaled $9.8 billion, a growth of 30% over the corresponding period in 2004-05. An industry study group estimates that remote (such as exports) and in situ provision (such as tourism, healthcare and education) of services can add 0.6% - 1% to annual GDP growth, and generate additional employment of between 20 and 72 million by 2020. The growth and quality upgrading (i.e. moving up from call centers to software or technology development and research centers) has been so fast that there are fears of an emerging talent crunch. The latest report from India's National Association of Software and Services Companies (NASSCOM) foresees a "potential shortage of skilled workers in the next decade or so, particularly in the BPO industry, [as] currently only 25 percent of technical graduates and 10-15 percent of general graduates are suitable for employment in offshore IT/BPO industries.

MGI (2001) finds that the labour productivity of India software companies is at 44% of U.S. levels and individual service companies have the potential to reach 100% of U.S. levels. In fact, best practice companies in India already match the U.S. average. MGI (2001) points out that the software industry grew at a rate of over 50% a year for five years to reach an output of $2.2 billion in 1999. With the worldwide IT services market growing at 8% a year and set to reach $910 billion by 2010, and demand from domestic end user industry expecting to grow at 30% a year for a decade, MGI (2001) sees a potential output of $46 billion by 2000 (more than 20 times its level in 1999) with exports absorbing $25 billion and domestic sales absorbing the remaining $21 billion. Like NASSCOM, it also recognized that the biggest bottleneck to future growth is the availability of good software talent.

Interestingly, India's success in software and China's success in hardware have generated interest at the highest policy making levels in a collaborative effort to capture a sizeable share of the global market for both. Former Chinese Prime Minister Zhu Rongji first pointed out this possibility during his visit to India in 2002. During current Prime Minister Wen Jiabao's Indian visit in 2005, a similar view was expressed in a report to the Prime Ministers of China and India by the India-China Joint Study Group.

INDIA FALLING BEHIND CHINA IN SOUTH ASIAN DIPLOMACY

India has always been a local superpower, being by far the largest country within South Asia, and is, in fact, the only one in the group that borders every other South Asian country except Afghanistan, which shares a border with Pakistan. But India's economic performance was stunted by years of state control of the kind now prevalent in Iran. Over the past 15 years, however, economic growth has been strong, enabling the country to have a much greater diplomatic reach than at any time since the 1950s when India briefly emerged as the leader of those countries that were being de-colonized by the European powers. Given this situation, it ought to have been the case that New Delhi would be preeminent in its own backyard. Instead, over the past two decades, India has lost the status of being the lead player in any South Asian country barring Bhutan, a country with which it still has a treaty relationship. In almost the entire region, China has overtaken India in that intangible quality - influence - especially in Nepal and Sri Lanka, while Beijing's existing alliances with Pakistan and Bangladesh are growing stronger.

This is not due to a lack of quality within India's diplomatic service. Instead, the Indian Foreign Service (IFS) has produced a modern corps of skilled diplomats, many experts in different regions of the world, and eager to do more to advance their country's interests. The wall they face is the ambivalence that has become second nature to the country's top policy makers, both within the political crust as well as the administrative backup. Phrases such as "going all the way" and "going for the kill" are inelegant. Yet they represent a reality that is that sometimes a country has to formulate and then determinedly implement a clear policy to be carried out till success is achieved.

In South Asia, such a quality was recently displayed by President Percy Mahinda Rajapaksa of Sri Lanka. He succeeded in wiping out the terrorist group known as the Liberation Tigers of Tamil Eelam (LTTE) where, over the past three decades, all his predecessors had failed. Unlike them, President Rajapaksa did not heed (well-meaning but disastrous) advice to slow down his offensive or agree to a cease-fire, the latter being a device that the LTTE used since 1987 to gain time to recover after having lost the initiative in the field. Once the LTTE recovered its strength, the ceasefire would be abandoned. This point was repeatedly made by Rajapaksa to the peacemakers who clustered around him, especially in the final months of the brief, brutal war against the LTTE that began with his coming to office in 2005.

Once India, because of political considerations such as the need to avoid alienating the country's sizable Tamil population, refused to give the Sri Lankan army equipment, Rajapaksa turned to Pakistan and China. Both countries opened their warehouses to him, and so built up immense capital both within Sri Lanka's

Sinhala most importantity as well as the country's policy establishment. Rajapaksa showed none of the half-heartedness that has characterized so much of Indian policy and, as a result, emerged a winner. In the case of India, the desire to win brownie points with key international players (by heeding their sometimes incorrect advice) as well as an aversion to risk ensured that much of Indian diplomacy was too watered down to be effective. This is especially the case in its immediate neighbourhood.

This on-again, off-again excellence can be seen in Indian diplomatic policy towards Pakistan especially in regard to the long-term pattern of instituting confidence building measures (CBM) being followed - usually after a mass terror attack - with strong rhetoric and a withdrawal of contact. The reality is that in the case of Pakistan, conventional war may have ceased to be an option. This is because the Pakistan army has itself lost control of many of the jihadis that it has trained, equipped and funded for so long.

Instead of reducing the risk of a terror attack, going after the Pakistan military would inflame a large segment of the Pakistani population thus making them susceptible to recruitment in the ongoing jihad against India. Given that situation, it may have been preferable for Indian policymakers to publicly resort to a conventional war except in the case of a conflict started by Pakistan, an unlikely possibility. The military option would work only if (a) the Pakistan army controls the jihadi networks and (b) is comprehensively defeated in battle. Neither condition exists.

A "No War" declaration by India would remove the Pakistani military establishment's most frequently used excuse to station more than 60 percent of its army along the India border, even as the force is engaged in a life-and-death struggle with the Pakistan Taliban. Instead, even though New Delhi has no intention of going to war, the prospect of one is deliberately kept open especially after terror strikes such as Mumbai 11/26-28. Thus, the benefits of India's "No War" declaration are denied, while the other side is aware that the mock-aggressive posture is a bluff and hence will not change its behaviour as a result of the threat. A glaring example of how promoting the idea that India would go to war over Pakistani provocations has hurt New Delhi can be seen in the 2002 standoff with Pakistan in the mountains separating the two. Ostensibly to scare the international community into putting pressure on Pakistan to call off its Kashmir jihad, the then-Vajpayee government mobilized two Indian army strike corps on the border, keeping them and their support units on a hair-trigger alert for the greater part of the year.

Aware that the Indians were bluffing, the Pakistan government refused to budge from its policy of helping jihadists active in Kashmir. The long Indian army mobilization created a perception of regional instability that affected India's status as a safe investment destination even as it exhausted the elite army units on the front line. Given the information that India would not attack, the 2002 mobilization came at a horrendous cost and no benefit. In a system where posturing comes easily to the higher levels of the Indian policy establishment, Prime Minister Manmohan Singh has thus far resisted jingoism and has made it evident that India would not be stampeded into military action. In the case of Sri Lanka, the policy was to intensify conflict until victory. What is needed is a clear policy that is carried out effectively, not a zig-zag routine that confuses the international community and results in a loss of credibility for India.

Military sales can become an effective instrument of diplomacy, were they deployed by India. Within the region, including in Sri Lanka and Nepal, the military is a significant component of the policy process, often the crucial player. Because of New Delhi's longstanding policy of not permitting foreign military sales save for exceptional situations, China has been provided an opportunity to fill the gap. Had Bangladesh, Nepal and Sri Lanka been more reliant on Indian equipment and training for their armed forces, New Delhi would have been in a much stronger position to influence policy in those places than it is today. Instead, the "weapons gap" isincreasingly being filled by China.

The mantra of "non-alignment" has in most instances become a cover for lack of action. Even during the period of the Cold War, when India suffered many of the consequences of being seen as a Soviet ally, not a single Soviet soldier was ever stationed in India or trained here, nor did any Indian soldier undertake any sort of mission in the USSR. In contrast, there are regular exchanges of U.S. and Indian soldiers and joint training exercises have become routine. The warming of ties is because there is a natural fit between the two sides. India has a significant pool of trained (and trainable) manpower, while the United States has abundant stocks of equipment that could be transferred to New Delhi rather than mothballed or left under-utilized. This is especially the case with naval vessels, where India is now being made to pay $3 billion for a secondhand Russian aircraft carrier that it is finding it difficult to float and move at the same time.

Progress in U.S.-India military to military relatives has been slow and is still far below its potential in substantial part because of the wariness of the Indian establishment over China's reaction. Compare this with Pakistan which has built up close military ties with both China and the United States, its friendship with one not affecting the other. In the military field, the choice is between going with the United States or going alone, because a military alliance with China is not an option. Beijing sees New Delhi as a potential competitor and has repeatedly shown through its actions its commitment to a strategic policy that inhibits the growth of Indian power. Unfortunately, in this case, Indian ambivalence is now being matched by the United States under the Obama administration, which has downgraded ties with India to a level much below that set under President George W. Bush. It seems inevitable, however, that both countries will, hopefully within the present presidential term, awaken to the need for a partnership that can ensure that Asia does not fall under the sway of any single power.

The persistent Indian ambivalence in policy was visible in Sri Lanka, where India simultaneously called for a cease-fire while backing the unity of the island nation. As a consequence of simultaneously conveying two contradictory messages, neither the Tamil nor the Sinhala zealots have anything other than distaste for India, while the abundant provision of military supplies has led the Sri Lankan military towards becoming as close to Beijing as are their counterparts in Pakistan.

In Nepal, after first helping to get King Gyanendra to abdicate, New Delhi threw its support behind the Maoists, who promptly reacted by threatening to scrap the India-Nepal agreement and replace it with a similar deal with China. After its embrace of the Maoists, which ended only after their tilt to Beijing became manifest (by the end of 2008), no other Nepali party is willing to trust New Delhi and see it as a reliable partner, even the once-friendly Nepali Congress. Meanwhile, in a show of deft footwork, Chinese diplomats have been active in Kathmandu renewing ties with the non-Maoist parties that today run the government (after the departure of the Maoists), so as to accelerate the growth of PRC influence in Nepal.

Today, there are almost as many radical training camps located within Bangladesh as there in Pakistan, camps whose specific purpose is to replenish the stream of jihadis into India. Yet, unlike in the case of Pakistan, the Indian government is not posturing as if was is likely. A hostile Pakistan, an unfriendly Bangladesh, and Nepal and Sri Lanka heading towards the PRC. These are the wages of a diplomacy that refuses to go for the jugular in the pursuit of objectives, but almost invariably crafts a compromise that gives much less geopolitical benefit. India presents an example of how a most important power that avoids a clear policy line or a better deployment of its assets gives way to the other who is ruthless and willing to complete the marathon rather than slow down and stop before the finish line. Such a policy is the delight of politicians and anathema to statesmen, who understand the need for not just vision, but for will and perseverance.

7

Sino-Indian Border Dispute and their Competitive Symbiotic Relationship

ANALYSIS

Recently, the Sino-Indian border dispute once again became a focus of for the world's mass media. A "tent confrontation" between the Chinese and Indian armies took place and continued near the Line of Actual Control (LAC) for several days. From the Indian point of view, the Chinese army invaded Indian territory, and this incident was "the most serious one in the past 25 years". Level-headed analysis will indicate, however, that China would not wish to provoke simultaneous conflicts with Japan and India, two major Asian powers. In fact, the Indian mass media's reports about Chinese incursions have been heard continually in recent years. Some reports that the Chinese have invaded India for more than 600 times in the past three years are ridiculous.

The Sino-Indian border issue is very complicated. It was left over from the time of British rule in India and has never been resolved. In the 1960s, a military conflict broke out between China and India over territorial boundaries. That conflict became the excuse for India to develop its armed forces vigorously, to get ready for battle, and to make nuclear weapons. The root reason cause of many of the "incursion" incidents reported by India is that the two sides have never reached a consensus on the position of the LAC since the boundary conflict in 1962. They have never delimited the LAC, let alone a formal border. It is therefore debatable to say the Chinese army invaded Indian territory.

Since 1993, however, China and India have signed two agreements and one protocol on the maintenance of peace and tranquillity and the establishment of confidence-building measures in the border areas. They have set up a working mechanism for consultation and coordination on border affairs. These efforts have helped ensure a durable peace and stability in the border areas. The possibility that China and India will come to serious conflict is very small.

Bilateral relations between China and India are very subtle; apart from the boundary problem, the issues of China-Pakistan relations, the Dalai Lama and water resources also hinder the promotion of China-India relations. These problems have given India a deep-seated distrust of China. Some Indians are gradually losing self-confidence as they observe the growing economic gap between China and India. The Indian mass media and some Indian strategic scholars frequently refer to a "Chinese incursion" and the "China threat" and propagate an attitude of no confidence in China's intentions. This situation provides opportunities for some Western countries to undermine Sino-India relations. With the US "rebalancing" toward the Asia-Pacific, the Sino-Indian relationship is undergoing subtle changes these days. Some Indian scholars promote an alliance under the US leadership to counterbalance China. For example, Harsh V. Pant, a professor of defence studies at King's College London, argues that India's strategic interests can only be realised by an Asia-Pacific arrangement in which the US retains its predominant status. The Indian Express columnist C. Raja Mohan similarly urges India to shift its policy of strategic autonomy and strategically cooperate with the US.

So far, India has concentrated on strengthening its "Look East" Policy to enhance strategic and security cooperation with countries such as Japan, South Korea, Malaysia and Vietnam. It has also taken a high profile in the South China Sea disputes. In

December 2011, the first trilateral dialogue between the US, Japan and India was presided over by the US. One of the discussion topics was China's growing military and political global position. It is no wonder that many think that India may abandon strategic autonomy to ally itself with the US and contain China.

Currently, Indian policymakers have a relatively clear view of Sino-Indian and India-US relations. India doesn't yet have the ability to directly confront China, and, as a country prioritising economic development, it is in need of a peaceful neighbouring environment. History shows that the US is not a reliable ally for India. Because of the effect of the economic crisis, the US is heavily burdened by its domestic economic problems, and there are doubts about how much money can be invested in counterbalancing China. The US anchors its hope on the strategy of "offshore balancing" to achieve balance with, or even contain, China by stirring up tensions between it and its Asian strategic partners. It is just taking advantage of India's strength to balance China, which, in effect, should kill two birds with one stone.

So, at present, we have the ironic spectacle of articles in both the US and Indian media trying to provoke each other into tensions with China. The Indian media highlights the idea that Uncle Sam is well-prepared to battle China, while the US media points out that India is engaging in military expansion in preparation for possible Sino-Indian boundary conflicts. India still maintains its status as a "swing state" in the international system. Although it has recently become more pro-US, since the US recognised India as a nuclear power despite it not being a signatory to the Nuclear Non-Proliferation Treaty (NPT), India will not abandon its strategic autonomy to ally with the US.

I have published articles that arguing that the Sino-Indian relationship is, in essence, a competitive symbiotic relationship. I say that for the following reasons: First of all, there really are some areas of competitions between China and India, mainly in geopolitics, trade and energy, etc. But that competition is not necessarily cutthroat and zero sum. China and India can cooperate if they have mutual trust. In fact, they do cooperate in fields such as energy and anti-terrorism.

In addition to the aspect of competition, the Sino-Indian symbiotic relationship can be divided into four areas: First, as two big powers that are rising simultaneously, China and India are in similar positions in the current international system. They are beneficiaries of that system, but at the same time, they are constrained by it and also suppressed by the dominant power in the system. They want to gradually advance the reform of this system. So, China and India have common interests on many global issues, such as the reform of the international financial system, climate change, and the WTO negotiations. China, India, Brazil and South Africa have organised the BRICS and BASIC groups, which promote the reform of the international order. If China, India and other countries cannot consolidate their views on these global issues, they could be crushed one by one by the dominant power in the system and lose forever the chance to rise again.

Secondly, in the trilateral relations between China, India and the United States, India's status will benefit from China's rise. China's growth is a prerequisite for India's rise. If India really becomes embroiled in conflicts with China, it's hard to say whether the US will stretch out a hand to help it. But if India surpasses China, it will definitely replace its neighbour as the target of the US.

Thirdly, as two neighbouring powers in Asia, both China and India need a peaceful and stable periphery to develop their economies. Statesmen in both countries know clearly that development is their primary task, and that development needs stable circumstances. So, China and India have a common task to maintain the stability of the region. This is the determining factor that encourages China and India to keep their border areas stable for at least 10 years.

At least, the Chinese and Indian economies are complementary. Since they are in symbiosis, they could, theoretically, nourish and assist each other's survival and development. Sino-Indian bilateral trade has developed quickly in the past ten years, and the trade volume has risen 20 fold. Although India complains that there are some problems in the bilateral trade structure, and the Indian trade deficit is too large, it is evident that Chinese goods, which are of good quality and cheap, raise Indian people's living standards. China and India have ample room to cooperate, especially in infrastructure construction. China has large amounts of capital and extensive experience in the construction of infrastructure; India on the other hand needs to improve its infrastructure facilities, but lacks finance. Sino-Indian cooperation in this field will benefit both sides.

Within India, the so-called "China threat" is a trick of Indian political figures to pull the wool over the eyes of their people and Western countries. From the aspect of domestic politics, by making waves in relations with China, Indian politicians can obscure domestic contradictions, bolster up national morale, pull votes, and the military can get an increasing budget. From the aspect of international politics, India can obtain advanced weaponry and technologies from Western countries. In fact, the major direction of Indian military expansion is the Indian Ocean - the Navy received the largest part of India's rapidly growing defence budget. India's military strategy on land is defensive in nature but in the Indian Ocean, India has another competitor that is much stronger than China. The so-called "China threat" is just a cover.

The direction of Sino-Indian relations is determined for the medium-term at least, but the border issue is still a hindrance to bilateral relations. India did undertake some domestic reflection on the Sino-Indian conflict of 1962 and Nehru's policy towards China at that time, but no consensus was achieved. The Indian government never released publicly the Henderson-Brooks report that summarised the reasons why India was defeated. Taking a coherent view of this history will play a decisive role in the peaceful resolution of the Sino-Indian border problem. We should not neglect the negative role of the Indian multiparty system, in which foreign policy is often hijacked by domestic affairs. The role of the opposition parties and mass media in the Sino-Indian border conflict of 1962 is a case in point. It is necessary for the Indian government to reveal the truth about the Sino-Indian boundary conflict to the Indian people, and for Chinese and Indian scholars to conduct joint research projects on some historical problems, to alter the longstanding misconceptions held by both sides.

SINO-INDIAN TERRITORIAL PROBLEMS

In terms of "the rise of China" and its "implications for India", the title of this book, the Sino-Indian territorial dispute represents an immediate arena in which India is having to face the uncomfortable implications from having an increasingly stronger neighbour. For India, the ability of China to deny India's hopes of territorial settlement on India's terms has become ever clearer in the wake of China's rise in military power in and around their disputed territory, which remains the biggest amount of land still in dispute in Asia.

As such, "the 4,056 – kilometre (2,520 miles) frontier between India and China, one of the longest inter-state borders in the world, remains ... not defined, let alone demarcated, on maps or delineated on the ground". Here, the judgement over a century ago of Lord Curzon, British Viceroy of India 1898-1905 still seems relevant; the most urgent work of Foreign Ministers and Ambassadors ... is now the conclusion of Frontier Conventions in which sources of discord are removed by the adjustment of rival interests or ambitions at points where the territorial borders adjoin", for "frontiers are indeed the razor's edge on which hang suspended the modern issues of war or peace, of life or death to nations".

Admittedly, the territorial issue has been officially decoupled from the wider Sino-Indian relationship; as with the PRC rhetoric that "China and India have already reached consensus on the border issue. Before it is completely resolved, both countries will endeavour to maintain peace and stability in the border areas and will not let the border issue affect the general picture of China and

India's cooperation". However, in reality their territorial issues do affect their wider relationship, in PRC terms "the existence of immense territorial disputes between China and India".

In dispute terms, this chapter argues that, in International Relations (IR) theory terms, the territorial disputes between India and China involve *classical geopolitics* entwined with *critical geopolitics*. Each strand of geopolitics, in their different ways, both involve the respective "position" that India and China hold for themselves and for each other in their immediate and extended neighbourhood.

Whilst each side argues from history, the chapter argues that in reality the evidence from history is rather ambiguous and inconclusive for both sides' territorial claims. Indeed, history is a sterile area to argue from, as one Indian commentator put it, "can we go beyond history to look at solutions which do not hark back to the past?"

The chapter argues that, from the outside, resolution of the issue seems feasible enough in terms of simple seeming territorial trade offs involving Arunachal Pradesh and Aksai Chin; but is complicated by smaller geographic issues surrounding Tawang, and wider geopolitical issues surrounding Tibet and indeed the balance of power in Asia between India and China.

The two main areas of dispute along this Himalayan frontier are the *Western Sector* (Aksai Chin, around 37,250 square kilometres/ 14,380 square miles); and the *Eastern Sector* (Arunachal Pradesh, around 83,740 square kilometres/ 32,330 square miles). On the one hand, Arunachal Pradesh is inhabited by over a million people, Indian citizens, and includes important Buddhist centres like Tawang. On the other hand, Aksai Chin is a virtually uninhabited bleak barren plateau with no permanent settlements. It is the place "where not a blade of grass grows" as Jawaharlal Nehru once dismissively said; but where China's National Highway 219 runs through Aksai Chin as a key geopolitical infrastructure link for the PRC between its provinces of Tibet and Xinjiang. One further complication is China's occupation of the Shaksgam valley;

around 5,180 sq kilometres/1,930 square miles, to which Pakistan relinquished its Baltistan-related claims in 1963, but over which India maintains its own Kashmir-derived claims. Smaller pockets of disputed territory are found, the *Middle Sector* fringes of Himachal Pradesh and Uttar Pradesh. Elsewhere along the Himalayas, lingering uncertainty over China's recognition of Sikkim's incorporation into India in 1975 is entwined with continuing PRC claims to the "Finger Area" in the north of Sikkim, with 71 supposed incidents reported of Chinese troop "incursions" in 2008. Nearby territorial disputes between China and Bhutan around the Chumbi Valley triangulation point with India are of further concern to New Delhi, given the Chumbi Valley's location looking down onto the India's sensitive Siliguri corridor which links India's northeastern states with the rest of India.

Wider nuances arise with India's Foreign Secretary (2004 – 2006) Shyam Saran, and his comments about *the logic of geography*. In front of one audience, it was a question for Saran of "geopolitical reality" in which "I would like to focus particularly on Asia, where the interests of both India and China intersect. It is said that the logic of geography is unrelenting. Proximity is the most difficult and testing among diplomatic challenges a country faces", where "to those who harbour any skepticism about this fact, it would suffice to remind that we share one of the longest [and disputed] land borders in the world with China.

In front of another audience, it was again a question that "it is said that the logic of geography is unrelenting and proximity is the most difficult and testing among diplomatic challenges a country faces"; with the following gloss that "frontiers with neighbours are where domestic concerns intersect with external relationships. This is where domestic and foreign policies become inextricable and demand sensitive handling", and in which "it is important for us to look at the [disputed] boundary question from the long-term and strategic perspective of India-China relations, rather than as a mere territorial issue. The territorial issues between India and China form one of the biggest land disputes in Asia, and are of significance not only for the size of area under dispute, but also because the two disputants are the big countries most evidently on the rise in Asia. Alongside this *logic of geography*, there is then what Neville Maxwell called "the logic of power"; a *logic of power* whereby powerful states "in their expansive phases push out their frontiers until they meet the resistance of a strong neighbour or reach a physical barrier which makes a natural point of rest". In geopolitical terms, the current point of rest is along the Himalayas/ Karakoram range, but in the long term where exactly is the "natural" point of rest between them? Amidst talk of mutual IR *security dilemma* dynamics, China's strengthening of military forces and related infrastructure in Aksai Chin and Arunachal Pradesh zones is now a spur to India's own more halting augmentation of military forces and related infrastructure. Meanwhile, both countries are seeking to expand their wider strategic space at a time when their immediate mountain borders remain unresolved.

ARUNACHAL PRADESH TERRITORIAL DISPUTE BETWEEN INDIA AND CHINA

International law never supports a country or a state which attempts to plunder the territory from other countries or states by threatening or warfare. Article 2 of The UN Charter clearly defines that "all Members shall refrain in their international relations from the threat or use of force against the territorial integrity or political independence of any state" (Reynolds 2004.) It is so-called a territorial dispute, which is "a disagreement over the possession or control of land between two or more countries" ("Territorial Dispute.") What leads the territorial dispute is not only relevant to the possession or control of natural resources such as oil, coals, fertile land or rivers, but also culture and religion. In addition, it has been said that "in many cases territorial disputes result from vague and unclear language in a treaty that set up the original boundary" ("Territorial Dispute".) Consequently, many territorial disputes possibly generate some conflicts between countries, and even worse, they can become a primary cause of wars and/or terrorism. A long time ago, before the territorial dispute between China and India emerged in Arunachal Pradesh, the first ancestors of the tribal groups migrated from Tibet during pre-historic period. Even though ancestors were there, little is known about the history of Arunachal Pradesh.

Recorded history is only available in the Ahom chronicles from the sixteenth century: the British Christened, originally known as northeast Frontiers Agency (NEFA,) took administrative control of Arunachal Pradesh and it remained under this rule until 1948. Arunachal Pradesh is northeast India's largest and remotest state, as it has railways and air services connecting only three of its town. Natives in Arunachal Pradesh used to eat "their food in uncooked condition ignorant about the discovery of fire" (WebDigitech.)

They were really isolated and not aware of the development and revolution which was occurring in this globalized world. The major cause of China-India territorial dispute, which deprived peace from Arunachal Pradesh, is from immediately after Chinese Revolution in 1911. At that time, Qing Dynasty, the last Chinese Dynasty, fell and the Emperor of Qing Dynasty resigned. As a result, China, Tibet and Mongolia became equal and separate countries. In these three countries, Tibet and Mongol tried to be approved internationally as independent states, and undertook to international society. However, on the other hand, Han Chinese Republicans started small war to subjugate reins of government of Tibet and Mongol. Therefore, they could not be independent states at that time.

In 1912-13, the British Raj made agreements with tribal leaders that defined the area that was known as NEFA. British rule could have very small impact on the isolated, self-sufficient in terms of economy and militarily uncontrollable tribal peoples. In order to arrange this conflict, in 1913 and 1914, the British administrator, Sir Henry McMahon, drew up the 550-mile McMahon Line as the border between India and China in Shimla, during a conference which also discussed the Tibetan and Chinese borders ("McMahon

Line.") This conference is called Shimla Conference. Regardless of this reconciliation, the McMahon Line was rejected by the Chinese government in 1947 ("Arunachal Pradesh.")

Following this dispute, the Chinese troops crossed the McMahon Line on the August 26th, 1959 ("Arunachal Pradesh.") They abandoned this in 1961, but in October 1962 crossed the line once again with force ("McMahon Line.") As a result, Sino-Indian War broke out. The Chinese extended their frontier as they intruded deeper and deeper. However, this war did not go on for a long time. In 1963, the Chinese agreed to withdraw back to the McMahon Line, and also returned Indian prisoners of this war at that time.

Environment Aspects

By losing Arunachal Pradesh located on the northeastern tip of India, bordering Bhutan on the west, China on the north, Myanmar on the east and the states of Assam on the south, either China or India would receive some damage in terms of economy. Both China and India are able to run good business because Arunachal Pradesh is a very good place for tourists from all over the world to visit. Evergreen forest, which covers more than 60 percent of the state area, certainly makes people feel comfortable to stay there.

From this fact, Arunachal Pradesh is known for its forest resources. Forest products and industries are considered as a lifeline in Arunachal Pradesh. In fact, 75 percent of its total workforce is engaged in agriculture (mainly shifting cultivation.) Therefore, if either China or India could obtain Arunachal Pradesh, it would be able to improve its economy by taking advantage of agriculture and tourism.

In addition to it, there are many fairs and festivals there such as Losar, the New Year's Celebration of the Monpas. Another famous festival there is called Reh, which is associated with the Idu Mishmis, the six-day celebrations' special attraction is the Priest dance. Fairs or festivals are held every month, thus tourists can visit there any time for sightseeing.

Conflict Aspects

In 1962, the Chinese had a claim on what India deemed its own territory called Arunachal Pradesh. China sent many well-trained and well-armed troops to the disputed region. On the other hand, India had only ill-equipped troops there, which made them more difficult to beat Chinese troops.

The Sino-Indian (Indo-China) War was started by China on October 16, 1962 on account of the territorial dispute against India. Chinese attacked India on October 20, 1962 because it was unable to reach political accommodation on disputed territory along the 3,225-kilometer-long Himalayan border. The Chinese did not invade farther, and on November 21, 1962 declared a unilateral cease-fire. They had accomplished all of their territorial objectives, and any attempt to press farther into the plains of Assam would have stretched their logistical capabilities and their lines of communication to a breaking point. Finally, the Chinese defeated India in 1962, which as a result led to the retreat of Indian Army in terms of doctrine, training, organization and equipment from the disputed area.

Environment and Conflict Overlap

Arunachal Pradesh dispute was classified as a territorial dispute, but both China and India had big enough territories on their own. Thus, this dispute was not really caused by a decline of resources (territory.) Therefore, the dispute is direct more likely than not even it has been argued for about one century long.

China and India had a direct conflict over the fertile land which certainly supports their economy by agriculture. Major crops in the area are, for example, rice, maize, ginger and potato. These major crops yielded 134,807, 48,346, 34,890 and 32,434 in hectare respectively (Gov't of Arunachal Pradesh.)

Because Sir Henry McMahon, the British administrator, clearly established the McMahon Line as the border, which could establish buffer zones around its colony in South Asia, between British

India and Tibet in 1913-14, the British have also something to do with Arunachal Pradesh dispute in terms of strategic interest.

China is also relevant to the territorial dispute. On account of various disagreements with the British, China refused to accept the terms imposed by Britain. As a result, China did not recognize the validity of the McMahon Line. China probably was mostly concerned about the loss of their essential resources such as land from losing Arunachal Pradesh. Therefore, British India and China were major countries in this territorial dispute with respect to strategic interest.

Even though both India and China found a peaceful solution to the border dispute in late 1980s, officials from two countries have met more than 15 times to argue the Arunachal Pradesh.

Chinese Foreign Ministry spokesman Kong Quan said that "As far as the incident mentioned, after investigations, we have found that the Indian side crossed the eastern sector of the Line of Actual Control (LAC).

At the request of the Chinese side, the Indian people who crossed the LAC, returned to the Indian side of the LAC" (Joseph 2003.) Thus, China still claims that "90,000 square kilometers of land in Arunachal Pradesh and does not recognize the northeastern state as part of Indian Territory" (Joseph 2003.)

Outcome of Dispute: Compromise

Arunachal Pradesh was part of the state of Assam until 1987 and was previously called NEFA. However, Arunachal Pradesh finally could gain statehood status on Feb. 20th, 1987 after making allowances for the security consideration in the east and Sino-Indian tensions ("Arunachal Pradesh.") India was satisfied with this outcome of dispute while China still does not admit the result.

Smoothening the India-China Border Wrinkles

The 17th round of India-China border talks (Feb. 10-11) in New Delhi passed off without any "free and frank" exchanges, that is, there was no disagreement. The first meeting was at the joint secretary level with military experts on both sides. The situation on the border was reviewed and apparently was found satisfactory. The meeting it appears, was constructed by both sides to ensure no negative vibration emerged.

The main meeting, the 17th round of talks between the Special Representatives (SRs) of the two sides was much wider in scale because matters outside the border issue were discussed. The Indian Ministry of External Affairs (MEA) statement said the talks were held in a "candid, friendly and constructive atmosphere". Mr. Shivshankar Menon, the Indian SR and Mr. Yang Jiechi, the Chinese SR are veterans in the foreign policy game and India-China relations. On the Chinese side they know the stakes they are playing with. They have in their pocket "something to give" on the border issue if need be. But no one can say for sure what that is.

It must be kept in mind that the old Chinese position "if India makes concessions in the east" has not become irrelevant. In China's foreign policy dealings, nothing once stated becomes irrelevant unless it is stated so officially.

The three-step process agreed to by both sides to resolve the boundary question was reiterated. The process has arrived at step-2 to reach a framework for a resolution of this question. This will be based on the Agreement on the Political Parameters and Guiding Principles for the settlement of the India-China Boundary Question. The SRs discussed possible additional Confidence Building Measures (CBM).

Other issues discussed, according to the MEA release included areas of mutual interest including cooperation in the East Asia Summit process as well as developments in West Asia and Afghanistan. Pakistan should have figured in the discussions, but it appears that the Chinese do not want it to be seriously included in the "India-China strategic partnership and co-operation". It is too sensitive a subject.

China made its general position on the border clear when reacting to Indian President Pranab Mukherjee's visit to Arunachal

Pradesh in November last year. Chinese foreign ministry spokesman Qin Gang urged *(Xinhua, Nov.30 2013)* India not to indulge in acts that complicate the boundary issue and work with China to create conditions for talks and preserve peace and tranquility on the border.

The *Xinhua* commentary went on to say "The so-called Arunachal Pradesh was established largely on three areas of China's Tibet-Monyul, Loyul and Lower Tsayul currently under Indian illegal occupation. These three areas, located between the illegal MacMahon Line and the traditional customary boundary between China and India, have always been Chinese territory." The commentary added that in February 1987, Indian authorities declared the founding of the so-called Arunachal Pradesh.

Before further meetings on the border issue the Chinese side drew the lines. That is, the basic Chinese position that the border lay along the northern banks of the river Bramhaputra; India set up Arunachal Pradesh illegally; and if India did not work with China and on its directions, China could revert to a hard-line position.

This is China's position on the eastern sector of the India-China border. It is, therefore, not surprising that even Chinese incursion into India's Depsung area in the western sector last year was generally kept outside the main agenda.

The focus is now testing out the Border Defense cooperation agreement signed during Prime Minister Manmohan Singh's visit to China last October.

With national elections in India barely two months away and opinion surveys emphatically suggesting that UPA government led by the Congress has little or no hope to return to power for the third time in a row, it was only right for Prime Minister Singh and National Security Advisor (NSA) Menon to take no new initiatives on the border and analyze the efficacy of Border Defence Agreement signed between the two countries last October. The new hierarchy in New Delhi will be well advised to consider relations with China on a much bigger canvas. While getting played by China on the boundary question, New Delhi must not lose sight of other strategic interests regionally and globally. The Chinese leadership including the People's Liberation Army (PLA) are full of hubris as the next global super power. On the India-China border, the Chinese attained confidence of military superiority, and would continue to play mind games. The Border Defence Agreement was proposed by China, and India agreed to it only after some critical amendments.

China went through with it but was not satisfied. The agreement could not put the Indian forces and border development in a strait jacket. It is going to come up with more CBMs on the border in due course. This is something Indian experts must look out for.

There was some speculation that because of support to Uighur separatists from extremist elements in Pakistan, China-Pakistan relations was becoming weaker. True, the Chinese were furious with Pakistan especially during the 2008 Beijing Olympics. But weak relationship? Emphatically no. Beijing is determined to crush the Uighur separatists as evidenced by the hard crackdown in Xinjiang.

Pakistan is of immense importance to China. It concerns Chinese interests in the Gulf and the Middle East with Pakistan being a Muslim nation.

Afghanistan now looms on the horizon, but it is a tricky issue. Certainly, China is discussing Afghanistan with India but all its cards on the burning issue remain hidden.

China's support to Pakistan on Pakistan's issues with India continues to be as strong as ever. On Kashmir, there has been no change in position though statements are deliberately muted. It has done nothing and said nothing on Pakistan sponsored and Pakistani based terrorism against India. Yet it high profiles the so-called "three evils" terrorism, separatism and religious extremism. China's cooperation against terrorism and extremism across the world remains a hollow trumpet till date.

A new worrisome development has taken place. The BBC reported recently that Pakistan had manufactured nuclear weapons exclusively for Saudi Arabia.

There were denials but not convincing enough. It is well known that China had supplied Saudi Arabia CSS-2 nuclear capable missiles in the 1980s. Obviously, these were meant for regional use. But nuclear capable missiles without nuclear warheads is an incongruous military doctrine. China has been modernizing Pakistan's nuclear weapons capability and fissile material production facilities.

The three countries tie up very nicely as the Saudis remain the mainstay not only of Pakistan's economy but of its military modernization. After all Pakistan, a Sunni majority country like Saudi Arabia, owns the "Islamic bomb"!

The above scenario is not an idle thought. The world is aware of the Pakistani nuclear scientist Dr. A. Q. Khan's nuclear trade network leading to major proliferation. China was a self-effasive but root player in this. The west let both China and Pakistan off lightly for their own geostrategic reasons. After Saudi Arabia and the US differed on the approach to the Syrian crisis the Saudis are moving back to engage China and Pakistan with more resolve. The Saudi crown prince was in Pakistan recently and his agenda included defence cooperation.

On the other end of the Indian Ocean is the issue of freedom of navigation in the South China Sea. China is increasingly trying to force control of the international maritime route through which around 50 percent of global trade passes. Using vague historical evidence mainly manipulated, China claims sovereignty of the Spratly group of Islands in the South China Sea. It is using the naval flag march here to intimidate other claimants. India is likely to get into conflict with China on its oil exploration with Vietnam in Vietnam's waters claimed by China. There are a whole range of issues that are likely to come up in India-China interface in the next five years. The new dispensation in New Delhi will have to deal with them.

How these issues are dealt with is another question. Prime Minister Manmohan Singh made non-conflict and warm relations with China and Pakistan his top priorities. He failed because such a relationship does not exist in the minds of either of these two countries. In the course of his policies, Dr. Singh bent over too much.

The foregoing are only illustrative examples of issues that India will come to face. It is not suggested that India should adopt aggressive postures against China. But at the same time, India should get out of the habit of rolling over to achieve what is not achievable.

Firmness on issues of national and strategic importance is imperative. Prime Minister Singh did this in the case of the nuclear deal with the US at the Nuclear Suppliers Group (NSG) despite China's opposition till the last moment. Unfortunately, the Chinese official criticism on President Pranab Mukherjee's visit to Arunanchal Pradesh did not elicit a suitable demarche from India.

DISPUTED TERRITORY BETWEEN CHINA AND INDIA

Arunachal Pradesh

Both countries retain their strong claims to the disputed territory, however, fueled by national pride and national security interests. China's "Go West" development policy and July 2006 opening of the Qinghai-Tibet railway have received mixed responses from Indian policymakers; those who favour expanded trade and people-to-people contacts have regarded the developments as positive, but some within the national security establishment have raised concerns that they will allow Beijing to extend its military power projection into Tibet and beyond into South and Central Asia.

Three rivers running through India—the Indus/Sengge Chu, Sutlej/Langqen Tsangbo, and Brahmaputra/Sang Po—originate in Tibet, a fact that has spurred Indian fears that China could use upstream dams and barrages to control the flow of water into

India. India, for instance, has blamed a series of flash floods along the Sutlej River in its state of Himachal Pradesh to China's reluctance to supply hydrological data to India in a timely manner or allow Indian scientists to conduct surveys of melting glaciers on Chinese soil. The absence of any water-sharing treaty between both states as a result of the disputed status of their borders contributes to these water tensions.

Regional Affairs

Regionally, Sino-Indian cooperation has been the exception rather than the rule. Beijing watches closely New Delhi's increasing engagement of East Asia, including relations with nations that have historically had particularly difficult interactions with Beijing, such as Japan, Vietnam, and Indonesia. At the same time, Indian strategists have expressed quiet concern over China's growing influence in the subcontinent, not only its maintenance of a robust political and military relationship with India's rival Pakistan, but also its extensive political, economic, and security relationship with Burma, growing relations with Bangladesh and Nepal, and increasing naval presence in the Indian Ocean. China's admission as an observer to the South Asian Association for Regional Cooperation (SAARC) in November 2005, with New Delhi's reluctant acquiescence, has been cited as further evidence of China's emergence as a player in India's backyard and the desire of India's smaller neighbours to draw China into the region as leverage.

India has viewed growing Chinese influence in Burma, which is strategically located along the eastern end of the Indian Ocean, with great suspicion. In the mid-1990s, India had been one of the most vocal and ardent supporters of Burma's democracy movement, led by Aung San Suu Kyi.

However, the combination of India's aim to forge closer links with Southeast Asia as part of its "Look East" policy, its need for Burma's support in countering insurgent groups in India's northeast, its desire for access to Burma's natural resources, including energy (often in competition with China), and its alarm over China's growing military ties to the Burmese junta led India to adopt a more conciliatory engagement policy with the Burmese leadership by the late 1990s to counterbalance Chinese influence.

Most notably, the presence of Chinese radar technicians in Burma's Coco Islands, which border India's Andaman and Nicobar Islands, has fueled concern in New Delhi (and Washington) that Beijing is monitoring naval activities in the region.

Furthermore, China's efforts to develop alternative overland routes to transport oil and gas imports through port facilities at Gwadar in Pakistan's Baluchistan province, which is at the entrance of the Strait of Hormuz, as well as through Bangladesh and Burma, have been viewed by India as part of a Chinese "string of pearls" strategy of economic and military encroachment into South and Central Asia. Indeed, China's senior-most leaders have openly declared Beijing's attention to placing priority focus on naval modernization, including greater power-projection capability. Indian policymakers fear that China's moves could undermine India's regional preeminence.

At the same time, India's joint naval exercises in the South China Sea — with Vietnam in 2000 and Singapore in 2005, joint patrols with Indonesia in the Andaman Sea beginning in 2002, and exercises off the Japanese coast with the U.S. and Japanese navies in April 2007, have sparked concerns in Beijing. The Indian Navy, the world's fifth-largest, has also set up a Far Eastern Naval Command (FENC) off Port Blair on the Andaman Islands to increase its presence in the Strait of Malacca and potentially monitor Chinese naval activities in the region. Such mutual suspicions could result in China-Indian naval rivalry in and around the Indian Ocean over time.

For their part, East Asian nations have increasingly looked to India as a potential partner in economic and regional security affairs, with some, such as Japan, apparently considering India as a potential element in a hedging strategy against China. South Asian countries have likewise begun to play the "China card" in order to counterbalance India's influence in their affairs or gain policy concessions from India and the West.

For instance, as relations have soured between New Delhi and Dhaka in recent years, China has become Bangladesh's largest supplier of military hardware and has replaced India as Bangladesh's overall largest trading partner. In Nepal, China defied international suspension of military aid and other support to King

Gyanendra's regime after the monarch suspended democracy from February 2005 to April 2006, calling the situation Nepal's "internal affair." King Gyanendra reciprocated by shutting down the office of the Dalai Lama's representative in Nepal as well as the Tibetan Refugee Welfare Office.

In the end, China and India each recognize the inexorable reality of the other's increasing involvement in its neighborhood. In response, the two nations are quietly balancing the prospects for cooperation and competition in their relationship without letting any residual suspicions, tensions, or mistrust derail their mutual desire to test the possibilities of political rapprochement, economic engagement, and confidence-building in the years ahead.

People-to-People Contact s

People-to-people contacts between China and India have increased in recent years, albeit from a low base. Regular direct flights were established in 2002, when China's tourism authorities designated India as an "authorized destination." More than 5,000 Indian students are currently studying in Chinese universities. In India, enthusiasm for Chinese popular culture is growing, and Indians tend to respect, if not envy, China's economic and political rise, which they would like to have their own country mirror. India dubbed 2006 the "Year of Friendship with China," and China declared 2007 the "Year of China-India Friendship through Tourism."

Nonetheless, while official interaction is on the rise and public opinion polls suggest that a majority of citizens and businessmen in both states hold favorable views of each other overall, popular interaction remains relatively minimal, restricted by the language barrier, cultural differences, and other factors. Chinese and Indian observers alike will note that the Chinese have more natural affinity with countries in East and Southeast Asia, while Indians are more comfortable in dealing with English-speaking countries and other South Asian states.

Mutual mistrust persists, particularly within India's older generation, whose memories of the Sino-Indian border conflict lead it to view China with suspicion. India's media and educational system have also nurtured the notion that China "stabbed India in the back" in 1962 and is sitting on Indian land. India's visa policy, in fact, is very restrictive and suspicious of the entry of citizens from China (among other nations, including the United States), further constraining popular contact.

For their part, the Chinese have expressed difficulty in understanding India's cultural and interpersonal style and have tended to be snobbish in their view of India and its state of development relative to China. While Indians may be focusing increasingly on China, relatively little Chinese popular attention is directed toward India. Few Chinese students study in India, for instance. Even at the official level, a similar lack of symmetry in the level of attention paid by China and India toward each other appears to prevail.

Negotiating Strategies

One repeated emerging criticisms of India's negotiating strategy is that "unilateral concessions" have been made too often by India, without similar concessions being made by China. When PRC military forces started moving into Tibet in 1950, the Republic of India quickly moved to (a) give up the Forward Rights inherited from the days of British India, which stemmed from the Simla Convention and Anglo-Tibetan Agreement of 1904; and (b) instead recognise Chinese control over Tibet in stronger terms than the hitherto used term "suzerainty". In effect, a "Tibet Card" was there to be played at a time of PRC uncertainties. A robust Indian intervention might have maintained Tibet as an effective buffer between India and China, or at least enabled concessions to be won by India on the Himalayan—Karakoram borders. This is the reverse logic behind recent Indian comments that "China has failed to appreciate that if Arunachal is claimed to be the southern part of Tibet Autonomous Region (TAR), India cannot accept Tibet to be within China. India's formal position on Tibet articulated in 1954 and 2003 is therefore a tentative and unilateral diplomatic offer that can only be sustained and the circle completed once China recognizes Arunachal as part of India". Reinvoking such a "Tibet Card" has been floated in some Indian circles in the past few years.

Having lost that opportunity, the next criticism of Indian negotiating strategy is that, faced with an immediate PRC military presence in Tibet and renewed Chinese claims over Aksai China and Arunachal Pradesh, Nehru ignored the chance of a trade-off seemingly offered by China in 1960; whereby Aksai China would have gone to China and Arunachal Pradesh would have gone to India. Instead, India refused to engage in sovereignty negotiations in the 1950s, maintained its claims to the fullest, neglected to build up its own military forces, yet still engaged in adventurist forward probing movements in the late 1950s. At the time, Nehru rejected the idea of territorial trade-off; India "will not concede one piece of territory in return for another in the same manner as a similar dispute between China and Burma was settled this year"; for "there is no question of barter in these matters … facts are facts".

His formal position was, in the formal *Indian Note* of June 16 1962; quite simply that "this boundary is well known and well recognized and has been so for centuries and cannot be the subject of any negotiations". The trouble was the precise boundaries were not well known, were not well recognized, and had not been in shape for centuries. The irony is that the territorial agreement reached between Burma and China in 1960 involved China following the MacMahon Line alongside other mutual concessions and swapping of territory; as did the 1963 Agreement between

China and Pakistan with regard to mutual concessions over claims and territory in the Karakoram reaches.

Nehru might have said "facts are facts" but the fact of the matter is that China's military superiority and continuing occupation of Aksai Chin created a very different subsequent set of facts in the wake of India's military defeat at the hands of China in 1962. The problem for consideration of negotiated resolution of the territorial dispute is that demands and offers have shifted. From the outside, an obvious trade off would be between the *Western* Sector and the *Eastern Sector*; which is where Noorani argued that "there is no territorial dispute which has been, and still is, more susceptible to a solution than India's boundary dispute with China. Each side has its non-negotiable vital interest securely under its control. India has the McMahon Line; China has Aksai Chin" In other words, China's *de facto* control of Aksai Chin could be reflected in agreed *de jure* sovereignty for China, and India's *de facto* control of Arunachal Pradesh could in turn be reflected in agreed *de jure* sovereignty for India. This had been Zhou Enlai's seeming suggestion in 1960, and was the "Package Plan" floated by Deng Xiaoping during 1980. The problem is that the Indian government has never taken up such trade-off offers, with Chinese comments made about the weakness of the Indian governments in taking any compromise deal to the Indian public. The separate *sector-by-sector* approach advocated by India when discussions resumed in the 1980s, rather than *overall package* trade-off deals suggested by China, has not worked, it has merely led the PRC to maintain its particular claims in all Sectors.

Another possible example of unilateral concessions was Rajiv Gandhi's visit to Beijing in 1988. Various concessions were made by him. He agreed that the settlement of the border dispute no longer was necessary as a precondition for improvement of bilateral relations, secondly he agreed that some members of the Tibetan community in India were engaged in anti-China activities, and thirdly he agreed that Tibet was an internal affair for China. Ganguly considered the results were "clearly asymmetric" as no support on the Kashmir issue was received from China, which "underscored the stark debility of India's negotiating capabilities vis-à-vis China". On the other hand, the earlier unequivocal support for Pakistan's case in Kashmir was moderated by a more neutral position by the 1990s, the PRC eventually announcing it was "not taking sides on Kashmir".

A final example of "unilateral concessions" came in the 2003 *Declaration on Principles for Relations and Comprehensive Cooperation between India and China*, in which India explicitly recognised the sovereignty of China over Tibet. A careful look at the text shows one-way agreement, one-way obligations, one-way concessions. On the one hand, it stated that "The Indian side recognizes that the Tibet Autonomous Region is part of the territory of the People's Republic of China and reiterates that it does not allow Tibetans to engage in anti-China political activities in India"; before going on to immediately say, on the other hand, "The Chinese side expresses its appreciation for the Indian position and reiterates that it is firmly opposed to any attempt and action aimed at splitting China and bringing about "independence of Tibet". As can be seen, there was no recognition of Indian territory (Arunachal Pradesh?) by China; not even return recognition by China of India's sovereignty claims over Sikkim, the Princely State reincorporated into the Republic of India in 1975, an incorporation which China had refused to recognise. Indian commentators may have read the accompanying *Trade Memorandum* designating Natu La as a border trade post as recognition by China of India's sovereignty over Sikkim, but that was implied rather than explicit, *de facto* rather than *de jure*.

Meanwhile, New Delhi has refused to lay out its formal position, other than the reiteration of its full claims of the Indian Parliament in November 1962, a unanimous vote to get China to vacate all Indian-claimed territories that China occupied. Specific territorial negotiations involving sensitive political climb downs or concessions might well be conducted in private out of the public gaze, yet there seems no indications of this either. India could then indicate some sort of territorial trade-off, short of this maximalist reiteration of its full claims which China is unlikely to accept. Of course, India indicating a territorial trade-off would not necessarily meet with Chinese acceptance, given Indian suspicions that China is happy enough to avoid definitive frontier settlement; but at least it would clarify the issue, and in such an eventuality enable India to more straightforwardly strengthen her own presence and power towards China along the border. In IR terms, if *engagement* proved unsuccessful in leading to territorial settlement, then India could go for a degree of *internal balancing* through building up its military presence and power in Arunachal Pradesh and Ladakh. Some Indian commentators have suggested that "when the Agni-III is finally ready for deployment, it is likely that the Chinese will come down to the table for negotiations and there is likely to be further progress on the border dispute". It could also go for a degree of *external balancing* with others vis-à-vis China but that is a much wider issue. It could try adjusting its bigger policy on Tibet, in effect playing a "Tibet Card" to engineer geopolitical shifts in the future; though would be a much more high risk strategy immediately bringing it up against China's perceived "core interest" of averting internal fragmentation.

If India's strategy over the disputed territories has been hesitant, this has been exacerbated by the very opaqueness, the "Chinese whispers" coming from Beijing. What exactly does China really want, what is its bottom line? For example, are PRC reiterations of claims over the whole of Arunachal Pradesh, re-invoked with greater vigour since the 1990s, just a maximalist initial tactic to end up with the Tawang pocket, thereby strengthening its control over Tibet, a line of argument by Chinese commentators like Ma Jiali and others. Are some suggestions in PRC circles of a different trade-off, Aksai Chin to India and Arunachal Pradesh to China, serious? Did China's acceptance in 2003 of Nathu La as an official border trade post between India and China represent full and definitive acceptance by China of Sikkim's incorporation into India; and what is the significance of rising "incursion" incidents into Sikkim during 2008 by Chinese troops; uncertainties that undermine Wen Jiabao's assertions in 2005 that "Sikkim is no longer the problem between China and India?" Is talk in the PRC that "China won't make any compromises in its border disputes with India" a tactical ploy by China to get India to make compromises? If it is, then a trade-off deal is likely at some point. If it is not, then indefinite deadline/stand off is likely, unless one or the other disputant state attempts to decide it on the military battlefield.

One emerging line from the PRC, with implications for India, is PRC emphasis and definition of a "core interests" diplomacy, reflecting the rise of China; "as the country becomes stronger, China is now on the trajectory to develop its own doctrine of diplomacy". This has been a development in the last couple of years, overlapping with rising friction along the disputed Himalayan reaches; generally what the PRC calls "the recalibration of its strategic focus in diplomacy to 'core interests'", over which it is taking a more obstructive/assertive line. This sense of "core interest" can be primarily seen at stake for the PRC in Taiwan and also Xinjiang. It can also be seen with PRC statements with regard to Tibet, whereby "Tibet related issues remain a core interest of China that refers to state sovereignty and territorial integrity. This is neither a religious issue nor a human right issue". The question is how far China's "core interest" framework may be "expanding". If such a "core interest" linkage is also invoked for Arunachal Pradesh (or in PRC eyes *Zang Nan* "Southern Tibet") as "Tibet-related issues", then one would have less expectations of territorial agreements being reached between India and China, and more likelihood of armed resolution in the future. Such trends were the spur for Barat Verma at the *India Defence Review* to warn that for the PRC "the most attractive option is to attack a soft target like India and forcibly occupy its territory in the Northeast...Beijing's cleverly raising the hackles on its fabricated dispute in Arunachal Pradesh to an alarming level, is the preparatory groundwork for imposing such a conflict on India"; a scenario dismissed in China as a "provocative and inflammatory illusion". Nevertheless, IR security dilemma dynamics may indeed lead to increasing military tension as both sides reinforce their military positions, and "war talk" about the disputed territories increases.

Concerned voices are easy to find as "tensions over a boundary dispute between the two sides are escalating". One reason for Indian concerns is the increasing number of "incursion" incidents along the border, though denied by China. The official India leadership downplays such trends, India's Foreign Secretary Niripuma Rao thus asserting in September 2009 that "there has been no significant increase in intrusions across all Sectors of the Line of Actual Control (LAC)", but that such India-perceived incursions were "because there is no mutually agreed or delineated border". This ignores the earlier increase the previous year, whereby the number of India-perceived "incursions" by the PRC has increased from 140 in 2007 to 280 in 2008, with a similar number in 2009. Such incursion incidents involved not just the *Eastern Sector* around Arunachal Pradesh but now also the *Western Sector* around Aksai Chin/Ladakh; a particular widening development that Indian commentators like Bhaskar Roy have found "sinister" and which Kanwal sees as "aggressive tactical posturing" on the part of China. Admittedly, such border incursions, reflecting different perceptions of where the LAC actually is, have often been trivial in themselves; for example Chinese troops painting rocks in red paint or cross-LAC sheep grazing. Chinese troop movements near and around the narrow Siliguri corridor "chicken's neck" linking north-east India to the rest of India do though cause immediate geopolitical concerns to India.

Certainly, a substantive military build up along the Aksai Chin and Arunachal Pradesh borderlines has also been evident. Partly this has been an infrastructure race, in which India has been belatedly trying to catch up and match China's better established road, and now railway, infrastructure in these disputed borderlands. It has also involved increasing military deployment, again by India to match China's already established forces in places like Linzi airbase. This is reflected in India increasing its ground forces in the border regions facing China. In the *Eastern Sector*, this has also involved the Indian Air Force (IAF) deploying advanced long range Sukhoi Su-30 warplanes to Tezpur for potential cross-LAC operation; complemented by six surface-to-air Akash missile squadrons. In the *Western Sector*, this has also involved the Indian Air Force reactivating disused high altitude airstrips like Daulat Beg Oldi and Fukche. Such reinforcements have been picked up in the PRC, and denounced as "unwise military moves".

Meanwhile, Brahma Chellaney asked the question in 2006 "will India — China border talks ever end"? He argued that "after a quarter century of unrewarding negotiations with Beijing, India ought to face up to the reality that it is being taken round and round the mulberry bush by an adversarial state that has little stake in an early border resolution"; in which "the more the talks have dragged on, the less Beijing has appeared interested in resolving the border disputes other than on its terms". His prognosis was simple, "it is time for it to draw the line, at least in the negotiations" and "to re-evaluate the very utility of staying absorbed in a never-ending process". Three years later, in the wake of the 2009 talks, his sense was the same, "the latest round of the unending and fruitless India — China talks on territorial disputes was a fresh reminder of the eroding utility of this process". The PRC may indeed wish to keep the issue open as a way of distracting and threatening India; but other dynamics may be leading the PRC to postpone decisive border negotiations. The PRC may well consider tightening its hold on Tibet itself as a greater priority, shaken during the disturbances that swept across Tibet and Tibetan areas in the spring of 2008? The PRC may also want to delay decisive border territorial resolution with India until it has resolved the Taiwan issue first? Garver also has wondered how far Beijing's apparent slowdown and readiness to avoid territorial resolution with India, is because of "understanding between Pakistan and China that neither will settle their territorial disputes with India independently of the other". Such a consideration point to the wider Pakistan—China—India triangle interplay around the disputed territories that stretch along the Himalayas from Arunachal Pradesh in the east to Aksai Chin and Kashmir in the west, which overlap with basic power balancing by the China—Pakistan "nexus" against India. The overlaps between the varied territorial disputes was shown in 2009 when China gave visas for the entry of Kashmiri separatists to visit China, in the wake of India giving permission to the Dalai Lama to visit Arunachal Pradesh.

What is certain is that any quick decisive territorial resolution between India and China is unlikely. Following rising border frictions, the PRC media reported "China—India border dispute turns sour", with hard hitting nationalist blogs being noticeable in the Chinese official and state controlled media in the autumn of 2009. Admittedly, the Indian and Chinese leadership did again reaffirm dialogue in autumn 2009. However, this reaffirmation was in cautious terms "to gradually narrow differences on border issues between the two countries … to continue talks, with the aim of incrementally removing the barriers to a solution that was fair and acceptable to both sides". Despite the euphemistic headline from the official Chinese media that the two countries had reached "concensus on narrowing border differences"; in reality this merely indicated the existence of a gap without showing how and when it would be resolved. Talk of "gradually" and "incrementally removing" barriers to a solution flags up the slowness of any likely process, whilst offering nothing on what solutions could then emerge once such barriers have been, incrementally, removed.

What of solutions? Could outside arbitration be one way forward? Nehru himself had offered such a route in the immediate aftermath of war in the shape of the International Court of Justice (ICJ) at The Hague.

However this was badly received in Parliament and Nehru then backed away immediately from this. In reality the ICJ seems ill equipped to deal with direct large scale territorial disputes between major powers, whilst China's reluctance to have outside bodies disposing of sovereignty issues is higher even than India's.

One bilateral solution which we can return to, involves a *logic of geography*, the "watershed/crestline" line along the Himalayas/Karakoram. It has a degree of clearness, "the advantage of having a border on such a prominent line as the high watershed of the Himalaya is that it is easily identifiable, historically traditional and politically neutral".

It may also be sellable to both parties. Thus, "as far as the Indian public is concerned, they have been brought up to believe that the Himalaya is the traditional boundary and they will be willing to concede any territory that lies beyond it without demur"; whilst "such a boundary should also be acceptable to China as it is based on the same watershed principle which they have accepted in defining their boundaries with Myanmar, Sikkim and Nepal.

This watershed principle was an angle suggested by Zhou Enlai in the abortive 1960 discussions. In effect, applying the watershed principle would leave Aksai Chin to China and almost all Arunachal Pradesh with India.

Admittedly, Tawang remains problematic. The Tawang District's 2,085 square kilometres is around 2.5% of Arunachal Pradesh's entire 82,743 area, and its population of 38,924 is around 3.6% of Arunachal Pradesh's 1,091,120 inhabitants (2001 figures), relatively small shares on paper. Neutralization of the entire Tawang subdivision pocket might be an option. Within the Tawang District, given that the Tawang Subdistrict and the District capital Tawang (27°34'47"N) itself lies north of the Se la Pass and the Ka crest line (27°32'26"N), whereas the Lumla and Jang Subdistricts lie on the southerly India-facing slopes of that crest line; could a division of Tawang District be carried out, with the Tawang Subdistrict allocated to China and the Lumla and Jang Subdistricts allocated to India? However, local opinion at the District capital Tawang, population c. 20,000, would probably vote in favour of staying in 'India' rather than going into the 'PRC', though an independent 'Tibet' option would provide an interesting third option. Having Tawang subdivision inhabitants relocate further south if they wished might be another solution, though ugly in political and human terms. Meanwhile, if the Dalai Lama's death was followed by any proclaimed rebirth at Tawang, a not impossible scenario, the situation would be still more complicated with the PRC.

Failing dramatic regime change scenarios of regime collapse/ democratization in the PRC, and re-establishment of a genuinely autonomous or independent Tibet, and Tawang notwithstanding; some sort of trade off involving Aksai Chin and Arunachal Pradesh seems the most likely way forward. In using relatively clear cut neutral geographic principles, the deadlocked politics and unclear history could perhaps be sidelined?

Such a trade off would give neither side too much geopolitical advantage, but also ensure a degree of security for each? A *logic of geography* for the future for the national leaderships that would enable these two neighbours to get past the inconclusive divisive *logic of history* between them, and would provide a mutually satisfactory *logic of power* in terms of geopolitical equilibrium outcomes. Failing resolution of their territorial issues, the grinding tectonic plates along the Himalayas will continue to have their geopolitical counterpart as the two Asian giants look at each other across these disputed areas.

INDIA-CHINA BORDER DISPUTE

On assuming power, the People's Republic of China (PRC) renounced all prior foreign agreements as unequal treaties imposed upon it during the "century of humiliation" and demanded renegotiation of all borders. The Sino-India border remains the only major territorial dispute, other than South China Sea disputes, that China has not resolved. China's growing assertiveness in its territorial claims, especially on Arunachal Pradesh, and its relentless development of infrastructure in Tibet will shape the prospects of Sino-India relations. The territory stretching from the jungles of northern Myanmar, westward to the Karakoram Range, and northward to the edge of the Tibetan plateau can be seen as a single geopolitical system referred to as the Himalayan-Tibetan massif. The ruggedness of this terrain makes movement of men and materiel extremely difficult, thus preventing Indian and Chinese civilizations from intermingling or projecting military power in these remote areas effectively. Not until 1962 did the Chinese and Indian armies fight each other over these desolate heights, thus altering the geopolitics of the region significantly.

Chinese President Hu Jintao met with Indian Prime Minister Manmohan Singh in Sanya City, south China's Hainan Province, April 13, 2011. Hu said China is willing to further push forward negotiations on border issues on the basis of peace and friendliness, equal consultation, mutual respect and understanding. The two sides should consider setting up a consultation and coordination mechanism on border issues so as to achieve consensus as soon as possible and to better maintain peace and stability at the border regions before the issues are solved.

China wants India to put behind the 1962 war as an "unfortunate" thing of the past and that the two countries should strengthen their military ties including formalising a border management pact under which their troops will not fire at each other. The Chinese assessment was conveyed to the Indian defence ministry team which visited Beijing on 14-15 January 2013 for the third round of the annual defense dialogue between the two countries.

Border tensions between China and India flared after New Delhi claimed a contingent of 30 to 50 PLA soldiers crossed about 12 miles beyond the Line of Actual Control between the two countries on 15 April 2012 and stayed there for three weeks. According to New Delhi, PLA soldiers frequently conduct border incursions (more than 600 times over the last three years) but do not usually cross more than a few miles over the Line of Actual Control nor stay there longer than several hours.

Beijing denied Chinese troops had crossed into Indian territory. A Chinese Ministry of Foreign Affairs spokesperson said, ''China has always acted in strict compliance with relevant agreements and protocols between the two countries on maintaining peace and tranquility in the Line of Actual Control area along the border... Chinese patrol troops have never crossed the line." Chinese Premier Li Keqiang attempted to downplay the incident and the risk of conflict. During a state visit to India, he insisted that "a few clouds in the sky cannot shut out the brilliant rays of our friendship." Premier Li did not directly address the alleged Chinese incursion, though he said "both sides believe we need to improve various border-related mechanisms that we have put into place and make them more efficient, and we need to appropriately manage and resolve our differences."

President Xi Jinping met Indian Prime Minister Manmohan Singh at the BRICS Summit in Durban, South Africa, 29 March 2013. Xi urged both sides to use special representatives to strive for a fair, rational framework that can lead to a solution to the border issue as soon as possible. India will abide by political guidelines set by both sides and seek a solution to the border issue with a commitment to safeguarding peace, Singh said. Since 2003, more than a dozen rounds of talks had been launched to resolve the border disputes. But ties have still been occasionally strained by the issue and overshadowed by closer India-US relations amid Washington's accelerating Asia "pivot" policy.

Bibliography

Ajey Lele: *Strategic Technologies for the Military : Breaking New Frontiers*, Sage, Delhi, 2009.

Amitabh Sikdar: *India and China : Strategic Energy Management and Security*, Manas, Delhi, 2009.

Anil, K.C.: *Military and Democracy in South Asia : Challenges, Politics and Power*, Sumit Enterprises, Delhi, 2009.

Asha Gupta: *Military Rule and Democratization : Changing Perspectives*, Deep & Deep, Delhi, 2003.

Bhat, T.P. : *India and China : Trade Complementarities and Competitiveness*, Bookwell, Delhi, 2008.

Chandra, R.: *Judicial System in Mechanical Warfare*, Lucknow, Print House (India), 1992.

Deepak, B R : *India and China : 1904-2004 : A Century of Peace and Conflict*, Manak, Delhi, 2005.

Donnan, H. and Wilson, T. M.: *Borders: Frontiers of Identity, Nation and State*, Oxford: Berg, 1999.

Evelyn Goh, *Meeting the China Challenge: The U.S. in Southeast Asian Regional Security Strategies*, DC: East-West Center, 2005.

Gao, Mobo: *The Battle for China's Past: Mao and the Cultural Revolution*, London, Pluto Press, 2008.

Gupta, S.: *Disrupted Borders: An Intervention in Definitions of Boundaries*, London: River Oram Press, 1993.

Hagström, Linus: *Japan's China Policy: A Relational Power Analysis*, London and New York: Routledge, 2005.

Huntington, S.P.: *The China Modernisation Military and the State*, N.Y., Vintage Books, 1964.

Ian Storey: *ASEAN and the South China Sea: Movement in Lieu of Progress*, Washington, D.C., Jamestown Foundation,2012.

Itoh, Mayumi: *Pioneers of Sino-Japanese Relations: Liao and Takasaki*. Palgrave-MacMillan. 2012.

Jagannath P. Panda: *China's Path to Power : Party, Military and the Politics of State Transition*, Pentagon, Delhi, 2010.

James R Blaker: *Transforming Military Force : The Legacy of Arthur Cebrowski and Network Centric Warfare*, Pentagon Press, Delhi, 2008.

Joon Ahn: *The Rise of China and the Future of East Asian Integration*, Asia-Pacific Review, London, Carfax Publishing Company, 2004.

Kapur, C.K. : *Chinese Military Modernisation*, Manas, Delhi, 2003.

Marie Lecomte : *Hindu Kingship, Ethnic Revival, and Maoist Rebellion in Nepal*, Oxford University Press, Delhi, 2009.

Mary, W.: *Military Space Force: the Cultural Dimensions of Authority*, Cambridge, Belknap Press, 1985.

Nayyar, K K : *National Security : Military Aspects*, Rupa, Delhi, 2003.

Posen, B.R.: *The Sources of Military Doctrine*, Ithaca, 1984, Cornell Univ. Press.

Prabir De: *India and China in an Era of Globalisation : Essays on Economic Cooperation*, Bookwell, Delhi, 2005.

Radhakrishna: *Military Ethics: Guidelines for Peace and War*, Sumit Enterprises, Delhi, 2009.

Raj Kumar: *Weapons and Military Technology*, Sumit Enterprises, Delhi, 2009.

Robert M Cassidy: *Counterinsurgency and the Global War on Terror : Military Culture and Irregular War*, Pentagon Press, Delhi, 2008.

Rosen, P.: *Societies and Military Power: India and its Armies*, Ithaca, Cornell University Press, 1996.

Samuel P. Huntington: *The Soldier and the State : The Theory and Politics of Civil-Military Relations*, Natraj Pub, Delhi, 2005.

Shaun Narine, *Explaining ASEAN: Regionalism in Southeast Asia*, Boulder, CO: Lynne Rienner Publishers, 2002.

Stuart R. Schram: *The Political Thought of Mao Tse-Tung*. New York: Praeger, 1969.

Wakamiya Yoshibumi, *The Postwar Conservative View of Asia*, Tokyo: LTCB International Library Foundation, 1999.

Wilson, T. M.: *New Borders for a Changing: Cross-border Cooperation and Governance*, London: Frank Cass, 2003.

Index

❑❑❑